AF590400

This book is dedicated to life.

I would like to give thanks to everyone who helped, encouraged, proofread, criticized or generally supported me in anyway whatsoever in this my endeavour, to bring my travels, trials and tribulations as well as the controversy and, hopefully enjoyment, to your lives.

Special thanks go to the two Michaels, my brother and MC, a friend as well as a colleague for many years who is brutally honest and hence keeps me honest. Dominic Riley who did a tremendous amount of work on the cover design to the exacting standards of us both deserves not only the gratitude for his work but also his patience.

In addition I would like to thank my wife for her patience and encouragement, my kids for their interest in my history and environment and finally all those who have encountered me on my road to where-ever. Thanks also needs to be extended to people in my life who have influenced me, negatively, as well as the positively as both have contributed to my journey. Finally to my extended family, some of whom I hardly know, many of whom have considered me the Black Sheep, Hippie or just a lazy sod, here is your evidence!

# RAMBLINGS

# OF

# A

# SCATTERLING

# Preface

This is story of my travels as a young man and also introduces my psychological development over the years, expanding on my beliefs which are often very strong. At this point I would like to make things quite clear that it is not my intention to criticize anyone or any group of people. I am just expressing my beliefs, sometimes strongly. I believe in debate, communication and the changing state of people, the world and the environment leaving me always open to discussion, which if done intelligently and with conviction may change my mind on some, or possibly all, issues raised in my ramblings.

I am a firm believer in equality for all people and I believe that all people have the right to live their lives as they see fit, as long as they extend the same curtesy to everyone else. This does not mean that I necessarily agree with some lifestyle choices but it is not up to me to decide how people should live. I am a Christian and I believe in the Christian doctrine. I can hear the many sighs from many sectors of society who only see the negative side of religion! Most religions I have looked at, however briefly, are peaceful and fanatics emerge on all sides and twist the doctrines to support their views.

Philippians 2:3 ESV

'Do nothing from rivalry or conceit, but in humility count others more significant than yourselves.'

Colossians 3:12-17ESV

Put on then, as God's chosen ones, holy and beloved, compassionate hearts, kindness, humility, meekness, and patience, bearing with one another and, if one has a complaint against another, forgiving each other; as the Lord has forgiven you, so you also must forgive.

You do not have to be religious to believe and try to live up to the preceding precepts, just human.

Lastly I would like to mention that various names have been changed for protection of all those concerned.

Thank you and enjoy my ramblings.

# Chapter 1

When telling or re-telling a story I have often wondered where to start and after sixty years of contemplation I have decided that the best place is the beginning. These writings are the progression of a simple person from birth to his current situation. They take us from his birth, as presumably a mindless infant, (other than genetic imprinting), to a grown man, still mindless but including society's imprinting. With a little thought this has led me to the question, 'who is insane, me or the world?'

My literature teacher at 'A' level, a beautiful and intelligent woman by the name of Liz Whittome, once asked the class a question: If by our current definitions in society we take a sane person and lock him in a room with 10 insane people, within that room is it easy to agree who is insane and who is not, but if no definition exists how do we know who is insane and who is not? This has led to my current predicament – Am I insane or is society insane? Insanity has various ´markers' or 'traits', however the dictionary definition is 'Insanity. *n.* *mental illness of such a severe nature that a person cannot distinguish fantasy from reality, cannot conduct her/his affairs due to psychosis, or is subject to uncontrollable impulsive behaviour'*. Surely this behaviour is present in many of our Presidents, Prime Ministers, politicians, army officers, school principals and other leaders of our communities and societies,

But I get ahead of myself, let's start at the beginning. I was born in a remote village in the western area of Northern Rhodesia among lots of black people with only my family and one or two other white families for hundreds of miles around, being the first second generation of British Colonial descent born in Mongu, which my mother never let me forget. Yes, I was born into privileged Colonial White stock but, at this early stage of life the black kids were my best and only friends. Later when I attended White Only Boarding schools, I was imprinted with the legacy that it is my duty to keep them in place as they cannot be educated and to eventually kill those of them who do not agree with our way of life and would endeavour to change it. I'm talking about conscription into the army which was prevalent among the British colonies and some ex colonies.

Growing up partly in the African bush and African cities is probably the best upbringing anyone can have! It is full of life and beauty and to this day I have no idea as to why society tells us that animals are dangerous. What a load of crap – animals are not dangerous – it is people who are stupid. Very few animals attack for no reason, they may be hungry, protecting their young etc., but few animals like human meat, (if all lions ate human meat why would we call the one that does a man-eater? Wouldn't they all be 'man-eaters'? Unless in the past we only fed them women and kids!!

Anyway Yay, my birth cannot be denied as here I am.

Well that is the beginning of the story but due to being a baby I cannot tell you much about the next few years, only what has been related to me. I had a nanny, I was a good baby, I lived in the Northern Rhodesian bush, I was nearly eaten alive by a marauding army of soldier ants.

I have no idea about when memories start, the selection or the chronology. My first memory is sitting up in a pram watching a game of tennis, somewhere in the African bush. My next one is toddling around Gaunt's Wood, my grandparent's farm in near Lusaka, and I suppose the real beginning of my story. This would be in the late 1950's and although only a toddler, impressions gained here have guided me in many aspects and ingrained my love of Africa. I was surrounded by my extended family, the farm workers and had the piccanines for playmates with an occasional trip into Lusaka for supplies. The farm was basically self-sufficient, fruit, veg, meat and a diesel run generator, thumping in the background all day every day from pre-dawn to 21:00. Our bedroom, my brother and I shared, was half way along a veranda, closed in with wire mosquito netting forming a corridor which overlooked the front oval shaped garden edged by small rocks behind a line of flower beds which fell away into the veldt beyond. Just out of sight to the east was the concrete swimming pool shaded by Mopane trees and my favourite, a Monkey Tree - not to be confused with the Monkey Puzzle tree of the Americas or Asia. Our bed time was 19:00 and even as a toddler I was in awe of the night sky which displayed all its glory every night. After the thump of the generator gave way to the silent sounds of the African bush I would fall asleep gazing at the wonder of the night sky. The night was alive, the heavens shone in glory and I was forever trapped in its beauty.

The days were spent either with my gran protecting me from the geese, one of whom in particular seemed to desire my flesh, or with my nanny around the house and garden. The geese hung out around the back of the house which was where the daily activity of the farm emanated from, the work shop, the generator the chicken coops were all clustered spaciously around the driveway which led from the gate, guarded by a blackened tree split in half by lightening, to the kitchen. The cars, my gran's grey Vauxhall Velox stood next to my granddad's black Volvo Amazon. (Funnily enough I cannot remember my parents' cars until they returned from an extended trip from Europe with a Peugeot 404 station wagon with three rows of seats - this was in the early 60's.)

My granddad's car was to me the best ever, black with tan leather seats, the sloping back, racing style and me standing in the back, my head not even touching the roof while speeding along the farm roads looking out for game and finally entering Lusaka and the lure of the big city! My gran's car seemed pretty normal except the indicator always fascinated me. The little lever on the steering wheel which when slid to one side or the other would activate a little arm between the front and back doors with a light in it. Whenever my gran left me in the car I would jump into the front to activate the arm which, to my dismay would never work for me. My gran had some type of magic! Some Saturdays were market days, I only remember because I was told, the days of the week had no meaning to me except market days and Sundays. On market days I would rise early to watch with fascination as one of the workers would round up some of the chickens and put them into a wire cage and haul them off to his tree stump seat and chopping block. His hand would reach into the cage, grab a chicken, place it on the chopping block and off with its head which would be dropped on the side of the chopping block opposite to the cage while the headless chicken would run around before dropping. I was always trying to count the how many headless chickens were running around at the same time! When he was really quick I counted up to three. When the job was completed he would then pick up the chickens and box them for the market while the heads were put into a sack and taken to the compound for the farm labourers. One of these chickens was reserved for our Sunday roast. Still the best roast chicken I have ever had. During the week while playing with the piccanines I was often drawn to the bloodied chopping block which held a morbid fascination for me. A stone's throw away were the chicken runs, not like runs today, but acres of free range chickens doing what chickens do.

Early in life I learnt the cycle of life, we grew crops which fed ourselves and the animals, the animals gave us eggs, cheese, milk and meat. The pelts were either given to the labourers or picked up by the tanning factory lorry once a week. These days of growing from a toddler into a young child were idyllic but the farm days came to an end as my dad was stationed in Fort Jameson, Ndola, Kitwe and Livingstone.

Fort Jimmy is on the Malawi border, Ndola and Kitwe near the Congo and on the Copperbelt, while Livingstone is on the southern border with Zimbabwe, so all in all my childhood gave me a large African playground. Fort Jimmy was basically a fortified boma and my dad's job was to keep the peace among the locals which included keeping predators away from villages and their herds, he was employed by the British Colonial service. It was here near Fort Jimmy that my dad, in his early 30`s, learnt one of the hardest lessons in his life and the decision he made haunted him until the day he died.

A local uprising was gaining pace due to a legal decision over stock theft. The tribal justice system demanded the life of the thief while the Colonial justice system sentenced him to six months in prison for the theft of one goat, which he admitted to stealing. His 'real' crime was that he was from a neighbouring district. The local Chief did not like the Colonial service interfering with tribal law. Skirmishes started, with the Colonial Service Messengers being attacked and beaten. My dad went to negotiate with the local Chief. He demanded that the thief be handed over for tribal justice. My father could not acquiesce and paid the Chief five cows, 7 goats and 10 chickens which the Chief accepted but kept them all for himself and offered the victim no compensation. The skirmishes increased, the Messengers were being killed. The Chief was once more approached and said peace would come about with the death of the thief. My dad refused. The skirmishes continued.

Armed with fifty African soldiers my dad approached the village to arrest those who had killed the messengers. He was met with over a hundred Ngoni warriors armed with shields and assegais crouching behind women and children. The warriors started chanting and advancing while performing menacing theatrics. My father shouted a warning to the warriors who could not hear him above the war cries and ululating while they continued to approach the men. My father had to make the decision whether or not to shoot into the crowd led by women and children; his decision was not to, the warriors ran into the soldiers, whom my father had ordered to retreat without firing a shot. However the warriors reached the line before the soldiers could disperse and 20 were killed with another 25 wounded. Still my dad refused to open fire on women and children. A week later he was ordered back with over two hundred troops and once again the warriors were crouched behind the women and children while advancing and ululating again with menacing theatrics. This time my dad opened fire to save the slaughter of his men. Even though the order was to only shoot the men to incapacitate, dozens of women and children were injured five children and three women killed while ten Ngoni warriors were killed and about twenty injured. The uprising was over. Meanwhile my father has to live with that decision for the rest of his life.

Africa is not only doom and gloom but a continent of vast contrasts; incredible beauty mixed with the savagery of man and beast. The next lesson started me on the road to question the savagery of the beasts, the cunning leopards, the man eating lions, the vicious attacks of charging elephants, etc. One morning as the sun was rising our servant, Julius, was making a racket waking up my mother, "Medem, medem, wake up medem! The bwana, medem! The Bwana, lion... uh medem the bwana, the lion eat him!

"Calm down, Julius, tell me what happened"

"The bwana, a lion eat him!!"

Throwing back the bed covers, revealed my father had not been eaten by a lion","See Julius, the bwana is fine. Tell me what happened."

" Uh uh eweh! But the bwana and the lion" and Julius, now a lot calmer, proceeded to lead us outside.

During the night my mother had heard noises outside and had sent my mostly asleep dad to investigate. He had picked up a knobkerrie and proceeded out the front door and into the driveway. As is quite common in Africa, the driveway was circular with a tree and bushes in the centre and my father heard noises coming from the bushes and started poking into them, telling the intruder to bugger off and after a few perambulations around the bushes the intruder disappeared up the driveway. In the morning Julius had seen lion spoor followed by my dad's. He had been poking the lion with the knobkerrie until the lion had had enough and wandered off! This was the first of many animal encounters, either relayed or experienced first-hand that planted the seed that grew into the love of animals who are so badly misrepresented, maligned and persecuted because of the ignorance of man. We have a lot to answer for.

It was also about this time that I became aware that domestic animals were not just things to tease, pull tails and chase. My mother was taking the four kids to Lusaka to visit our grandparents - back to Gaunt's Wood, a place I loved. Meanwhile my dad was a free man for a while and went to meet his drinking buddy, the government vet. As he approached the building he bumped into a man taking his Alsatian to be put down. The dog was still young and everybody in the boma knew the dog. He had been chained up to a tree since birth, ate under the tree, slept under the tree, pissed under the tree, crapped under the tree and tried his best to maul anyone who came near. The dog finally was turning on his master, and hence the need to put it down. My dad decided that he would take the dog, and off he went with this vicious Alsatian trying to have him for dinner while walking him home. That evening while at the local drinking club my dad started to boast about the vicious dog who was already befriending him. The dog was known to everyone and my dad was considered, not only mad, but also stupid for taking an animal like that into a home with four young kids.

One of my mum's friends phoned her in Lusaka, no easy job in those days, probably an hour of waiting by the wind up handset before the connection could be put through! Anyway my mum was FURIOUS, holiday cut short, grandparent's tongues wagging about the irresponsibility and onto the next plane to Fort Jimmy. Arriving home my mum started laying into my dad. Us kids left the house and went out back to get away from the shouting which was still a background din from the rear garden. My sister, Margaret went straight up to the dog, let him out of the kennel and he started playing with all four of us and when my mum, eventually entered the garden still bitching and decrying the whole situation, was suddenly dumbstruck, and I guess fearful, but nevertheless we kept the dog who became a firm family friend.

We soon moved to Livingstone where I started school. School started when you were seven and before I started 'big' school I spent a year in nursery school, where I was supposed to learn to read and write, but as my mum had already taught me, I was allowed out to play more than the other kids. This allowed me to become quite popular with my sisters' friends who would give their 'cute little brother' fruit, sandwiches, sweets and drinks over the fence from the "big" school. I lapped up this attention! All too soon I started school and my life started to change. My first day at school was quite memorable in that I had a name change. I was baptized John Anthony, but I had always been called John Ant or Ant and I was only called by these names. When the teacher was asking our names I replied "John Ant".
The teacher repeated "John".
Politely I responded "No Miss, my name is John Ant",
To which she responded "OK, thank you John, you may sit down now." From that day forward I had two names, to the people I met through family I was John Ant or Ant and people through school I was John. This pattern continued through my work and study life, so today my extended family and friends met through them I am Ant and people I meet through work or study I am known as John.

Livingstone was also my first real introduction to the Catholic Church and here I need to introduce my parents and their basic background as it helps put my upbringing into perspective. My father was about to enter to a Catholic monastery to train as a priest with the view to a ministry in the military when he met my mum. My mother was a strict Catholic who considered a career as a nurse when she met my dad. My religious route was set for my siblings and myself.

In the 50's and 60's Catholicism was undergoing change and for me it was quite a rapid change as Africa was way behind in everything and then caught up almost in one go. My first memories of Mass are of everything in Latin, (besides the sermon). By the age of eight I could recite the whole Mass in Latin, sing all the hymns in Latin and as an altar boy could even ring the bells at the right time. The biggest problem was I had no idea what the mass was about. Once a month (or so it seemed) we had a High Mass, also in Latin, but all this meant to me was an hour longer of participating in this ceremony of which I had no idea of its objective.

I had been going to mass all my life but now I started to belong to the church. Scripture studies, altar boy serving and the church itself, which was a massive cathedral, considering my young age. Christmas time brought religious plays at school, but I never really featured in them, acting wasn't my thing. I remember serving at my first Christmas midnight mass at the age of six. My brother, 5 years my senior and the head altar boy, was to help me through this first really important serving event of my young life. After a short time of kneeling on the top steps leading to the altar and watching a priest dressed in fascinating ritual garments alternating between talking and singing in Latin, with Latin responses coming from a men's choir somewhere way back in the cathedral, boredom set in. I started fidgeting, looking at my watch, fingering my chaffing collar, moving from knee to knee to get comfortable while the droning of the Latin chorus went on and on and on..... I spotted the triangular bell my brother was put in charge of, it was between us. I started to edge towards it and slowly attempted to move it towards me. A quiet whisper from my brother stopped me. A few minutes later another attempt resulted in a smacked hand which led to a whispered argument. Once more peace reigned until I grabbed the bell and rang as vigorously as I could. I now had the full attention of my brother who was trying to grab the bell away from me as I moved further and further away from him, both of us sliding along the top steps on our knees until my brother caught up with me at which point I turned and fled with the bell ringing out for all the congregation to hear!

Livingstone was a wonderful place for a young child to begin their journey in life. It was a city! It had a population of about 5,000 people! It is also incredibly beautiful. On Sundays we would cross the bridge into Southern Rhodesia to have a family lunch at the Victoria Falls Hotel. Just before the bridge was large rock on which a baboon who imitated my dad's sitting position to a tee and made my dad the butt of Sunday jokes.

The Hotel Garden overlooks the Gorge and we would play in the gardens and walk along the paths admiring the power of the falls, the mist, such a contrast to the heat, the rainbows which can be seen from miles away, the gurgling of Devil's Cauldron drowned out by the thunder of the falls. The elephants walking up to the river for their afternoon watering, lions ignoring the buck while lounging under the shade of the trees in the mid afternoon sun, monkeys staring while waiting to create a moment of havoc, the baobabs sprinkled majestically stretching to the horizon. However my favourite spot was back on the Northern Rhodesian side. My mother was a member of the Police Force, the NRP and the Police Club was situated on the banks of the Zambezi, not far upstream from the falls. Motor boat racing was held regularly on this part of the river and we would sit under a wonderful monkey puzzle tree and watch the noisy boats and play along the bank.

One day while the adults were sitting there chatting, drinking and doing the things adults do under the Monkey puzzle tree, my dad got up to go to the toilet and, as if on cue a monkey walked along the branch until directly above my dad's beer and peed with amazing accuracy into his beer mug. Boy did we laugh as my dad turned around, saw what was happening, started to shout at the monkey who continued with total nonchalance until he had finished and then scrambled up the tree to join his mates!

One day we packed up and headed to the capital, Lusaka. However Lusaka had not always been the capital, Livingstone had been until 1935 when the colonial government deemed it too dangerous for our health due to the intense heat and malaria mosquito. Anyway arriving back at Gaunt's Wood was always joyful and when my parents went on an extended European trip I wasn't even aware that they had left. Being on the farm again was great, playing with the picannies, being spoilt by grandparents, listening to the thump thump of the generator give way to the quite sounds of the African bush while falling asleep under the scintillating starry starry nights. All too soon my parents arrived back with a brand new Peugeot 404 Station Wagon with three rows of seats and whisked us off to Lusaka and back to school!!

My older brother, Patrick, was back at boarding school at St Michael's in Southern Rhodesia while my sisters and I were newbies at the Dominican Convent in Lusaka. This was where I started to become aware, with thoughts and attitudes which began me on the road to my individuality. As a colonial I became aware of the phrase 'back home' referring to Great Britain, a place my family left 200 years ago, my parents had visited once, my grandparents on my mother side a few times and my father's side never and us kids never. How could that be 'home'? My mum put me into afternoon elocution classes, at school, so I could learn 'The Queen's English'. I also became vaguely aware of politics as my granddad was quite a well-respected politician. However my life revolved around holidays and weekends.

We moved into a house my dad had built in Olympia Park, a new suburb way out of town (in those days) which is still the best house we lived in! My dad was strict and Julius, our cook / houseboy took a liking to me and became a saviour from my dad's wrath when I misbehaved. In the morning my mum would give instructions as to what was to be cooked for dinner, but Julius would override my mum's menu and asked me what we should have for dinner! There are various vegetables I really don't like and those were always changed by my choice. My mum soon noticed that certain vegetables were never cooked and on some occasions would insist and then Julius could do nothing. These became times of torment for me. I would sit at table shoving the food around the plate until bed time when we all had to kneel on a coarse knitted hessian mat to say our prayers before going to bed. The next morning I was given last night's uneaten dinner for breakfast, lunch, dinner, breakfast, etc. until I finished it, with no other food. Julius would sneak me food until my dad realized that I was cheating and would then give me anywhere between 3-6 cuts with a sjambok.

We had a nice garden sloping down and terraced, where we had a slip and slide, a long plastic sheet with a hosepipe attached and we would run and dive onto it and slide to the end and start again. The garden also had mulberry bushes running down the length of the garden. Oh the joy of belly aches from stuffing yourself with too much fruit! This was also the house where I learnt to ride a bicycle. My brother had a new bike and as he was away at boarding school most of the time I begged him to teach me to ride when he was home for the holidays. So during the following holidays he kept his word. I got on the bike, hands too small to pull the brakes, legs not long enough to sit and pedal and my brother holding the bike upright with me perched on top with a nice steep driveway across the road and another road carries on downwards with a rise at the end of a cul de sac. Well, before I knew it Patrick had let me go and there I went bumping down the dirt driveway and went headlong into a thorn bush at the end of the driveway. Undeterred Patrick came and extricated me, put me on top of the bike, bleeding from thorn pricks and all, manoeuvres me across the road to the top of the cul-de-sac and once again lets me go. This time I loved it! The bike was gaining speed and going down the hill faster and faster. I got to the dip and started up the other side slowing down until the bike was virtually stopped when I realized that I couldn't stop or get off the bike and fell over onto the tarmac road grazing my arm and leg. Patrick came ambling down, while I got up and righted the bike and when he reached me I was grinning like a Cheshire cat, my first ride on a bicycle! Patrick looked over the bike not approving of the scratches, gave me a clip over the earhole, mounted his bike and rode home. I walked up the hill still bathing in the glory of my first ride.

My dad liked to listen to Opera and we had a mono record player and every evening before 7pm bedtime, he would play some Opera before we had to kneel down and say prayers on the dreaded matted green hessian carpet. To me, a double torture. While saying our prayers, if any of us moved to try a more comfortable kneeling position, another prayer was added on to the daily bedtime prayers, this was a torture we learnt to endure as not only were the prayers extended but my siblings would take it out on anyone of us who extended the torture!

Animals also played a big part in my life here. When we moved to Lusaka my mum moved to the dog division of the C.I.D. so all our dogs were well trained. My mum's favourite was a bitch called Gypsy, but she was just known as Bitch ( long before the word became common usage as a swear word). The dog that adopted my dad was Prince. He was police trained, specializing in break ins. One day Patrick and I were playing cowboys and Indians. When Prince took offence to the cap gun, he grabbed my brother by the hand and without hurting him too much forced him to let go of the gun. He then took it to his basket and lay on it, not allowing any of us to retrieve it. When my mum arrived she went to retrieve the pistol but Prince wouldn't let her. A while later my dad arrived home and before the car had even stopped Prince had got off his bed and was waiting next to the car to hand the pistol to my dad as he exited the car. My dad then took the cap gun, handed it back to Patrick and told Prince that it was OK and we never had a problem playing cowboys and Indians again.

Prince amused us once again when we went on holiday to Beira in Mozambique. We were staying in Chalets and meeting some friends of the folks there. Well, one day we were all on the beach having a normal sunny holiday when one of the ladies, Charlotte, needed to go to the toilet. Well, there were no public toilets and the friends were in a hotel up the road, so my dad gave her the keys to our chalet and off she went. About an hour later someone noticed that she had not returned so my dad went to investigate. On arrival at the chalet the door was unlocked and in he went calling for Charlotte. He found her still in the toilet but sitting on the closed lid with Prince not letting her out and growling each time she tried to leave. Us kids found this hilarious but the adults took some time before they could appreciate the humour of the situation.

Cats were also a large part of our upbringing. At this time we had two. One whose real name I can never remember but was called Crackers by all and sundry. He was actually mad. You could not walk across the room without him attacking your ankles. He would also run up the curtains and sit on the pelmet and when you walked below he would drop on you from above. The other cat, Fluffy, did not like dogs, not afraid of them but always caused trouble for them. He had a habit of killing snakes and bringing them into the house and plonking them down on my dad's chair, a gift for his return from work! Unfortunately Fluffy came to a horrible end. Both our neighbours had large dogs, boxers on one side; ridgebacks on the other and, with our Alsatians, fights were always breaking out often with Fluffy as the instigator. He would go to the fence on one side and rile the dogs up and then do the same to the dogs on the other side. One night the dogs found a hole in the fence and Fluffy got killed in the ensuing dogfight. R.I.P.

Once again during the holidays and, as was normal, we siblings were fighting. Margaret had been teasing my other sister, Kathleen or Kay, about what I don't know but I heard the squabbling and decided to join in. Kay was quick to rise to the bait, always was and always will be. An easy mark for teasing. Anyway, I joined in just as she flew off the handle. Margaret came charging up the veranda stairs and through the door into the house, I saw Kay chasing hard and decided to turn and run as well, following Margaret into the lounge and slammed the door behind me and Kay ran straight into the door, which happened to be glass and she had her arm straight through up to her upper arm which was badly cut with blood pouring out. Ambulance, stitches shame and regret abounded. Well, we all knew it was sjambok time no matter how we spun the story. However Julius had a different idea and the sjambok could not be found and was never seen again but that did not stop my dad from using Birches. Corporal punishment was a part of home and school life.

We had to rest between 14.00 and 16:00 every afternoon. It didn't matter which bedroom we were in, as long as we rested. Boys had one bedroom and girls another, but for rest time we went where we wanted. One afternoon I was in my bedroom with Margaret on Patrick's bed, Patrick and Kay were in the girls' room. Patrick walks into our bedroom and tells Margaret: " Out, I want my bed." Margaret refuses. Patrick goes the cupboard and gets out his Diana 16 pellet gun, loads it, returns to the bottom of his bed and once again says "Out, I want my bed." My sister lying on her back draws up her legs, " No, I was here first", Patrick aims: "Out". Margaret: "No". BANG, shot in the knee with a plastic pellet. Clutching her knee she jumps up, hurriedly hobbles over to Patrick still standing at the end of the bed with the pellet gun, pummels him shouting, "You bugger, you bugger". Fortunately besides the pain no real damage was done, even though she has the scar to this day!

One day Patrick and I were playing with little lead die cast figurines of the second world war. We would set up our figurines at each end of the corridor and use a soft rubber ball taken out from golf balls (we used the elastic to make fly catties) and roll it down the corridor to knock your opponent's pieces down. On one occasion, as was often the case, the ball rebounded off the door and back up the corridor. Both my brother and I sprang up to chase the ball and during the ensuing battle for possession the ball split open shooting a white liquid all over us. It stung like a bitch! The ensuing commotion drew the attention of my mother who got the gist of what was happening, rushed to phone the hospital who insisted that we take a bath in cold milk! Apparently the acid from inside the ball was neutralized by the milk. A bath I shall never forget!

Weekends were a great time. My dad used to take Patrick fishing and I continually begged him until one day I was given a brand new rod. I was overjoyed to be fishing at last. The whole family packed up for a picnic and off we went. Patrick, my dad and myself were spread out along the banks of the Kafue river, a couple of hours out of Lusaka. Excitedly I baited the hook, with help from my dad and cast off. Time and time again. It felt like hours before I got a bite and a struggle ensued and I eventually landed my catch and rushed to grab it to release the hook when I heard my dad shout, "NOoooo ", running towards me. Too late. I had grabbed the fish which happened to be an electric barbel and I was suddenly buzzing and vibrating with 350 volts running through me and thrown onto my bum!! This incident put me off fishing for life!

Weekends were also a time to visit the Msamba club - a country club that seemed hours away off the main road heading east out of Lusaka along a dirt road. This club was both enjoyable and a place us kids disliked. Again it was either a Saturday or Sunday outing. It was well out of town on the main road and then heading off onto a dirt road for another 15 minutes' drive. It appeared much like a converted farmhouse. Bar, dining room, veranda, swimming pool, etc. Us kids would play and swim most of the day while my parents sat in the bar. As the coolness of the evening would set in we would retreat to the veranda where we talked and played darts while the resident African Grey would chirp up with "you're cheating", and various other colourful expletives learnt from the vast pool of darts players. Then dusk would display its beauty and night would set in. We would periodically and rotationally enter the bar to plead for an end to the day, we were tired and wanted to go home. We were sent to the car to sleep, which was impossible. The periodic trek to the bar would continue, as would the dismissals, occasionally being bribed with drinks and snacks. This routine was the first indication that my parents had a drinking problem although I was too young to realize it at the time. Eventually we would get home and flop into bed.

We were also members of the Police Club in Lusaka which was another institution of frequent visits but mostly during the week for sundowners. The Police Club was where serious family talks happened. My mother had been operated on and could not have another child and yet at the Club we were informed that my mother was once again pregnant and that it was a life threatening pregnancy. For us kids it was a confusing and difficult time but the pregnancy went quickly as my parents had only informed us once we had noticed that our mum was getting 'fat'. This period brings two memories to mind.

Margaret and Patrick had become fascinated with matches, showing us all sorts of tricks, how to make match sticks walk, how a match can burn twice, shooting flaming matchsticks etc. One day they disappeared into my mum's cupboard only to come out screaming a short time later with a blaze starting in the cupboard. Patrick and Margaret were screaming about how to put the fire out while my mum's clothes went up in flames. The fire was eventually put out but not before it had claimed some of the clothes. This was such a serious matter that Kay and I were not privy to the discussion or punishment awards, although sore bums were the order of the week!! The second memory is the birth of our baby brother. Patrick was away at school when my mum went into labour at home, in what seemed the early hours of the morning. My panicked dad unintentionally woke the family. He had already phoned for an ambulance but the baby was coming too fast. Margaret was put on the phone to a doctor while my dad delivered the baby, with instructions and updates shouted and relayed up and down the corridor as mobiles and cordless phones hadn't been invented yet. Eventually our baby brother Michael William Jefferys was born, my dad was awarded a Midwife beer mug and now 13 years separated the youngest from oldest with an 8 year gap between Michael and myself, now the second youngest.

It was soon after this that I went off to boarding school at St Michael's in Southern Rhodesia while my brother went up a school to Hartman House. It was a Catholic boarding school, quite strict, and along with this came not only daily mass but the beginning of my studying of the bible. My routine was busy but I enjoyed this period of my life, which must be left for another time and place. We rose at 5 am, had a communal shower and then attended mass at 6 am, breakfast at 7:30 am, school 8-3, sport 3:30 to 6 pm, shower and dinner at 6:30 pm, homework until 9:00 pm and lights out 9:30. Weekends had their own routine. No morning Mass on Saturdays but confession and penance, at least 1 decade of the rosary if I had been a good boy. Interschool or House sports from 9 am to about 3 pm including a picnic lunch, 4 to 7 pm homework with letters to and from family and friends, then dinner and lights out at 10 pm.

Sundays always had an extra-long Mass, but other than that we were generally allowed to do as we pleased, within the set boundaries and visiting hours in the afternoon. Once a month we were allowed out with family or pre-arranged friends for the day. However, as my family and friends were over a thousand miles away, I often ended up alone at the school with half a dozen other kids in the same situation. This sometimes led to a bit of mischief. The birch was a popular punishment, and, as far as punishments went, my one of preference. It was over quickly and it also brought respect from my peers, I still do not understand why, but there you go.

One Sunday when the school was deserted except 4 of us, the nuns and priests cloistered away, other than Sister Philomena, who was on duty but busy in her room. The four of us wandered around the school, played a bit of football, French cricket, going for the posts with a rugby ball until we really didn't feel like doing anything. Walking around the school grounds and bored to death we happened upon the orchard... it had always been there, but out of bounds. The fruit looked so tempting that our desires got the better of us and we spent the next few hours gorging ourselves and then engaged in a fruit food fight. That evening the four of us were as sick as could be. The next day the game was up and for the first time I could remember we were not punished. The Head explained that the school made its own jam from the orchard and as there was no fruit left the whole school would have to go without and at the next school meal everyone was informed. Even without a punishment the consequences were dire!

St Michael's also ignited the fever for sports in me. I was in the swimming team for crawl and backstroke as well as the relay race. I was in the cricket and football teams and won various medals and certificates in athletics. My parents made it to one of the inter-school galas when I was swimming for the school and I got first place in backstroke and second in crawl and it was one of the proudest moments of my life! All in all this was a period of joy. School was great, as were the holidays when I would go back to my family with the term's gossip and news.

Around this time my parents decided that they were not compatible. Frequent arguments erupted, drinking increased and one horrific day while at the Police Club my parents informed us that they were getting a divorce. The shock did not stop there as our parents then asked us collectively and then individually who we would choose to live with. Over the next few months this question became a repetitive factor in our lives with our parents pulling us in two directions and a constant discussion between us kids.

For the first time in my life politics influenced my life. Zambia gained its independence, we watched an amazing ceremony of the NRP and the Army finishing off with an amazing retention of The Last Post echoing through the African bush while the British flag was lowered for the last time followed by fireworks - still the most impressive I have seen over 50 years later!

The new President of Zambia did not like opposition and a kill order was put out on my grandfather and so my grandparents had moved to Salisbury, where we spent happy holidays and Christmases with cousins, uncles and aunts. We were a close family and although we lived all over Rhodesia and South Africa we always came together for Christmas and many a Sunday lunch. One particular Sunday my Dad had decided it was time for Michael, who was only about six months old, to learn to swim. All the adults apart from my aunt Rosaria, were on the porch overlooking the garden and swimming pool and as usual all the kids were either in the pool playing games or sunbathing next to it. My dad ambles up to the pool holding Michael in his arms and starts talking to Patrick who then nods to my dad who then throws Michael into the pool! The silence was deafening. The disbelief at this was soon overcome as all hell broke loose. My mother and grandmother rushed down the stairs towards the pool, my granddad stood up to observe the commotion, my aunts and uncles looked totally stunned and all us kids just stared at Michael swimming towards Patrick who picked him up and took him back to the side of the pool and handed him back to my dad. Michael has not stopped swimming ever since! Needless to say my dad was not in anyone's good books for a while. It was this same holiday that my grandfather informed us he was joining the Government of Ian Douglas Smith, who had just declared UDI in November 1965, and would be the Rhodesian Ambassador in South Africa.

A short time later the kill order on my grandparents extended to his family so we had to leave as quickly as possible. The up side of this was that it once again united the family. This exodus happened rather quickly. I was back at school after the holidays asleep in the dorm when the lights come on and in walks Sister Assumpta with my dad. I get hustled out of bed, dressed and whipped off in the car to pick up my brother at Hartman House and off to the airport and put on the midnight flight to Pretoria, my brother Patrick arguing all the way as to why we had to leave Rhodesia. Arriving at Jan Smuts Airport in the middle of the night we were met by my mum and granddad. Upon leaving the airport we came across elephants wandering along the road and I wondered where the hell we were! Back at my grandparents' house, or the Ambassador's Residence, brothers and sisters were reunited.

# Chapter 2

The change from Lusaka to Pretoria was massive. Lusaka was a small place, albeit the biggest I had known, Salisbury didn't count as all I ever saw was school, my grandparents' house and a shopping centre called Highlands which I thought was the centre of town. But Pretoria, the Administrative Capital of South Africa, half an hour car ride into town, sky scrapers, massive parks, suburbs for the super-rich, Church Square and with the Voortrekker monument looking over the city. I was bedazzled! However all the glitz and glamour was distracting and I started to fail at school. I started to attend Christian Brothers College, once again a strict Catholic school. The school was great, massive area for field sports, cricket, rugby, tennis, hockey etc. The school was from year one until matric and was divided into three sections: the school with its classrooms and a field used for any and all sports and school activities: across the road behind the school classrooms were the boarding houses; and adjacent to the classrooms across another road were the sports areas and the Brothers' College. All in all a BIG school. Here I started Standard 3, got onto the cricket team, started rugby although football was my preference and followed Patrick's footsteps in trying to learn the bagpipes, which I failed at miserably, never getting off the chanter!

This is the only school that I ever had a physical fight in, but not of my choosing. I made a friend, a guy called Van der Merwe. Both our parents were continually late in picking us up by at least an hour every day. So we would play football on the rugby fields near where our parents picked us up and we slowly got to know each other that way. However Van der Merwe was cheeky to the seniors and they wanted to teach him a lesson. So they approached the Brothers informing them that we wanted a fight. At CBC this was acceptable and arranged as a proper boxing fight, ring, ref, rounds, the whole lot. Once this was arranged my brother and his mate came to inform us that the fight was arranged. Both Van der Merwe and myself objected, but seniors always got their way. The few days before the big fight my brother and his mates trained me and in the evenings Van Der Merwe and I tried to find a way out. However being 'chicken' was worse than losing the fight, so eventually we agreed to it.

The big day came and after lunch the ring was set up, ref arrived, informed us of the rules, crowds of seniors gathered all supporting me as they all wanted to see the cheeky bastard Van Der Merwe go down. The fight lasted only a few seconds. Van Der Merwe came in hard and fast and soon I was against the ropes and down on the floor! I couldn't believe it and neither could the seniors who rapidly drifted away really disappointed with my performance! That evening while Van Der Merwe and I were waiting for our parents we discussed the fight and he apologized and informed me that his father had been a boxer and now a promoter and that he had been boxing since he was five!!

My dad started working at ISCOR, the largest iron and steel company in the region. We moved out of my grandparents' house and moved to the other side of town, Rietondale. It was a nice house. Good size garden, swimming pool, double story with lower story split level, fish pond that went under the stairs and outside next to the front door, five bedrooms, Patrick and I were in the pool house with our en-suite. A terrace next to my parents' bedroom made a great diving board into the pool below. Out back were the servants' quarters and a great natural rock garden that was fascinating for its lizard and insect life. Overall a nice place to live.

With this move came a change of schools. I was moved to Waterkloof Junior School where I spent the last two years of my primary education. The last days of the holidays were a nightmare for me. I had always been to male-only schools since leaving the convent and Waterkloof was co-ed. The only girls I had in my life up to now were family and I spent many nights without sleep imagining the evils of girls and the male minions who belonged to them. The days leading up to my first day were terrifying!! When the day arrived I reluctantly went off to school. I was really worried and begged my parents not to send me there, all to no avail. Arriving at the school I refused to get out of the car and my dad lost it. Shouting at me to get out of the car and telling me he should have dressed me as a girl as that was how I was behaving. With tears in my eyes I got out of the car found my way to the hall for assembly and on to my classroom, where doom awaited me as I entered a room half full of girls! As an 11 year old I learnt quickly that girls were not so bad if you stayed away from them and I soon settled in. However there was one girl in the class who scared me no end. She was the daughter of one of the USA Embassy personal and she wore winklepickers with which she threatened to kick any boy in the balls if we displeased her and boy was she true to her word! I kept well away from her!

Once again I got involved in sports and expanded my skills to include tennis and I was quickly on four teams, cricket, tennis, swimming and football. Break times were spent playing marbles, stingers or red rover, all of which I became a master of and hence eased my position at the school. Even though I have always been a shy, quiet person I got on with others and never had any problems; even the girls started to greet me! I soon joined the Scholar Patrol squad at school and shortly thereafter became a Corporal and was designating duties. The down side of all this was that my studies were neglected. I had a full day rising early to catch the 6 am bus into Pretoria city and then another bus from Church Square to school. All in all the bus ride including changeover took an hour and forty minutes. The school day was long, starting at 8 am and finishing sports etc. at 5 pm and then the ride home. The up side was that Malvern House, my grandparents' residence, was only about a five minute walk from the school and I had lunch everyday with my gran and great aunt (more on her later).

I soon fell behind on my academic work and consequently failed the term. Without my knowledge my parents and grandparents agreed that I should spend term time with them and I ended up sleeping in a little bedroom annexed to my grandparents' bedroom. This started a new study routine for me. My grandfather was scary! He never gave me reason to be scared of him and I wasn`t scared of him as such, just in awe and afraid to disappoint him, which I'm sure I did often. He was a good man and I had grown up close to him but the most aggressive thing I ever witnessed was after an obviously long and tiring day and we were all in the family lounge and five or six kids being noisy and my granddad used a slightly lower gruff tone and higher volume to say "SHUT UP, all of you, go and play in the Bamboo lounge", and off we scuttled.

Malvern house was big and beautiful, I loved it there. Other than the two lounges, there was a third one, the Red Lounge, where Embassy events took place, adjoining the Bamboo Lounge and nice double glass doors into the garden. The dining room had a massive dining table with places for 24 people, overlooked by a massive portrait of Admiral Sir Ernest Gaunt, our Great granddad. Another forbidden area in the house, but nevertheless acted as a magnet, was the stand that held the swords belonging to our great-grandfather and the chest full of his medals. No warnings or punishments could keep me away from the wonderful daydreaming that these invoked!

My granddad realized that I was not as stupid as my school reports were claiming and turned to bribery at the end of year exams, he offered R5.00, a lot of money for a kid in those days, for each exam I passed with over 75%, needless to say I passed them all except Afrikaans!

A character trait I inherited from my granddad was the love of gadgetry! Today you may wonder what gadgets were available in the '60's. Well, the one that I really liked was my grandfather's radio, about the size of a matchbox. However it was totally forbidden for us grandkids to touch it and even looking at it one felt guilty. Well, one day my curiosity overcame me and I snuck into my grandparent's bedroom and located it on the chest of drawers and was admiring it when in walked my granddad. As quick as I could be, it was in my pocket, and I could replace it as soon as grandpa left. However this was not to be. It was a Friday and I was to be taken back to our house by the Embassy Driver, Goodall. Without a chance to replace the radio I was ushered out to the car and off home. I started praying that grandpa would not notice its absence before Sunday when I returned to Malvern House with the family for Sunday roast. Before our night routine I changed into my pyjamas and went to say goodnight to my dad, who noticed I was not my normal self. To my utter dismay he discovered the radio. Instead of getting into his normal punishment mode he removed the radio and sent me to bed. A really difficult night for me and I was up early nervously prowling around my parents' bedroom. This only added to my anxiety as on Saturdays my dad never rose before 11 or 12. Once he was ready after his morning ablutions he summoned me into the study gave me a lecture which seemed to last hours and then had 'six of the best'. I never touched anything of my grandparents again!!

An uncle, Hugh, had moved to South Africa before us and was living at Halfway House, about half way between Pretoria and Johannesburg. He was married to Shelagh and at that stage had only given us two cousins, Susan and Judith. We often spent weekends together and occasionally Patrick and Margaret would babysit us all while the adults went out. On one of these occasions Judith and Susan were in bed and we siblings were chatting, sleeping, etc. downstairs while waiting for the folks to return. Suddenly an earth shattering scream from upstairs interrupted our peace and quiet. Patrick and Margaret hurried upstairs while Kathleen and I ambled along and hung around the bottom of the stairs. Susan, Patrick and Margaret were trying to console Judith who was cowering from a pink elephant in her room! Patrick, all business like was trying to inform Judith that it did not exist. Margaret was trying to calm Judith down, but she was adamant. The scene that developed was Patrick and Margaret pushing this imaginary pink elephant down the stairs and out the front door. Kathleen and I were in stitches which didn't really help, but eventually the elephant was ejected, Judith returned to bed and peace was restored. One of the best things Hugh did for me was to get me into Formula 1 as a spectator sport. Hugh was a Petroleum Engineer working for Esso and at that time the petrol being used at the South African Grand Prix. So off we would go to watch the Grand Prix, grandstand seats and pit passes, it was great and started my lifelong love of Formula 1 racing!

Soon Primary School came to an end and I was sent to Pretoria Boys High School to join my brother who was in Standard 9, his second last year. For some reason I did not work at school. I never did my homework, I bunked regularly but I had fun. I enjoyed the sports and was still playing cricket, swimming and tennis. It was during Std 6 that I got my Bronze Medal in Life Saving, my only real achievement that year. A few other significant things happened, both at school and at home. My best friend Daryl lived down the road from us and so we would ride our bikes to and from school together. His older brother Brian, was a friend of Patricks', and they came from a family of five strong boys brought up by their mother, I never found out what happened to the father. One morning on our ride to school Daryl was really quiet. Eventually we stopped by the side of the road and he told me Brian was in hospital, he had had a car accident over the weekend. Brian had a Mini and with one of his friends and their girlfriends they had gone out, as teenagers do, looking for something to do on a Saturday night. He was speeding and took a corner to quickly and rolled the car down a five metre embankment. Brian was in hospital and the only survivor of the accident. Over the following weeks Daryl withdrew into himself, he started missing school, would not answer his door and his mother informed me that he didn't want to see anyone. After about a month or so Daryl started to become himself again, but I had learnt my first lesson in tragedy, even though not directly related to me, I witnessed it second hand. School was fine, I still was not working and failing all my subjects except Woodwork and English, which I suppose, I was just good at because I did not put any effort into those classes either. My home and social were great, after all I had no homework or study to do, just have fun! I had a friend, Cliff, a bit of a naughty boy and his dad did research on snakes, one of my phobias at that time of my life. Anyway one day he brought a Cobra to school, he milked it just before classes started and put it into the teacher's desk. The teacher was our music teacher and a little man with a high voice, effeminate, just the right type for annoying. He could not discipline a class and would run off to the headmaster for any little infraction. He hated Cliff with a vengeance and hence this was Cliff's revenge. The teacher opened his desk and out popped this swaying cobra's head, the teacher jumped up and ran screaming out of the classroom. Cliff jumped up, grabbed the snake put it back in his container, rushed outside and hid it on the kopje behind the school to return just in time before the headmaster, Father Abernethy, arrived with the music teacher. After the usual interrogation whereby no one in the class mentioned anything about anybody, the standard reply being, "I was looking for my books and didn't see anything until Mr Mathews screamed and ran out of the class. I had no idea why." The whole class got 2 weeks detention, but no one said anything and we got another music teacher.

On the home front, we had just moved house to New Muckleneuk and met various neighbours, George, Mathew and Neil were my brother's and sisters' friends, while I spent most of my time with Daryl. Margaret, to my knowledge had her first boyfriend Neil, a bit younger than her, but so what, it gave me hope for some of the older girls. In the meantime Patrick had a crush on one of George's friends while George had a crush on Margaret. George and Patrick were found often to be negotiating and planning a swop, George's friend for Margaret. Needless to say Margaret was not too impressed when she found out what was happening but she started to like George anyway. Around this time I learnt the hardest lesson of my life up to that time. My dad used to send me up to the corner shop regularly for basics, milk, bread, cigarettes etc and I had, and still have, a craving for biltong. The best meat in the world!! On one occasion I decided to pocket a packet and returned home to devour it with relish! The next day when I returned home after school there was a big notice stuck on my bedroom door. My bedroom was off the lounge so anyone coming into the house could see the note which read, 'I AM A THIEF.' This mortified me. I was embarrassed and angry. I was also punished with the birch and lines. Not the repetitive kind but 200 lines chosen at random from the encyclopaedia, the first subject on the page was Michelangelo. So I wrote my 200 lines and gave them to my dad. Who read it, took the encyclopaedia away and my lines and told me to précis it in 150 words. However the punishments weren't the problem, the note on the door was. It stayed there for a week and all the friends, friends of brothers, sisters, and parents as well as relatives all became aware of my ill deed. I had well and truly learnt my lesson.

Soon enough my first year at Secondary School came to an end and with all the fun I had coupled with the work not done, I failed the year with a grand score of 29% , including 9% for Latin!! This is when it hit me, school work needs to be taken seriously. However I was saved the embarrassment of re-taking the year at Pretoria Boys High as we moved back to Rhodesia.

My granddad had been recalled and had moved back to Rhodesia about a year previously and so when we arrived back in Salisbury we stayed with them and then a while later got house two doors down. My granddad had been appointed the Chairman of the Board of Censors which gave us various advantages, watching films in the cinema with us as the only patrons, an introduction to Playboy and Men

Only and other girlie magazines, (by sneaking into his study after school), that were banned in Rhodesia. I started school at Oriel Boys High and my sisters went to the sister school Oriel Girls High. Patrick had elected to stay in Pretoria with my uncle Dennis, aunt Rosaria and cousins John and Robin. We did not see much of Patrick for a time after this as he had set out on his own path in life. I was put into Form 1, the equivalent of the year I had just failed in South Africa. However about a week later I was taken out of class by the Headmaster Mr McGrath and placed into Form 2. My mum had worked some magic on him! School wise that year was probably one of the best. I did my work, passed all my exams got into a few sports teams - cricket, rugby, swimming and hockey. During the year my granddad died of a heart attack at 65. It was a sad time for all of the extended family, brothers, sisters, cousins, uncles, aunts and, as I discovered, the country, as my Granddad was a well-known politician and was very popular. A chance eavesdropping on a conversation between my gran and my mum was the actual start of my interest in politics. They were discussing the fact that my grand dad had died of a "broken heart". At this time I had no idea what it meant but I kept my ears open around adults to learn more. The funereal was attended by a lot of the Rhodesian politicians, Ian Douglas Smith (who on an occasion signed my homework book when I was at Waterkloof) and Clifford Dupont among them.

Things changed after my granddad's death. My uncle Robert and his family of four kids had recently been moved to New Serum Air Force Base in Salisbury and he moved into the house my granddad had bought just before he died with my gran and great aunt moving into a granny flat attached. The Sunday family get togethers became less frequent and my parents were drinking more and more, however I continued to get on with my grandmother and visited her regularly. She soon moved into the Avenues in Salisbury where it was easier to visit as I often rode my bicycle into town, a good 14km ride! During this time my schoolwork was not great but I was managing to scrape through. Sport wise I concentrated on tennis, hockey and rugby, football was not an option at High Schools in Rhodesia or South Africa, although we often played during PT, now called PE. I started to have discipline problems after Mr Macgrah was promoted and left and was replaced by Mr Trediglejo, or nickednamed Trigger Joe, ( easy to set off), for his penchant towards the cane. He and I were at total odds. I became his greatest antagonist resulting in a friend, Alan, and myself having a bet as to who could get the most cuts in one term. The term 'cuts´ refer to when the caning is below the short trousers which were our school uniform, and the cane would literally cut you, making you bleed. The 'Thank you Sir' that I left his office with would drive him insane and on the next occasion I would be beaten even harder. I did not commit any infractions of violence or verbal abuse. My cuts were for mundane things like, no garters, hair touching my ears, not attending sporting events, etc. Towards the end of the year Trigger Joe would call me out at the Monday morning assembly to go to his office after assembly where I would receive 'six of the best' as a warning for the week ahead. Needless to say I won my bet with Alan receiving approximately 350 cuts in the last term with an average of 5 a day, Alan came in at 200 with an average of just under 3 a day. However I still enjoyed my school life and although I was constantly in trouble, (even being kicked out of Maths for a whole term), I stayed in school until I finished my COP exams. (These are exams for students who have no desire or ability to do further studies). However Trigger Joe informed me that I was too stupid to do 'O' and 'A' levels but my parents insisted and so I was enrolled for another year.

About this time another tragedy struck. My best friend, Bernard, and I were going to the farm for a while during the holidays. We had a great time, shooting, capturing a vulture who needed rehabilitation, walking among the animals of the African bush, even carefully checking out a Leopard's cave. My future brother-in-law used to breed Great Danes and one night in the early hours the kennels erupted in chaos and Mike ran outside and a leopard had killed all the dogs with the exception of one, Genoit. Obviously upset, Mike grabbed his rifle and set off after the leopard. It was still dark, but soon dawn started breaking and Mike bumped into a labourer who warned him that a leopard had backtracked and was waiting to ambush him. He decided to give up the chase. During the work day his job took him close to where he believed the leopard had its den and decided on a detour and he found the den in a cave on a kopje. There he discovered a female leopard feeding three young cubs. He was glad that he had not pursued it earlier that day. This also educated me into the cunning of leopards and the danger they can bring. This was the same den Bernard and I were visiting but with binoculars and at a safe distance. One day while out hunting the three of us in a line on a path, me being at the back, Bernard in front of me suddenly jumped back into me as Mike ducked and jumped forward. A boomslang was right in our path twirled around a branch a just the right height for somebody walking to brush the ‘branch’ out of the way! The bite of a boomslang can kill a person by attacking the blood system and then die from internal organ failure and internal bleeding. Not a happy death but anti venom for them is easily obtained and most farmers in Rhodesia would have it on hand. But what a heart stopping moment!!

This holiday Mike also introduced me to his double barrelled shotgun, one given to him by his father. He loaded both barrels, and gave me the shotgun with both him and Bernard standing well behind and either side of me, and told me to shoot at a tree. I lifted the weapon aimed, touched the trigger and BOOM!! Both barrels discharged, the shotgun kick slamming into my shoulder sending me flying 10 feet back. When I got up both Mike and Bernard were in stitches, and Mike informs me, ‘sorry I forgot to warn you about the hair trigger’. Bernard declined his shotgun lesson and we returned home, me with a throbbing shoulder and sore bum!

The holiday came to an end all too soon when my sister Margaret came out to the farm for a few days and then took us back to Salisbury. Soon after this Bernard fell ill and I stood by helplessly as my best friend withered away to the ravages of leukaemia and died within a year.

This was one of the worst years of my school life as Bernard and I were really close. We spent weekends at each other’s houses, were a great mini soccer team, (table football to the Brits), played a lot of pinball together, started puberty together and for a large part of that last year of his life I would visit him two or three times a week and watch him wither away. At one stage it got too much for me and I stopped visiting and started hanging out with other friends. Guilt soon set in and I visited again and then watched him until he died.

The holidays over and I was sent back to school, I had just turned 16 and if I didn't go to school I would be conscripted. Old enough to die for my country but too young to drink. Well I bunked school for the first week until Trigger Joe asked my parents if I was returning to school, and thus they found out that I was bunking. Luckily my dad was away working in Botswana investigating the accounts of Barlows Rand to find where money had been 'leaking'.

Anyway after telling my mum about the misdeeds of myself and Trigger Joe, who had said that I was too stupid to go further in my education, we compromised and I went to a college in town, Commercial Careers College, which did various vocations as well as 'O' and 'A' levels.

CCC, as it was known, had good teachers but the onus was on the individual to work. However along with this my parents became more relaxed in home discipline, which was not always the best thing!! When it came to church I still had to go, but it was up to me where and when I went, anytime from midday Saturday and all day Sunday. This left me free to discover the different Catholic churches in Salisbury. I attended the various Saturday afternoon and Sunday morning services, all much the same and to be quite honest quite boring to a 16 year old teenager. I started skipping and lying to my parents and visiting mates instead. One Sunday I was in town with a mate while I was supposed to be at mass and who do I bump into, yes that is right, my parents. As well as one of the usual punishments my dad, who was in Salisbury for the weekend took me to the Black African Mass at the Cathedral, 4 o'clock on a Sunday afternoon. I was quite angry but had no option. During the service my mind was racing, thinking about what was going to happen, how do I get out of here with nobody seeing, the only white people in a cathedral full of blacks? Due to the politics of the time this mass was not only a punishment but an embarrassment to a white teenager and was packed to overflowing with people I had been brought up to believe they were dirty and inferior! I hated my parents at this moment and vowed to go to war with them. This was not to be. The Mass was held in Shona, which at that time I barely understood, and was a sung Mass. The whole congregation was pouring their soul into these beautiful songs praising The Lord and having a wonderful time doing so. The African Church Choir with the richness of various tones interspersed with the ululations, call and response, rhythmic clapping and the congregation singing out in joy, the whole church was alive! This was not the TV Baptist type singing or show singing but the hymns we sing every day (I could recognise some of the music) coming from a thousand souls sung by a Church full of people praising The Lord in the way they knew best.

This experience opened my eyes politically and gave me a whole new take on religion. It wasn't just solemn ritual, well versed passages and thumbed pages of a larger text. Religion was alive and over the next ten years into early adulthood my journey had been set. My age of rebellion was beginning.

I made friends with blacks, Indians and coloureds and as I started my last few years at college and due the fact that we literally had nowhere to go due to the segregation laws, we were spending more and more time on the streets of Salisbury and pinball alley. This made me an easy target for the Police upholding the 'Morality' laws. The first encounter, which had a major effect on me, happened when I was 16. After College I was going to meet some friends, Sam, an Indian and Ish, a coloured (mixed race), in the centre of Salisbury at the pinball alley. After chatting a while a white van drew up and 3 C.I.D inspectors got out, separated us and took us one at a time into the back of the van. I was called in first questioned about drugs, theft, inter racial sex etc. After what seemed ages, I was given a thorough strip search, all clothes removed and gloved hands probing in private areas. I was then released into a uniformed Policeman's custody who drove me home and chatted to my mum for over an hour while I cowered in my bedroom. I was forbidden from ever socialising with those agitators, delinquents, drug addicts etc. Sam and Ish were just kids my own age that I happened to get on with, but were the wrong colour. Later in the week I asked Ish where Sam was and what happened. Both of them were beaten, evidence still remained on Ish and Sam was in hospital. I was furious and after meeting a few other black and Indian kids I learnt that this was a normal every day event for them. So my rebellion spirit was fed. Just a side note here, I was not really a rebel, I never took up violence in any way, I was just objecting to the injustice of my society in the way I could.

I started questioning everything, the police had lied to me, my parents were brainwashed by the Rhodesian propaganda machine – which I still believe to be one of the best ever. The whole Rhodesian system was geared to the propaganda of school, army, work, army, life, army. The communists had to be beaten - at all costs. My private rebellion took me to places that conformity couldn't. I snuck into the black townships, attended black rallies, went and saw black bands with traditional African music. I loved the people, the atmosphere and their honesty, even in their hardships. Then life in the white community, my safe haven was falling apart. Home, church, school and white friends, were full of lies, hatred and ignorance generated by an impossible belief of 'a thousand years of white rule in Rhodesia'. This lead me to examine the other lies that this society propagated, banned films, like Woodstock, banned music, like the Rolling Stones and then even drugs. I no longer believed anything I was told. I wanted out. Fortunately before this could happen I had to finish 'A' Level otherwise I would have been conscripted immediately. During my college years, I hung out with a 'gang' of white students most of whom knew nothing of my relationships outside of the white community (with the exception of Charlie who introduced me to Sam and Ish) and were not aware of my friendship with other races and slowly they started to hang out at parties that were held at one or another of our houses when our parents were away. One weekend my mother was away with my little brother visiting my dad in Botswana and my other siblings had left home already, so the house was mine and like a good little member of the 'gang' we had a party at my house, all weekend! This party revealed to me the impuissance of this type of relationship as these are not really friends but acquaintances who are feeding their narcissistic side. During the weekend some of my mum's jewellery went missing which my mum discovered shortly after her return from Botswana. The police were called in and the whole weekend party came out. I was reluctant to give the police names of who came over during the weekend, but they immediately assumed it was Ish or Sam, I knew it wasn't. Loyalty to a group of people is very tricky ground and when one of my friends started buying me records of my favourite groups I grew suspicious, but said nothing. The police had me in the police station every day after college questioning me, but I told them nothing sticking to my story of ignorance. The group of friends carried on as if nothing happened. After three weeks of spending my afternoons at the police station, I confessed but the police didn't believe me. Unbeknown to me they had recovered the jewellery from a high street jeweller and had a description of who sold it to them. By the description I knew it could be one of two people, but one of them wore glasses and it couldn't be him. I still did not rat out my friend, the one who had been buying me records. As I was still attending the police station every afternoon, being picked up from college I couldn't speak to anyone other than a few of the group who were in my classes. A short time later, the one guy from the description who was not the culprit was leaving for the UK forever. I was tired of the situation, I was in bad books with my family, some of my friends heard that I had confessed and believed it and so my friendships started to fracture, so I blamed it on Stephen who had left for the UK, never to return. The police interviewed his parents and the whole episode came to an end. But it didn't. It came back to bite me in the bum. Stephen didn't like England and returned a week later to be arrested for theft. At this stage I was forced to acknowledge the truth and turned in the culprit. Every single one of that group of friends turned on me. The excuse that Stephen was not to return to Rhodesia and that I protected one of our group all the time was of no consequence. Some blamed me for throwing the blame on Stephen and some for ratting out Bullet, (a nickname due to the shape of his head), the culprit. No one understood or cared that I did my best to protect Bullet. I was an outcast and after a few days I realized that I had made a mistake right from the beginning and should have had the truth out immediately. The only friends who stuck by me were Sam and Ish. I had learnt my lesson and I also learnt to choose my friends carefully.

However High School and College were great times for me, apart from a few incidences. I hitch hiked all over Rhodesia, rediscovering the beauty of Africa as a teenager, Kariba, Mana Pools and the Zambezi River, Chipinga, Umtali, Victoria falls, Wankie and the list goes on. However my favourite place was my future brother-in-law's farm. It was a large farm, 300,000 acres with large cultivated areas, cattle and lots of wildlife. We would go hunting often, shooting for food and not for fun or trophies. The game we shot was mainly Guinea fowl, pheasant and various types of buck, springbok, sable, duiker etc. This was plucked or skinned, some taken to make biltong, some put in the freezer for us and the rest given to the farm labourers. Mike, was always the first up at the crack of dawn and we would join him when he returned for breakfast at around 8am, after his early morning farm duties and then spend the day out with him and Genoa, the Great Dane. Genoa was also a good hunter, not normal for this breed but he had been going out with Mike since he was a puppy and loved it. He loved it so much that it nearly caused him serious injury on one hunt. Mike was out and got a sable in his sites but the sable got spooked as he fired and hence missed his shot. Genoa did not like this and chased the sable, jumped onto its back and slid round and down its neck just as the sable thrust his head back, his horns just missing Genoa while a perturbed Mike managed to bring the sable down with a second shot. For those of you who are not aware of what type of antelope a sable is, it's about 1.5 metres high at the shoulder, 2.5 metres long weighs about 220 kilos and has arched horns up to 1.6 metres long. Quite a feat for a single Great Dane!!

Baboons and bush pigs are the scourge of farmers. They get into the mealie fields and destroy acres of maize within minutes, baboons at any time and the bush pigs usually at night. The baboons were such a scourge that the government offered a reward of 50 cents per tail. This helped supplement pocket money for many teenagers. However shooting bush pig is another matter. They are reasonably small, about a large dog size, built like a tank and are fearless especially when wounded. One night the alarm went out, bush pigs in the fields. Grabbing the rifles and rushing out to the fields we heard them soon enough and the spotlights picked them out. When they see you, they charge. This was the case for Peter, Mike's younger brother who only had a 22 rifle. Although he was a great shot and hit the Bush pig straight in the forehead the bullet just bounced off and it carried on its charge. Fortunately Mike was in the next row and witnessed what was happening and brought the charging bush pig down a couple of metres from his brother!

The farm was great and I loved being out there but Rhodesia as a whole is a beautiful country and Kariba is a favourite for all inhabitants of the country. We would hitch hike up there for weekends but borrowing a parent's car was the best. We usually ended up camping on a beach while spending our days in boats, canoes or just wandering around. Wild life was plentiful and care had to be taken when camping. One evening we returned to the tents to find we had been raided by baboons, clothes and tinned food lay scattered all around while only the remnants of fresh food was to be found. Campfires are a wonderful thing but unfortunately they attract snakes that like to warm themselves before moving on, often into our sleeping bags, so you needed to check carefully before slipping into them for the night.

One potential visit to the farm ended up with my first experience of a prison cell. Mike had come into town to visit my sister not long after they had gotten engaged and was returning to the farm with Peter and myself on Sunday evening. Mike's mum lived in the 'Lanes' of Salisbury, which was basically flat land and a few of the old houses. We were leaving from there to go to the farm so at about 9pm we left Mrs Breen's flat but once outside Mike said Pete and I must wait there while he takes Margaret home. So there were the two of us sitting in the well-lit lanes with a 22 hunting rifle. We sat on the kerb and talked, we walked up and down the street always keeping the flat in view for when Mike came back, remember no mobile phones in those days. We got bored midnight came and went, 01:00 came and went and at this stage we decided on a competition to keep us amused. We chose a spot and I shot first at the nearest lamp. One shot lamp out. Pete then took out the second lamp, one shot, I took out the third, all from the same spot. The fourth proved a bit elusive and after a few more shots each the police arrived and down to Salisbury Central Police Station we went. Pete phoned his mum who picked him up. I phoned my dad who told the police to throw me in the cells for the night and he would pick me up in the morning. So I spent the night in the cells with at least 20 drunken Africans a few of whom were activists and so I sat huddled in a corner scared shitless until my dad picked me up at 10:00am. I was so glad to be out of there even into the wrath of my father!

Another great place which was visited often on Sundays and public holidays was Mermaid's Pool. Situated about 35km from Salisbury, the last four or five a terrible dirt road which led you to a small river flowing gently over a beautiful rock with the smooth gradient of a slide and about 200 metres long ending in a pool about 300 metres round. The river was constantly flowing so bilharzia and other water borne diseases were not present. Any way most people would acquire a tractor or aeroplane tyre inner tube and start running down the rock holding the tyre then dive onto it slide down the rock, hit the water at the bottom and skim across to the other side. This is not as easy as it sounds. First running down gently flowing rock surface is dangerous and kept the medics on duty busy, next hitting the water with the tyre held at the right angle is an acquired skill causing many people to enter the water at the wrong angle and get thrown in the air like a rag doll. Those not brave enough to attempt this sport would start about half way down and stick to the water's edge, although this had an obstacle of its own in the form of a 5 to 7 cm high by about 1 metre bump, called Humphreys bump, which if you hit, it give you a real pain in the bum and sent you flying into the water! The other main attraction was one of the highest foofie slides I have ever seen. If you drop too late you end up in the rocks, if you drop too early you end up in the rocks but as it is about 300 metres across and the rocks are only protruding a few metres each end it is only dangerous for those who are too scared to drop the 5 to 10 metres into the pool and the daredevils who wanted to drop as close as possible to the rocks.

As I said earlier High school and college were great, I had a great time, played a bit, studied a bit and got politicised a bit. On the day of my last 'A' level exam I had my backpack outside the exam room, picked it up and my mum was kind enough to give me a lift out of town and onto the road to hitch hike to Botswana to visit my dad, who, luckily was in Botswana on an assignment and the Customs officials knew him well, so I had no problem leaving the country. I felt free of the shackles of Rhodesia but a sadness accompanied it.

# Chapter 3

I spent about two weeks with my dad who was determined to send me back to Rhodesia in order to do my military service. This time was mainly one of conflict although we got on, on various things and I managed to get my driving licence. I had been driving since I was a young teenager although not much on the roads, just farms, around the neighbourhood empty plots etc. My dad was a friend of the driving examiner and arranged a test virtually immediately and for a few days he paid for an unemployed man with a driving licence, to sit in the car while I drove around. The day of the exam came and off I went. The examiner got in, started giving me directions and after about 5 minutes asked how long I had been driving and I replied about five years. He just said lets go back to the centre and he gave me my licence.

Eventually I made an agreement with my dad, one I knew I was not going to keep. Seafaring is prominent in our ancestry and so I was to stay in Cape Town with family friends who had moved there from Zambia and join the South African Navy. This got me out of Botswana. I got on an overnight train from Francistown to Gaberone, travelling 3rd class with the poor black population and not the privileged classes. I must point out that at this stage Botswana was an independent country free from the shackles of apartheid and racism hardly existed, but it was a poor country and the poor classes were mostly the blacks. My comings and goings to Botswana during my teenage years engendered a love of the country and its peoples.

Arriving in Gaborone I set out immediately for South Africa and Pretoria as my first destination and to catch up with my brother who was doing his Articles in Law. I was really worried about crossing the border into South Africa as the Immigration Department were co-operating with the Rhodesians and not allowing males within conscription age into South Africa unaccompanied. I needn't have worried I went straight through and started hitch hiking. I arrived in Pretoria later that day as it was not too far, about 350km or three hours' drive in those days. I went straight to Patrick's office as it was nearly lunch time and I phoned him and he said come and meet him. He was put out immediately when he saw me. Dirty from the road, rucksack on my back and my hair starting to grow, (from short back and sides, the Rhodesian school regulations). We hurried out to lunch where he questioned me on my future plans advising me to return to Rhodesia to complete my Military Service. This was the first of many political discussions we had which sometimes got quite heated. Patrick had stayed in South Africa after we left for Rhodesia and so had been living there since he was 13 and considered it his home, but due to his circumstances he managed to avoid conscription in South Africa and I considered these conversations a little hypocritical. Politics aside, he considered me a dirty hippy, but being family we got on quite well although he could not put me up as he was living in bachelor apartments with strict regulations about visitors and advised me to go and stay with my Aunt Rosaria and my cousins John and Robin. Rosaria is a wonderful person who led a hard life as her husband died early in their married life and she sacrificed her life for her kids before returning back to her own life. At this stage, Denis, her husband was still around but not very well and had an addiction to drugs, what drugs, Prescription drugs.( Another failing of the system). However she did not like surprises like wayward nephews pitching up on her doorstep. Patrick had not warned her and I arrived without notice. She was a Bank Manager for Standard Bank, ran her household and was a carer for Dennis and I added to her burden as I arrived with little money no work or work prospects, but I only stayed a few days before I moved into a residential hotel and found a job selling televisions door to door, on a commission only basis. This should be an easy job. The church in South Africa, The Dutch Reformed Church had enough control in the government to not allow the evils of television into our homes until the early to mid-seventies. When I started selling TV's the test programs had just started broadcasting a few hours a day while the system was set up and tested, with the launch the following year. It should have been an easy job, selling TV's to a nation that had no TV's but broadcasting starting soon. Well this is when I discovered that I was not and, despite various attempts throughout my working career, never would be a salesman. In one month I sold exactly one TV while other salesman were selling 5 -7 an evening. I gave up, but fortunately one of my brother's friends, an Afrikaner putting himself through University, had a job with a catering company, catering to weddings, barvitzmahs, engagements, company do's etc. and he managed to get me a job as a waiter on the wedding events. The tips were great but the official pay was virtually non-existent and I managed to survive.

On the social front I met 2 young newly qualified engineers on contract from the UK and I furthered my belief that the

English who come over to work or live in Africa quickly become the biggest racists of all. Without going into racism, which we can tackle later, white Africans are racist, often denying it but they also respect the boundaries of decency. Sure they didn't allow non-whites to shop in places reserved for whites, use toilets, benches, busses etc reserved for whites, but aside from political violence, crime between non-whites and whites was rare. However the uneducated class of white Africans often considered the non-whites a threat and this has resulted in crime. The Europeans who come to Africa for work on a temporary basis quickly become extreme racists. In the case of the engineers mentioned above, I met them in a Hotel bar close to where I lived. One evening a pretty black waitress walk passed our table, she looked away while the engineers started giggling. Suspecting some sort of illicit relationship between one of them and the young waitress, I asked them to spill the beans. It was a terrible story.

A few nights previously they were drinking late and the place was nearly empty. The waitress was on duty and among her duties was cleaning the toilets. The two engineers followed her in and both of them raped her. I was struck dumb and astonished. They immediately thought my reaction was because I couldn't conceive of white on black relations and started justifying the fact that she was 'just a black kaffir nanny'. I was still speechless and got up to leave and hopefully persuade the young woman to go to the police. As I approached her she cringed and backed off. I assume that after seeing me the with the other two she probably thought I was after some of the same. I left and went home utterly disgusted and the following day went to the police station. A black constable was on duty at the front desk and I started to relate the story to him, he interrupted me saying that he needed to call in a white officer. I was shown through to an office where two officers sat asked me to sit down and relate my story, no notes being taken. At the end they asked me if the woman was black or white, and upon my reply of her being black I was informed that there was 'nothing we can do'.

A few days later I embarked on the 1461 Km hike to Cape Town. Anyone who knows the Afrikaners knows them to be an extremely generous group of people, politics and religious beliefs aside, and the hike to Cape Town takes you through the heart of Afrikanerdom. My first day hiking was not that successful and I reached the Southern side of Bloemfontein on the National road going south. The sun was setting and a gorgeous yellow to pink sky was slowly turning to red then purple and dusk set in as the sun disappeared over the horizon. As darkness was setting in I was mentally preparing to spend the night in the roadside bush and looking around for a suitable spot to lay out my sleeping bag when lights appeared in the distance and approached and eventually stopped. A bakkie with a couple in it spoke in a thick Afrikaans accent asked 'Where you going?'

'Cape Town'

'Not tonight' he chuckled, 'jump in the back'. In I jumped and off we went. A few miles down the road he turned off the main road onto a dirt road that led to his farm. We jumped out of the bakkie and headed into the house, his wife showed me to a bedroom, gave me a towel showed me to the bathroom and stated 'supper in half an hour'.

After emerging clean and refreshed into the lounge, Koos introduced himself, offered me a beer and we started chatting about Rhodesia, me, his family and farm etc. After dinner we had another drink and headed to bed with a parting , 'breakfast at 7'.

I was awake at 4:30 when Koos rose and left the house to attend to farm business. Just before 7 I heard him return and I headed out to the dining room to be greeted by a proper Boer breakfast. Fresh orange juice, porridge, egg, bacon, tomato, mushrooms, boerewors, toast and finally rooibos tea. I then started my farewells and asked the way onto the road. Koos said 'don't worry hop in the bakkie and I take you to the main road'. So off I went and when he dropped me off he gave a picnic lunch prepared by his wife. This was the first of many experiences of the hospitality offered by Afrikaans strangers. Many of these encounters were in later years when I had grown my hair and was considered by many, 'a dirty hippy' and yet although the Afrikaners did not like my lifestyle they still offered their hospitality with no judgement offered. I am aware of the evils of apartheid, but I still hold the Afrikaners as one of the most hospitable people in the world and all they have ever wanted is to be left alone. This is another discussion left for another time. Two days later I arrived in Cape Town and headed to the Wheelers, (Friends from Zambia), in Rondebosh.

I had no intention of joining the Navy but the family were in contact with my parents and so I had to go through the motions, which I did and discovered that Simonstown was in a beautiful area at the end of the peninsular near a protected nature reserve and the South African Navy is a bustling community involved in protection of South African waters and apparently doing a good job. I also started looking for a job and after a couple of weeks I moved out of the Wheelers and into a boarding house on Main Road, Rondebosche. A great area of Cape Town 10 minutes' walk from the University and opposite a university residence. I got a job as a Disc Jockey in a new night club 100 metres down the road. My only qualification for the job was that I had great taste in music, not pop or disco music but good rock, blues and Jazz that went down so well at Universities in the 70's. It was quite a success and I had students there every night and often arriving in the afternoon asking if they could just sit and listen to music. I was easy going and I said yes. So the afternoons started to fill up as well. The owner was a butcher making an extra income and also a nice guy, so I was left alone most of the time.
During this time I had my first spiritual experience.

One of the things I packed in my back pack was my parents' family bible. I hadn't opened any bible since the incident with Sam and Ish and I do not know why I took the bible with me, but I had it. One night after work I picked it up, probably 2-3am and started reading, to this day I do not remember what I read only the feeling that slowly overcame me. A feeling of dread started to creep over me, I tried to stop reading but I couldn't, my hands started sweating, my heart was thumping and I was convinced that I was going to die. I couldn't stop and the more I read the more fear filled me, and yet I still could not stop reading. After turning yet another page, this was it, when I reach that section over there, referring to the next chapter on the opposite the my eyes kept jumping to, something dreadful is going to happen, I tried to stop reading, I couldn't, I was reading but not knowing what I was reading, re-reading again and again, not wanting to reach that point chosen - I don't know why, but I could not stop reading, the dread was overwhelming as I reached the chosen spot.

Suddenly a warm glow overflowed my body and my mind and I floated off into tranquillity knowing I was safe in the hands of God and fell into a deep and restful sleep. I know a lot of people will attribute this experience to a panic attack or other psychological problem, but the relief at the end with the wave of warmth and safety sweeping over me with the comfort of Christ enveloping me was a real religious experience that I will never forget.

For some reason after this event I started smoking marijuana. The students who came to the club were mostly smokers and so I started smoking with friends I knew from Rhodesia. A lot of the Rhodesians there were studying in order to avoid conscription, tertiary education was a route to either avoid conscription altogether or join afterwards as an officer, considered an easy option. All in all we had similar ideas about Rhodesia.

One day after scoring some marijuana I cleaned it at home and left mid-afternoon to have lunch and walk to work. Having the marijuana seeds in my pocket I decided to sow them along the route, some in garden beds and some in flower pots outside restaurants and other shops. A week later I noticed some of them had started to grow. Outside one restaurant, the white management not knowing what they were cultivating, thought they were beautiful plants and were tending them with care. I had to laugh to myself. Slowly I noticed that the marijuana plants were disappearing, the restaurant last of all after a visit by the police!

It was about this time I met Richie, a friend of some mates from Rhodesia. He was studying architecture and was a brilliant chess player, at the time I met him he was the top player at UCT. One day when visiting him in his room before going to dinner, (Cape Town University had a really large dining room for the students and tickets could be bought for visitors and as it was a good cheap meal I ended up there often), Richie offered to play chess with me and help me improve my game, so we started and a few minutes later Monique, a mutual friend came in and watched. Richie lost all his main players except his King and pawns. I still had all my pieces minus a few pawns and I was feeling in total control of the game. Then the tide changed and Richie gave a running commentary on the game, I lost, he had beaten me with just his pawns! Monique burst out with laughter 'both of you were obviously communicating but not a word was said'. Richie and I looked at each other in disbelief, we had been talking! Monique insisted that only intensive looks passed between us. I had been smoking marijuana but Richie neither smoked nor drank and so we could only conclude that some form of telepathic communication had taken place. I know most of you will not believe it possible, but we had no other explanation for it. I have not spoken about it since. Unfortunately my newly found preoccupation with marijuana led to my dismissal as the owner walked in one night while I was smoking a joint with friends.

While hitching from Rondebosh to Fishhoek, about 25km, I was picked up by a nurse, Clair. We started chatting and she asked if I would like to move into a house rented to students over the holidays and so I moved out of the boarding house into a student commune in Claremont and found a new job selling ballpoint pens, all in the space of two days. Selling again proved not to be my thing. However on the social side with the students was good. Aside from Clair the house had three medical students, John who I didn't meet until after the holidays, Jenny and Dante both of whom I got on well with. Dante and I had music in common. Jenny and I had Shakespeare and literature in common. So after failed days of trying to sell pens I would end up listening to music or attending a stage production in the open air stadium or at the Varsity stage. Life was good, until I started to run out of money. Cape Town, on this occasion happened to be the instrument of a young mans' dreams and desires – I lost my virginity. One evening Dante held a barbeque with friends from University and some siblings. A woman, slightly older than me showed interest in me, the flirting started and off to bed we went. I couldn't believe my luck, a beautiful young woman interested in me!! We undressed quickly and jumped onto the bed, foreplay commenced and as I entered the desire and dreams of all boys and teenagers, shoot, it was suddenly all over! How embarrassing, an unlucky start to my sexual life, I turned over and went to sleep hiding my embarrassment. The next morning when I woke up she was gone, what a relief! Getting dressed I went to the kitchen for breakfast and Dante was there, and so I asked ' What happened to Michelle?'

He replied, 'My sister is getting married today and has gone home to get ready', this made me feel sorry for the poor girl who had had a disastrous last fling!

This also coincided with the news that South Africa was picking up all the Rhodesian draft dodgers and sending them back to Rhodesia. I packed up and hitched hiked to Windhoek in South West Africa, with less than R100 in my pocket.

# Chapter 4

Once out of Cape Town the road north had little traffic and after a couple of hours I got a lift with an Afrikaans farmer to Port Nolloth, just south of the South West border. The next day was even worse, managing just about 250km to Grootplaas, not too far across the border where I spent the night in a rundown flea pit which didn't seem to have more than two or three guests a year. The next day I was on the road by 6am and was lucky enough to be picked up by a guy called Dawie, a young Afrikaaner who had driven through the night from Durban approximately 1,500km. In those days that was easily done. He was going all the way to Windhoek, another 700km, I was in luck. About half an hour later, after the small talk on a long trip had worn out, he pulled off the road and said he needed to sleep, I was welcome to wait or try my luck with other cars. Due to the lack of traffic, and what traffic there was, was likely to be local farm traffic which basically meant that lifts are going to be from farm to farm, being tiring and time consuming, so I decided to wait. A few hours later he woke up and we set off once more. Dawie was a David Bowie fan and the trip to Windhoek was blasting David Bowie from an eight track all the way, while driving in one of the best sports cars available at the time, a Mustang 390 GT. Shortly before we arrived in Windhoek he asked if I would like to travel on up to Swakopmund, for the weekend, as it was a Friday. So we carried on through Windhoek and camped on the beach. It was basically a small fishing with lovely friendly people who kept buying us drinks all night. It was a beautiful place in the desert on the Atlantic coast. The only road out went to Walvis Bay, a dead end enclave belonging to South Africa and one of the largest fisheries in this part of Africa.

Over the weekend I asked Dawie why he came to Windhoek. His reply shocked me.
"I was born on a sugar farm near Tongaat in Zululand. The workers were good people and we lived a peaceful life until the political violence of Inkatha and the ANC spread into the farmlands intimidating the local labourers. During the week things seemed peaceful but at weekends when the farm labourers would have their get-togethers with plenty of umqombothi and soon the agitators would arrive, with knobkerries, knives and broken bottles. At first it was just threats and propaganda but later turned to violence. The labourers were afraid to even go to hospital as they were controlled by the ANC, so they stayed at home and helped each other. Through this I decided to become an ambulance driver and a medic, and I got a job at Queen Nandi Hospital. We were understaffed, overcrowded and lacked funds. There were only 3 whites working at the hospital and a lot of aggression was directed at us, but little violence. One night in the previous week we were called out to a woman in labour, myself and two other black medics. When we got there the woman's waters had broken and as we were getting her into the ambulance with locals gathering around somebody shouted in Zulu, I did not understand what but the two medics turned to me and stated that they would not take the woman into the ambulance as her family were Inkatha members. I argued with them while the crowd grew restless, and then I was pushed aside and held down while the men started to rape the woman while she was giving

birth. This continued for about half an hour while cheering crowds started ululating, dancing and generally encouraging this heinous act. We finally got this woman into the ambulance and rushed her to hospital. Word had already got around and the hospital staff had been threatened that if they help this woman their families would be killed. One doctor said to me very quietly take her to the Lutheran Hospital, they have agreed to help her. The baby died and the mother is going to recover physically. This, for me, was the last straw in a long line of Zulu violence which I had watched helplessly, so I decided to move here for a fresh start.''

Sunday afternoon we returned to Windhoek, which was a small capital with about 75,000 people. I was directed to a German boarding house where I settled in for the duration of my stay. Monday I picked up a newspaper and went through the wanted ads. Applying for an interview at various institutions I obtained an interview at Barlow Rand the next day. I was interviewed for the position of Trainee Account, which I got, due to good bullshit and a father who had a reputation as a great troubleshooting accountant. The work my dad was doing in Botswana was for Barlow Rand. So my career in accountancy began and ended three months later when I moved on into Angola. Windhoek was small enough to be able to walk everywhere but hot enough to make the longer walks uncomfortable. The German boarding house was comfortable, good food, good company, clean and cheap, so the money I earned stayed mostly in my pocket. Before leaving I had my first encounter with the cholera vaccination, not as painless as it is today. There were two vaccinations about 7 days apart and were only valid for three months. The first one is like any other, a needle in the arm and off you go. The second one is the same until about an hour later when PAIN hits in massive doses! You can hardly move your arm which appears bruised and as I hadn't yet given notice at work I phoned in sick. Fortunately only a weeks' notice was required and that day I bought my air ticket to Luanda, as the borders were closed due to the bush war between the various Angolan guerrilla groups, with UNITA, on the southern border being supported by South African troops. The whole northern border with southern Angola was one of Southern Africa's hotspots, with the Caprivi Strip one of the most intense areas of these independence wars. Five countries meet at the Strip, Angola, Zambia, Rhodesia, Botswana and South West Africa. Three of them involved in Independence wars with Zambia being a refuge for the Guerrilla groups and Botswana as Africa's Switzerland.

Anyway the next day I gave in my notice and a week later I landed in a chaotic Luanda. The airport was chaotic, people bustling in urgency to leave the country. Angola gained independence in November 1975 and it was now March. In theory the war and ended and the parties were 'campaigning' for the elections. Three main parties were contesting for leadership, the FNLA, MPLA and UNITA, while the Portuguese troops were slowly withdrawing. FLNA was not considered a real contender and formed a union with UNITA and the people I spoke to seemed to think that UNITA had more followers but that the MPLA had a stronger military presence with Cuban Troops and Soviet Union supplies in Luanda and the surrounding area and would probably win the elections through corruption and intimidation.

The city was incredibly busy, all the roads were choc a bloc but it seemed to be a laid back activity, everybody was going somewhere but nobody was in a hurry. I got to my hotel settled in then headed to the beach. Luanda has a unique beach. There is a bay with the town on the one side and as you pass the old castle and come round to the other side of the bay it is just a long finger shaped beach about 6km long and 500 metres at its widest point but mostly less than half of this. The beach is lined with grass hut beach goods shops, restaurants, ice cream places and bars and a really jovial atmosphere. Within less than two minutes dozens of people had greeted me with a few of them having longer conversations. The language barrier was not much of a problem as quite a few people spoke English. I was soon in a political conversation about the upcoming elections and on the beach opinions varied considerably with all parties being represented and there seemed to be no animosity between the groups as they played football, swam, talked drank, flirted and carried on with life. Around 16:30 to 17:00 the men started disappearing and my curiosity was satisfied when I was told they were mostly UNITA and MPLA soldiers going to their barracks to get ready for the nights peacekeeping activities. A short time later gunfire could be heard coming from the castle and when I enquired as to what it was about, I was told it was political executions. About 18:00 an air raid siren sounded throughout the city and everybody started to pack up and I was informed that the curfew would start in half an hour, so I went back to the hotel. All night sporadic gunfire could be heard in all directions and through the bedroom window tracers could be seen streaming across the landscape. After little sleep that night I headed down to the beach to the same jovial scene that had greeted me the day before. One of the guys I had had a good conversation with on the previous day was not there although he said he would be there this morning and so I asked one of his mates what time he would be here. The answer was "never, he had been killed in action last night." This really struck me hard. Such a jovial and friendly country being torn apart by war and yet the death all around didn't seem to have any effect on them. This was really troubling and I had difficulty trying to reconcile this attitude in my head.

The next few days I started to explore the city and found the people beautiful in spite of the war, its presence and consequences all around. Road blocks everywhere, one with Portuguese troops, later with MPLA, and UNITA further along down the road. After a few days I was enjoying the city and discovered a nightlife that began with the start of the curfew and ended with the end of the curfew. The few places I went to also had a room of beds, for an extra charge. The night clubs were full of life, a combination of live and recorded music with local music mixed in with western rock and Portuguese heavy metal, alcohol and marijuana abound and everybody dancing, talking and drinking. When the siren went off bleary eyed and staggering patrons made their way home, work or where ever they needed to be. After about ten days I started thinking about moving on. The road north was in armed conflict and I was strongly advised to forget about that route as Northern Angola was in the state of full on guerrilla warfare. Once out of Angola, getting to Europe would be clear of major conflict areas, so I made up my mind to fly to Libreville in Gabon and proceed overland from there. Nowadays it would be a crazy trip with various countries have military problems and a callous attitude to human life but in the mid-seventies the 'wave of independence' had been completed in this part of Africa, obtaining independence in the late fifties and early sixties. However I was ignorant of the politics and just wanted to travel through Africa and into Europe with England as my final destination.

I bought my ticket and three days later at midmorning I was on my way down the hill and loaded with my rucksack to the airport bus pick up point when a guy approaching suddenly crouched down in front of me and I was pushed from the back and flat on my face and held down while my rucksack was rifled. Everything was taken, clothes, money and passport. I didn't know what to do. I wandered around trying to figure what to do and where to go, where was the Police Station, would they help? Where was the British Embassy? I decided that due to the chaos the Police would not really be helpful so I sought out the British Embassy. As I had just renewed my passport before leaving Cape Town the British Embassy representative decided that I had probably sold my passport, told me it would take a week to investigate and replace and bade me leave. The Embassy was next to the Fort and with the sound of the firing squad I forlornly trudged the streets. No money, no clothes, an empty rucksack I had no idea what to do or where to go, when I heard, 'Hey friend, what's wrong?'

Looking up I saw a hippy looking teenager about my age standing in front of me. That was how I met Walter. An Angolan of Portuguese descent I could not help but pour out my troubles. He took me home, introduced me to his mother and sister, his father was away on business. The whole family were great. They immediately let me into their family, I had a roof over my head, food and a bed until things were sorted out. My mood swung from one of dejection to one of glee and gratefulness. Walter was more than a friend, he took me around town introduced me to his mates, bought me clothes and a tent, ( this was a disaster relief tent, dropped daily by aid agencies and ended up for sale on the black market), took me out to the cinema and various tourist attractions while explaining the politics of Angola. Due to the curfew films were all matinées with a little time afterwards to get home before curfew began. Walter took me to see the film 'Shangri La', which I thoroughly enjoyed, even though it was a total flop for the film industry. I later found out that the film is from the novel 'Lost Horizon' by James Hilton.

Walter also re-introduced me to marijuana and enquired into whether I was interested in LSD. Grass was had been around me all my life but this was the first time I smoked anything so powerful. Angolan grass is pretty good although at this stage of my life I was not in a situation to know. So my days were spent in glassy eyed euphoria and the nights in a happy family environment. While waiting for my passport to come through I managed to get my ticket to

Libreville, to be confirmed when my passport came through. It took nearly two weeks and worryingly, due to lack of funds, I started wonder what would happen. When I was leaving for the airport Walter's mum gave me two things, her sister's address in Lisbon and US$100. In today's currency this does not seem much but had the buying power of $440.00 today and Africa is pretty cheap, so it could go a long way. It was a sad farewell to Walter and his family and I was sure I would see them again and so I left for Gabon. Without even leaving the airport I hopped on a flight to Yaounde, where I decided to continue overland to save money.

The next portion of my trip I saw very little of the people, the culture, cities or anything really. I just wanted to get to Europe. I set off hitch hiking to Port Harcourt in Nigeria. I had been made aware of unrest in Gabon, was assured that the problems were minimal and would not affect tourists but decided to bypass it. I set out on the about 500 mile hike, comparing the distance to similar distances in southern Africa where this type of hike could be done in a day. Boy was I wrong! The roads were terrible and in parts not more than a track. However traffic was quite plentiful and the lifts were short hops with local rural, (rich), farmers taking me a little further up the road. Four days later I arrived in Port Harcourt, after being told dozens of times I was crazy, this phrase about the only one I could understand in the rural districts I went through as few spoke English even though English and French were two official languages through colonialism and French was the dominant European language. Even then most people in the rural areas only spoke the bantu languages. Conversations were short and repeatedly reverted to hand signals and place names. One thing this trip did do for me was to reaffirm my belief that the average African is a great person. I never went off the road, mostly sleeping in my tent by the roadside.

Arriving in an English speaking country was a relief and I immediately felt at home. Two things I learnt in Port Harcourt is that the Delta is really beautiful and huge and Nigerians have a tendency to violence both physical and verbal. Beggars try to molest you and when you do not contribute they verbally abuse you, me being white usually got the full on racist fascist monologue degenerating into threats. Those that could get up usually tried to throw a punch but I moved on quickly.

I spent two nights in a flop house getting my strength back after the tiring hike before starting my hike to Lagos, a 600km drive which I was assured that even though the roads weren't great they were good enough to do in 7 ½ to 8 hours. After spending a few hours on the road only getting short hops I finally got a lift about half way to Lagos. The driver was an older gentleman who was a salesman of agricultural machinery doing his rounds of rural Nigeria which would take about 10 days. After discussing my plans of getting to the UK he told me that after an overnight stop in Abuja he was going straight to a farm north of Sokoto and I was welcome to stick with him until then. I agreed and spent the next 3 days learning about Nigerian politics. At this time a conflict was brewing, which I had been totally ignorant about and sure enough soon after I left a coup took place which placed Murtala Muhammed, who continued the Military dictatorship until he was assassinated the following year, in power. However I was informed by Adek, (the salesman), that although he was originally a Northerner, as is Murtala, he did not support Military governments and had hopes for a bright future as Nigeria could be a rich country if the corruption could be stopped. 'Typical of African States!'

Other conversation revolved around the people, countryside, his family and advice about travelling through Niger and Mali. We arrived in Sokoto and the farm Adek was going to was an hour north but he decided to drop me off at the border where we had a farewell drink and he went on to his business of selling farm implements. As we had driven the landscape turned dry and semi desert with a marked decrease in population and with the prospect of traversing the Sahara I was becoming apprehensive, especially after some of the stories Adek had told me about the slave trade route running west to east with the camel trains, however I had passed the point of no return, bit the bullet and crossed over into Niger.

Niger had recently been through a Military Coup, but the country was on the road to economic recovery even though the government would not tolerate dissent. The people were really friendly, but suspicious, it took all day to let me through the border and I was questioned for hours about the South African stamp in my passport, but in the end I think they let me through because they wanted to close up and go home and didn't want to bother with me. They gave me a ten day visa, and warned me about 'suspicious' action.

Added to the fact that conversation was in broken English with French as the main language, communication was difficult, as it was throughout Niger. My intention was to find the nearest train station and traverse the country a rapidly as possible.

Finding the station was a linguistic nightmare. My knowledge of French was non-existent and I found myself mimicking trains and their sounds which proved entertaining and hysterical to the local population. Eventually I discovered that no trains existed in Niger and so I returned to the campsite to contemplate my next move. I was advised of a truck stop café that was hauling goods from Nigeria to Mali and Senegal. After hanging around for two days I eventually got a ride to Gao in Mali with a Gambian truck driver, Suma, who also spoke English, much to my relief. He intended to drive straight through with five or six hours sleep at mid-day and early afternoon. I slept under the truck, but the burning hot sun left me with little sleep. Gao was only about 900 km but with the heat and roads more like tracks in some parts the journey took 5 days.

The Sahara is an amazing place. The southern part was savannah and reminded me of parts of southern Africa although vegetation was more bleak and the sun was killing. The local rondavels were similar to the Zulu rondavels but had animal skin roofs and some had really low entrances. A little north of Naimey we started to drive parallel to a river and glimpses of lush vegetation got thicker the further north we travelled. Subsistence farming was all along the river. The river got larger and larger, finally I was informed this was the

Niger. Yet the contrast in the landscape was really extreme, the left, (or west), was lush with trees, shrubs, animals, gulleys, farms and generally a hive of activity. The right, (or east), just disappeared into the distant horizon of sand and massive rocky kopjes with the odd sight of distant mountains. The closer we got to Gao the larger the river got.

Although I studied geography at school and new roughly where the Niger River was, I was not prepared for what I saw, it was the largest river I had ever seen! Boats navigating up and down the river with fisherman plying their trade, ferries offering transit at various places. This is not what I expected from a land locked Saharan country – a beautiful surprise.

We finally arrived in Gao and as I didn't want to spend time in a city I made my way to the north of the city where I found a cheap hostel and settled in for the day. I soon discovered that I was on the northern road close to where it branches off to Algeria and Timbuktu. Timbuktu is a place, which, as a young boy, I believed was fictional. Whenever my dad went out and any of us kids asked 'where are you going?'. 'Timbuktu' would be his reply. As a youngster I believed it to be an imaginary magical place and as I grew up I believed Timbuktu to be an old abandoned city, only now, excuse my ignorance, I knew it to be a real active city. I wanted to go. This was a decision quickly made although it flew in the face of my urgent desire to get to Europe ASAP!

Entering Timbuktu I was awestruck! It is a lot larger than I thought it would be and what strikes you immediately is that it is ancient, and its adobe, (clay and straw), buildings are absolutely beautiful. The Sankori Mosque and the University of Timbuktu are large landmarks with the University dating back to 973 AD. It was a place of learning for the whole Arabic world and the teachings of its' three great Mosques were integrated into the University study program. The mathematics taught there in the 16th century was on the second year Universities syllabi in France in 2002! Timbuktu rose to prominence due to its location near the Niger River and the trade routes of the caravans. It became a rich and important trading centre along with its scholastic appeal. Europeans used to attend University there in the 18th and 19th centuries. In its heyday it had a population of about 100,000 with 25,000 of them being students. Gold, salt, ivory and slaves were the main trading goods from about the 10th century. Timbuktu became a ´false gold rush' after the Malian Emperor made his pilgrimage to Mecca in 1325 when he lavished gold at so many places it was thought that gold was found all around Timbuktu! Alas, it was only due to the trade.

Learning the history of Timbuktu shocked me when I looked at it in the present day. Many buildings are in disrepair, empty and the population has halved, leaving ruins around the city but due to the shifting sands a lot has disappeared but the locals proudly tell their history.

Trying to find a Hotel or Hostel proved really difficult. Not many people visited this area and the hospitality industry had all but disappeared. I was eventually put onto the Malian equivalent of a bed and breakfast. It was a large adobe house with the family living downstairs and numerous rooms for the guests upstairs. The family was extremely polite and quiet, so quiet that I thought that they were out all the time! I stayed there for two nights and then headed out to resume my journey. While at dinner with the family on the night before leaving the family enquired as to where I was going, I replied to England through Algeria and Morocco to which I was told that the husband's brother- in-law was taking a lorry full of cotton to Marrakesh and I could catch a ride with him.

The terrain was fascinating, going through sand, over rock, down valleys, over hills and mountains, all the while hot and sticky. Few travellers on the road and passing fewer animals while drinking tons of water made the journey both interesting and boring as it was slow going. The villages we stopped at were only to fill up with diesel and water.

Seydou, the driver did this trip every two months and spoke English haltingly but could make himself understood and after a few days I could communicate with him quite well. We slept under the lorry during the heat of the day and travelled about 16 hours a day and 9 days later we parted ways in Fes.

As tired and dirty as I was, I carried on up to Tetuan which only took an afternoon as we were back on 'good' roads. That night I splashed out and spent the night in a cosy Hostel and went to public baths where I spent a few hours getting the grime off my body and the grit out of my orifices!

The next day, feeling fresh and really relaxed I took the ferry from Ceuta to Algeciras. I was in Europe!! I was in Spain! First time ever and I was euphoric, nearing the end of my journey. I got straight onto the road and headed to Lisbon to stay with Walters' cousins, who had been informed of my arrival. Arriving in Lisbon I went to the address given to me by Walter's mum but only the cousins were at home as the parents were away on business and the letters sent from Luanda had not arrived, the chaos of civil war. Fortunately I had a letter from Walter which I handed over and left. Before I had left the building Cristiano, Walter's cousin caught up with me and invited me to stay a few nights.

The next couple of days was spent in the local Communist Party Office as Cristiano was heavily into politics, but as I knew nothing about Portuguese politics I just went along for the ride. Apparently this was an important election as this was just after the 'Carnation Revolution', a Military Coup backed by popular support. It was an interesting few days but I soon hit the road again as my finances had become virtually zero. I needed England and a job.

Hitch hiking in Spain I got picked up by a French national going to Paris. He had already picked up another hitcher, Andy, from Yorkshire, attending Coventry Polytechnic. Alain, the Parisian, spoke very little English, my French was non – existent and Andy had a smattering, so we could actually communicate. Alain had just been released from a 3 year stretch in a Moroccan prison for drug smuggling and was anxious to get home.

We stopped off in Toulouse for about an hour while Alain left us in the car and he went off into a house to score some hash. The rest of the journey to Paris was in a smoke filled car with hash being continually smoked. Although I did not partake, I did not know what that was, as I had only had contact with marijuana, I still got high on the second-hand smoke.

Arriving in Paris was phenomenal. I was in total awe, the city was huge, the buildings old, the people gay and chatty, sidewalk cafes numerous and then we arrived at a market near the Eiffel tower. Alain found a gap between two cars and proceeded to park by nudging one forward and the other back until he had created a space big enough for his car. When we stepped out of the vehicle the two cars in front and the two cars behind had been pushed into each other with Alain's battered Citroen DS parked perfectly between them!

We said our farewells and Andy and I set off for England, after I persuaded him to visit the Eiffel Tower. He was reluctant as he was also running short on cash. However he noticed my enthusiasm and childlike awe of being in one of the major capitals of the world. So the two of us with the appearance of long haired dirty hippies, (we were not hippies), complete with rucksacks, trudged up the 670 steps to the second platform. What a view! A long green stretch of grass with paths on both sides and a grass circle in the middle of the promenade leading up to the tower itself, the river breaking the city into two as they both disappear into the distance and the ant-like people hustling around on the ground. We finally had to leave, back down the 670 steps and off to the Gare du Nord train station to get the ferry train to London.

After the African trains the Paris underground and French trains were modern but uncomfortable, however the speed made up for a lot. The ferry was quite comfortable and the crossing smooth. Then I arrived in the UK for the first time in my life and a feeling of euphoria and curiosity overcame me. Compared to the French trains, the English train was a bit old, rickety and even more uncomfortable, if possible!

# Chapter 5

During our trip Andy had asked me what my intentions were and other than getting a job I didn't know. As he had a spare room in his house he invited me to stay, to which I informed him that I had no money for rent etc. until I got work. To which I was absolutely astounded to be told not to worry the government would pay me while I looked for work! I couldn't believe it, my first day in England and I had been introduced to the dole!

The trip through London was basically the underground, I didn't see much with the exception of the bustling underground of central London, the wind being forced out the tunnel and onto the platform as a train approached, the click clack of train on the rails and the squealing of the brakes as the train ground to a halt, 'Mind the Gap' blaring out the speakers and written along the edge of the platform, the pouring out of impersonal, blinkered and hurried human forms stepping off the tube and rushing along the platform while the next group stepped into the tube to disappear into the shooting sardine can to await expulsion at their destination. To my relief the tube slowly emptied the further into the London suburbs we went. On the way to Cockfosters Station Andy pointed out the options of getting to the M1 as we were going to hike to Coventry. We could take a bus which takes about an hour and a half plus a bit of walking, change onto an over ground train which would be about the same time, or walk which was about 7.5 miles. I chose to walk, we got to the Motorway in about 2 hours.

The motorway was something else new to me. Three lanes in each direction, cars choc a bloc on the roads, services scattered along the route. Coventry was not far, about 80 miles or so and we got there in about 4 hours and two lifts. I was astounded that 80 miles could take 4 hours, back home that would be under an hour! The activity of the motorway kept me occupied while the green pastures of the English countryside fascinated me. We were dropped in central Coventry and a short walk brought us to what was to be my home for a while. A feeling of relief and disappointment overtook me. A long row of terraced houses stretched before me half of them dilapidated and starting to fall into ruin. Andy's was the first house next to the deserted row. Entering the house we went straight into a lounge with mattresses on the floor for couches, a doorway past central stairs led to a kitchen come dining room, with a back door leading to a patch of a garden with a toilet at the end. Upstairs had three mini bedrooms, the largest for Andy and Lynne, the other two for myself and another guy who was away visiting his parents. I settled into my room and soon got sociable with Lynne and Andy who showed me around the area, laundrette, corner shop, supermarket, Fish and Chippy, town centre, etc. I settled in and I realized that Coventry was going to be a seat of learning for me and what a quick and intensive course it turned out to be.

I suppose that a certain amount of Culture Shock was inevitable but I never felt shocked, only awed. Other than the physical surroundings which were both incredibly beautiful and extremely ugly, side by side, the culture was really at the end of the hippie culture, music, drugs, long hair, colourful clothes, liberal sex, burn the bra, racism, eastern philosophies and so the list goes on and on. Of course I had seen clips of the culture in the movies and a few hippies who had passed through Rhodesia, but the reality was totally unexpected. Rhodesia had had strict censorship and one of the most powerful propaganda machines of the modern age. Other than the more obvious rhetoric, hippies were communists and were to be fought as such. My street education in Coventry put me on a road whereby I became an observer of people and society.

The people I met were all warm and friendly and I had to revisit all my beliefs which I had been brought up with. This, as we now know, started with my questioning of politics in Rhodesia and was now spreading to all aspects of humanity and life.

Soon after my arrival in Coventry Andy and Lynne went off to visit their respective parents and I was left alone in the house. One night I was going to the Fish and Chippy and while eating them on a bench I noticed that the local cinema had a midnight show that evening. As it was getting towards that time I decided to go, bought my ticket and some popcorn, which to my disgust was sweet and ended up in the dustbin, and then took my seat in the cinema. The next hour and a half I sat scared out of my wits watching THE EXORCIST. The walk home was the scariest walk ever and the streets were still new to me as I had been in the UK for less than a week. The dull yellow lighting in the deserted streets was eerie, the shadows down the alleys and doorways were chilling while my active mind was in overdrive and I jumped at everything that moved. When I arrived home I could not sleep and was pacing up and down the lounge until sunrise when I went for another walk swearing that this was the first and last horror film I would ever see! I returned home and slept like a baby.

Although I had signed on and was receiving the dole I still wanted to work and spent the rest of the week looking for a job. Andy and Lynne came home at the end of the week with the other housemate, James, who was also studying at the Coventry Polytechnic and came from an upper class family, the first real 'Toff' accent I had ever heard!

I was offered some acid. I had no idea what it was and Andy explained what it was and the hallucinogenic properties and the fact that these would last for at least 8 hours with a whole day needed for the trip. At the weekend we dropped the acid. It took a while to take affect and then wham!! I was not prepared for what was happening. The wall paper started running in spirals around all the walls, the music was alive and I could get 'into it', floating around within the notes. Andy, Lynne and James were round and I could see their whole bodies, front and back at the same time. I wanted to go out for a walk. Andy said that we would be going out to watch the sunrise in a couple of hours. I sat back down and checked the time, 3am. I got back into the music and the notes floating around the room for about an hour, checked my watch again, 3.01am. I couldn't believe it!!! Checked that my watch was still working, asked Andy the time and was informed that time becomes warped during a trip. I got back into the music accompanied by hallucinations of colour and notes swirling around the room. Another hour went by and I checked my watch, it was going backwards, I thought I was travelling back in time, I took it off and threw it against the wall! I started to freak out, strange place, am I really in England? Is this whole thing just a trick of my mind? I started to pace getting really paranoid, feeling my heart beat getting faster and louder when suddenly Andy was next to me calming me down. Reassuring me that things were alright it was just the acid.

All of a sudden the sun was rising and we went for a walk to a forest just outside Coventry. My spirits rose and I started running through the forest when I came across a field of flowers, bluebells as far as the eyes could see!! I started rolling around and crawling amongst the flowers when suddenly I came across a pride of miniature lions, not more than 6 inches high! I was fascinated and didn't want to leave when the other three informed me it was time to go, we would be coming down soon. So off we went. Back at the house the boys sat down while Lynne went into the kitchen re-appearing a few minutes later with a carving knife in her hand and dripping with blood. We all jumped up shouting to each other, trying to figure out what had happened and then Lynne shouted out 'SHUT UP', which brought us all to our senses and Lynne was totally normal just asking what we wanted to eat. We had had a common hallucination. This particular hallucination has stayed with me for years along with the question of all three of us seeing the same thing. The horror of the bloody figure disappeared quickly as the phenomena of mass hallucinations occupied my mind for years.

Soon after this I heard from Walter, from Angola who had informed me that he had sent some grass to the house next door, which I had informed him was empty when writing to him on my arrival in the UK. This was totally unsolicited and I had got a job in a Hotel as a sous chef, with accommodation in Stratford-upon-Avon and so I said my goodbyes, promising to come back on days off.

Before moving on to Stratford I would like to think about what I had learnt since my arrival in the UK. Music! Rhodesia had primarily promoted pop music and although there are pop songs which I enjoyed when growing up they were not songs that had any depth to them. Some of the 'heavy' and 'underground' music got through and I enjoyed bands like Deep Purple, Yes, Emerson Lake and Palmer, Credence Clearwater Revival, Procol Harem and to a degree Rick Wakeman and Mike Oldfield, but this was just the surface of what has become, probably my biggest passion – music. Andy, unwittingly, taught me the difference between music and songs, which up until now I believed was reserved for Classical and Jazz music. The music I was introduced to varied from groups like Frank Zappa and the Mothers of Invention, Captain Beefheart, Steve Miller Band, Commander Cody, Allman Brothers, Bonzo Dog do da Band, Bob Marley, James Gang and so the list goes on and on. I learnt that music is for listening to and not singing along – that is what pop songs are for.

The freedom within the UK was also something that struck me. No government looking over your shoulder, no conscription, little censorship, (and that mostly as guidelines to protect children), I mean you could go into any news agent and buy Playboy! Along with this came the press which was, (is), ridiculous! It took me months to find a newspaper that I could read and believe, at least with a bias only and not outrageous lies. It is still a mystery why the media lies and twists the truth so much and this leads on to the negative aspect, from my point of view of the new wonderful society I was integrating into. The masses are kept in the dark about what is really going on (although all the information is available if you want it) but also kept happy through the trivialities of life. As an example during the late sixties and seventies Rhodesia was in the news on a daily basis and yet the majority of people I spoke to were not aware of where it is, what was going on and some not even aware that it was a colony of the UK! While the newspapers that were gobbled had headline news of 'Alien Abduction', 'Teenage Virgin has Twins', ' Monster Ravishes Bride' and so on – you get the idea. This is not to say that all people were not aware as a lot of people I met were at university and they were quite intelligent and aware of the situation in Rhodesia and educated me into a worldwide political awareness which was different to the view I had been brought up to believe. This contrast opened up my mind, maybe a too much in the early days, but lead to an understanding of what was happening in the world. However I came to the conclusion that the majority of the English population are sheep following selfish desires fed by the Government and big business.

The last item, for now, that I learnt was that the English Government gave you money to stay at home and do nothing. To this day I believe this is wrong. The Government is blamed by the unemployed people and some people I met had been unemployed for years and still blaming the government! I arrived in the UK with no skills, admittedly took a short break, but within a week of looking for a job I found one, and one that I had no skills in but was willing to learn. Onto my time in Stratford.

Being a Sous Chef is boring. Making the salads, desserts and other side dishes is boring, but I met some nice folks at the hotel. A couple of guys from Durham shared a room next to mine and we became friends. The barmaid also received a lot of attention from me. It was through my association with her that I learnt that I had a sympathetic ear. This barmaid, who I shall call Jane for reasons of privacy, had been living with a serial rapist Paul. They were both from Yorkshire. Jane had no idea that her boyfriend was a rapist and she had been living with him for three years, until one early morning the Police awoke her with a loud crashing of the front door and rushed into the house looking for Paul. He worked the night shift and was not at home. Jane was taken into custody and questioned for hours. The Police would not believe that she was unaware that her boyfriend was a serial rapist and accused her of being aware of his crimes. Jane was totally unaware. She worked as a barmaid from 11-2 and 5 -11. Paul was a night shift nurse at the local hospital. Jane discovered that it was a lie. He was not at the house in the evenings when Jane got home at 12 or so and would arrive back home at about 9am and they arranged to have their days off together. They had a happy and fulfilling relationship, as far as Jane was concerned. Later the same day, the time Paul usually got home from 'work', he was arrested and taken into the same Police Station as Jane. With the evidence against him, he soon realized that he was caught and asked for a lawyer. Jane was still in a state of disbelief, the Police eventually believed her and released her 24 hours later.

She went home. When the newspapers released the coverage the next day, Jane's life became a living hell. Reporters after her, friends and family deserted and ridiculed her, legally she changed name and moved to Stratford upon Avon where, at the time I met her, was still too afraid to form relationships either as lovers or friends. I was the first person she had ever told of this frightening time of her life, still having psychological scars. We became good friends and a sexual relationship was never considered. I left Stratford a few months later and never saw her again but I still think of her horrific experience and pray that she is alright and living a happy and fulfilled life. My sympathetic ear had been opened and over the years a few people took welcome advantage of it.

Stratford had a great side to it and I visited all the Shakespeare haunts and I believe some that have been added on over the centuries. The canal was a favourite spot for me and I spent many hours along its meandering banks. On one such occasion I met Alfred, an older gentleman and his wife Dorothy who were living in early semi-retirement in a caravan site along the River Avon. They were circus people, Alfred was the animal trainer while his wife had been the administrator of the circus. Due to public pressure the circus had closed its animal shows. Alfred and I had many sundown chats and was quite a clever and switched on guy. Of the animals he had and trained at the circus, only two lions remained, and this I could not believe, Alfred offered me a job ' because you are an African you must have had a lot of experience with lions. Would you like a job taking care of mine?' I was gob smacked!! An intelligent person with such ignorance! I could not believe it but it led me onto a good few amusing situations later on.

The Durham boys and I smoked a bit of hash occasionally and then one day Andy phoned to say the grass from Walter had arrived. My next day off I went to Coventry, ignorantly walked into the post office and asked for the parcel, which was given to me. On the way back to Andy's house paranoia sent in. Looking over my shoulder, ducking around corners, hiding in alleys and finally arriving at Andy's, we opened the parcel and proceeded to get thoroughly stoned on good African grass. Andy, Lynne, James could not believe and commented on how 'trippy' the grass was and I could not believe that hash was a concentrated form of tetrahydrocannabinol, (THC), the active ingredient in grass and hash. Hash, to me was a little more than a slight high and made me sleepy which is why I usually smoked it just before going to bed. In my mind there was no relation between the two drugs. When I left for home that evening I left half the grass with Andy and took half with me, the Durham boys had the same reaction as Andy when I lit up a joint.

With the summer beginning and a letter from my mum reminding me that I had been invited to visit some second cousins, the Hemerys, living near Brighton, I decided to hand in my notice. The Durham boys arranged a little party and we took a microdot of Acid. In the early hours of the morning we decided on a walk down to the canal. Almost as soon as we stepped out of the Hotel a Police car pulled up. This was my first confrontation with the Police while tripping. One of the boys told me to keep quiet and let him do the talking. OK, fine by me. While the other two were talking to the Police I noticed that the Police car starting throbbing, like a heart and actually had a heart beat! It was pulsating like crazy when one of the Policeman turned to me and when I looked at him he started pulsating just like the car and his helmet and face were merging with each heartbeat. I heard vaguely in the distance behind me 'whaaaat isss your naamm?' I turned round with a rainbow of streaming light following my gaze and managed to mumble out my name, to which the Policeman responded, 'are you drunk? Whereupon one of the Durham boys interrupted that we had had a leaving party and we were just out getting some fresh air. The Police being satisfied jumped into their pulsating car and drove off. This relieved me as I stated how glad I was that they did not arrest us as I was not sure I would be able to squeeze through the artery into the vehicle!

A few days later I arrive in Newick, Sussex, meeting some extended family, none of whom I had met before. My uncle,( actually second cousin once removed but as he was in my parents age bracket, considered an uncle), was a gracious host but like all family asked about my intentions for the future. I had no idea and found it difficult to answer the question. I was an 18 year old youngster who had run away from doing Military Service in Rhodesia, had no idea how to pursue studies or further a career and had not even thought about it.

My aunt offered to put me up for a week while I found a job. I was put in the outhouse, which was great and as it contained the 'kids lounge', I settled in and got to know most of my cousins, the younger two were considered too young. Cathy and I got to know each other quite well, while with Sue and Les we basically formed a friendship. Sue was going out with James who lived down the road as did Pete and Crimp, who were long time neighbourhood friends. This tight circle and a beautiful English summer created a wonderful time for me. At the end of the week, I hadn't bothered to look for a job, I found myself camping in a vacant lot in Haywards Heath, a 20 minute bus ride from Newick, with Cathy and Les visiting regularly and bringing me food, as my money had run out.

I quickly got a job as a kitchen hand at the local lunatic asylum. Although the work was monotonous, I really enjoyed the atmosphere. The Doctors and Nurses were snobbish and looked down on us kitchen staff, the porters and maintenance staff were friendly and this is where I met Staffy, who became a lifelong friend. Upon finding out that I was camping Staffy informed me that squatting was permissible and that evening I moved into an empty house on the main road, almost in the city centre. I took showers at work and ate in the staff restaurant, incredibly cheaply. The work was shift work so I ended at Joe's Café for one meal a day. Anyone who knows Joe's knows that the toasted sandwiches are the best to be had anywhere. You tell him what and it is cooked right in front of you.

The house I was squatting in was part of a row of condemned houses approved for demolition. At the pub on the corner I met Ron and Don, two porters at the Hospital, who were also squatting on the same road. After a couple of days of associating with them they offered me a room in their squat, which had electricity, bath kitchen, etc. and I jumped at the opportunity. Ron and Don were English upper class but refused to rely on their respective families and travelled extensively, returning to the UK in summer to work to finance their next year's travel. We had a great time! Ron taught me the guitar and even bought me one as a gift. Don had a really good sense of humour.

My days off I spent with my cousins whose parents were glad that I had obtained a job and so always welcomed me for Sunday lunch when my shifts allowed. Everybody remembers the summer of '76 but the summer of '75 was also a great summer and I enjoyed it tremendously. Ron, Don and John became a phrase used by workmates, friends and teased about in our local pub.

One early morning Ron, Don and I had the munchies and decided to walk to the train station which had the only chocolate machine in town when we got stopped by a policeman.

'Good evening and what are you three doing out at 3am'?
'Just a stroll to the train station to get some chocolate,' replied Don.
'You haven't been up to any mischief?' continued the Policeman.
'No sir.'
'Well I'm going to have to take your details just in case,' said the policeman, while drawing out his notebook. Pointing to Don he continued 'I'll start with you'.
'Actually we are brothers,'
'OK, what is your surname?'
'King'. The policeman writes it down.
'First names'
Don points to me and says 'he's John', then he point to Ron and says 'he's James and I'm Alfred'.
The police mumbles while writing, 'King John, King James, King Al... you taking the mickey son?' By this time we are all supressing laughter, even the Policeman had a smile on his face as he continues, 'On your way then and don't let me catch you making mischief.'

On another occasion I was hitching to Newick to visit my cousins when Don decided to accompany me as his mother lived a bit further along the road. A lorry stopped to give us a lift.
'You look familiar, have I met you before', enquired the driver.
'Probably not, but I am famous so you may have seen my picture somewhere,' replied Don while nudging me in the ribs.
'OK, who are you then?'

'Eric Clapton'
'No, really? Why are you hitching if you are so rich?'
'It is my way of keeping in touch with the people and writing music that is down to earth'.
'Oh really, that's great. My missus isn't going to believe this!'
So the conversation went on and Don had convinced the driver that he was Eric Clapton. We reached Newick and we both got out and laughed. I went on to see my cousins and Don caught a bus to see his mum.

On another occasion while hitching with Don we jumped into this car and on the spur of the moment Don decided that he was dumb and I ended up being the interpreter in a bizarre conversation which I had to make up as we went along. That was Don, always having a laugh.
Ron was a little more serious but also an interesting and entertaining guy. He had just returned from a trip where he had ridden a bicycle to India. Yes in the seventies you could still go through Iran, Iraq, Afghanistan etc. His picture of travel reignited my desire to see the world.

Meanwhile life at the Hospital continued. Staffy pitched up at our squat one day and said that he and a guy called Rodger were moving in next door and could they run an electric cable until their electricity was switched on, which of cause we agreed to do. Little did we know at the time what these squats, a row of ten or more houses were to become.

Well the summer ended, my cousins went back to school and work carried on as usual. Staffy and Roger became friends and this introduced me into a criminal environment.

Staffy was quite a moral person whose only criminal activity was hash. Rodger had spent time inside for armed robbery and was going straight but he still had friends who were active criminals. At this stage I heard little about criminal activities as I was an outsider.

One day my cousins wrote me a letter asking me to bring a ¼ ounce of hash to them at boarding school with a time on Sunday when they were allowed out of school. I decided to go along and visit them and replied that I would see them on Sunday and I would do what I could. I enjoyed the afternoon with them, spent wandering around Maidstone in Kent, my first of many to this beautiful small town. I did not take any hash for them but had a bit to smoke during the afternoon, but this action was to lead to future problems with family.

Winter was moving on and I wanted to as well, with home in mind. I had saved a decent amount of money and with the naivety of an 18 year old youth I reasoned that I was a British Citizen, albeit a colonial, with a new Passport issued in the UK and my place of birth was Zambia, so a visit to Rhodesia should be no problem. I paid a deposit for passage on the SS Helenas to Cape Town. However my restlessness got the better of me and with three and a half months to wait I did a lightening 10 day tour of Europe and set off to India.

# Chapter 6

In 1975 it was still possible to reach India overland. Leaving Europe over the newly constructed Bosporus Bridge was the first glimpse I had of Asia and the realization of a totally different culture previously only hinted at in geography and history lessons at school. The reality is striking! From the architecture to the scenery, to the clustered houses huddled in splendour along the strait dating from the 16th century I was intrigued and wanted to stay but re-enforced my will to continue to India, a country that had intrigued me for years. My family history has had contact with India as my great grandfather was the Commander-in Chief of the East India station from 1917 to 1919, as well as being the Commissioner at Wei-Hai-Wei and the Administrator at Lui-Kung-Tao, both places in China, places I have yet to visit.

So with this in mind I spent the night and headed early the next morning for the road to Iran. As luck would have it I got an early lift with an Arab trucker taking goods from Germany to Pakistan. It was a really lucky ride. Hitch hiking was so good in those days, cheap and easy – except when you get stuck!

Not much really happened on the ride except at one truck stop in Iran I met two Australian girls who begged me to convince the driver to give them a lift out of Iran as they were having a really hard time with Iranian men who wanted to marry them as second or third wives. The driver agreed and so the three of us set off out of Iran. Along the way the driver took a fancy to one of the girls and asked me to sell her to him. I was utterly shocked! I was gobsmacked! Didn't know what to say. I explained that the girls did not belong me and therefore I could not sell them and furthermore our culture would not permit it and I could go to jail. This discussion went on for a while, all the time the girls listening in silent horror. The driver just could not understand why I couldn't accommodate him. In the end I just said that I wanted to marry them both and that was the end of the conversation, he could respect that. What a learning curve a new culture can be!

The driver was sleeping about 5 hours a night, with him and I sleeping under the lorry while the girls slept in the cab and we made Karachi in 6 days where we parted ways. The girls were going to Delhi while I was continuing on to Srinagar, so we decided to bus together as far as Delhi. We said farewell to our driver who dropped us off at a family hostel which cost the three of us about 100 rupees (about 25 pence) each which included dinner, bed and breakfast.

The Pakistani people are amazingly friendly and go out of their way to help you and keep you comfortable, informing us about the local area and sending one of the young children along to escort us and make sure we don't get lost. The tourist trade was slow and generally safe, no rip off artists although many, many sales people trying to sell you everything from clothes and food to exotic animals, like snakes, birds etc. However they were not as pushy as today's vendors. After a casual walk around and a cup of chai we returned to the hostel where I had a cold shower in an outdoor grass walled bathroom. After a vegetable curry dinner I went to bed as we had to rise a 5am in order to catch the daily bus to Delhi.

The bus depot was crowded with dozens of busses heading off in dozens of directions, we bought our tickets and it took us about half an hour to find our bus which was a hive of activity! People on the roof receiving baggage which was being tossed up by workmates on the ground as passengers hustled to get their belongings and livestock secured on the roof before entering the bus to claim their seats. We got seats towards the back on a two person bench where the three of us were crammed in. The bus quickly filled up with maybe 100 people in a 60 seater and with a laden roof we set off on our '18 hour' trip to Delhi. The first few hours leaving the city and slowly getting into the countryside had me continually staring out the window at the ever changing the greenery, the slow dissipation of motorised traffic giving way to donkey carts, loaded pedestrians, cows and buffalo. Peasants working the fields with the men dressed in drab grey or dirty white with their turbans, the women more colourful sporting hijabs with the rare sighting of a niqab. The passing of the countryside soon faded into drooping eyelids and eventually a bumping doziness as the bus battled the potholed roads. Hours and hours passed until we finally reached the border. We all got out at the request of the emigration officers who paid more attention to the foreigners than the rest of the bus put together! It was not aggressive attention but curiosity which resulted in a passport stamp in less than 30 seconds and a myriad questions about Australia and Rhodesia which held up the bus for half an hour or more. On the Indian side of the border the Customs Officers inspected everything on the roof, so everything had to be taken down and then repacked again, making the border stop well over three hours.

We set off again and after a further 15 hours of a bumpy, painful cramped ride we arrived in Delhi 29 hours after setting off! I could not believe it! Out of interest I asked the driver why it was advertised as an 18 hour trip but it took 29 hours, he shrugged his shoulders and said that that is the company rules, he was very jolly, though for someone who had spent 29 shared hours driving and smiling he parted saying that he needed to sleep before the return trip tomorrow. As I was going up north I said farewell to the girls and found my way to a hostel near the train station. The next day I went to enquire about transport to Srinagar. A train could take me as far as Jalandhar and then I would have to bus it again. Aside from the fact that the train was packed, including the roof, the changing scenery on the journey was monotonous. Changing onto the bus for the last leg was the onset of fatigue. This is something I have never understood – how can you sit on your arse for days, alternating snoozing, stretching and looking out the window for days on end and then feel exhausted? Other than the exhaustion the trip was uneventful with the added attraction of the Himalayas slowly getting high, higher and then massive half white, half grey brown green mountains creating incredible beauty all around you. However I still snoozed a lot.

We arrived in Srinagar at 06:30 approximately and I went and flopped down in a small café serving breakfast to workers starting their day. I was approached by various friendly people all offering one thing or another, but mostly conversation. Slowly they dribbled off to work and I was left alone with my kulcha bread and a salty pink tea for breakfast. The kulcha was fine but the pink tea was disgusting. I spoke to the owner asking for somewhere to stay for a few months and he gave me various options, one being a houseboat on a nearby lake, I decided to look into this option. As the day was only beginning I asked if I could leave my rucksack with him while I took a look around and I set off around the town. It was obviously an historic town and up until now I knew nothing about it, just a point on a map that I decided to travel to, totally at random. The buildings were a mixture of ramshackle dwellings and amazing buildings constructed four or five centuries ago, to me obviously eastern, mixed with British Colonial architecture. During my stay here I was to learn more than that.

I returned to the café and a couple were there to greet me and the café owner explained that they had a houseboat to rent. We started negotiating the price, but I was so shocked that not much bargaining took place. The couple wanted American Dollars, which I had, and the princely sum of a dollar a day, two dollars if I wanted meals! I told them that meals would be on a day to day basis to which they agreed, but also it was all dependent on viewing the boat. We set off in a donkey cart for Dal Lake. Approaching the lake was awe inspiring, the beauty of the massive mountains reflecting in the lake persuaded me to accept the offer before I had even seen the boat, although I said nothing. We arrived at the boat and it was a small colourfully decorated wooden boat and not a fixed mooring but could be moved. It had two bedrooms, toilet, cold shower more like a mounted hosepipe) on the deck, lounge and a small patio garden – I thought it was great! Once I had paid my first month's rent with food, $60, I was asked where I wanted to take the boat, ie: where I wanted to live. As I didn't know the area I ask them for a secluded area within walking distance of town. They towed me to a place on a sort of promontory on the lake with a western view of Hazratbal, a developing area with a little development and the Eastern view over the lake towards the majestic view of the mountains. Town was about an hour's walk away although a few shops were closer. It was ideal, as there were also donkey carts taking produce to the town markets that also act as taxis.

After a good night's rest I woke up early the following morning feeling refreshed and went onto the patio and looked out over the lake to the mountains and just took in the view. Slowly a flotilla of boats came floating past. These were market boats, and I soon discovered that these boats follow the sun as with the mountains so high and near, a large part of the day was in shade, and as we all know vegetables need sun. Later in the day they returned to their mooring on the Nageen Lake, which is connected to the Dal Lake by a narrow strait. Nageen Lake was where the floating market took place.

I spent two months in this tranquil setting, mostly near the boat, venturing into town a couple of times a week to talk to locals in the cafes etc. The history of Srinagar is coloured and at times has been really strained. The first known settlement dates from the 6th century. From there we know that various cultures have ruled, Buddhists, Hindu, Mughal, various Afghan tribes and of course, Britain. All these cultures are visibly present in many ways, mosques and Christian churches, Buddhist monasteries etc. The vast majority are Muslims and are extremely friendly and generous. The flora and fauna is phenomenal, colourful flowers abound but the Chinar tree takes the prize. 25 metres high and a 15 metre girth!! How is that for a tree! The fauna is mostly small but there are bears, of which I have still never seen one, but stag abound with a decent population of the snow leopard.

The tranquil two months came to an end, a hairy bus ride, a crazy train ride and a flight took me back to Heathrow and Haywards Heath. I went back to the squat with Ron and Don, worked another month in the kitchens at St Francis Hospital and booked passage on the HSS Helenas to Cape Town.

The ship sold off tickets cheaply; I paid just 90 pounds, as it was going to Cape Town to start its summer season in the southern hemisphere. This was my first trip on an ocean going liner and I was looking forwarded to it. We left quite late in the evening and went straight into a rough Bay of Biscay, the dining room was deserted with most people on board being seasick. Funny thing, although I was never seasick, when walking along corridors I noticed that I could not walk straight in semi rough and rough seas, I walked as if drunk. The reputation of ship romances came true for me. The first night at dinner, when most of the ship was sick, I met a few other young adults but I caught the eye of an English girl, Sue. I say I caught her eye as I was, and still am, a quiet person particularly with new people and females. Sue was brought up by her grandmother as her mother died when she was young. She had spent her school days boarding in the UK and holidays with her grandmother who had moved to Rome after the Second World War. I never really learnt much more about Sue as she had a voracious sexual appetite and we spent most of our time indulging in satisfying it. Although we did have other fun on the ship, shows bars, movies, crossing the Equator party and so on as well as socialising with other people we had met.

The principle acquaintance was a guy, Adam, a South African who had just been released from jail, after a five year stint for drug smuggling. Unfortunately he took a fancy to Sue and followed us around like a puppy. Sue indulged him and I didn't think he was too bad, even though he was stoned and tripping all the time. At night he would drop acid and sneak to the front of the ship just under The Bridge and would watch the ship plough into the sea, especially in rough weather, he loved it there. He invited me to join him on a few occasions, but I refused, preferring to continue with my sexual education. A fortnight later we arrived in Cape Town and I returned to stay with Jenny and Dante. Saying goodbye to Sue was difficult but as she was going up to Rhodesia, I gave her my mum's phone number and agreed to meet up. A few days later I started hiking up to Salisbury, with a backpack and approximately 100 vinyl LP's. That was heavy going! Hitching 2,500 kilometres with two LP cases, a backpack and a guitar – I think it was the most luggage I have travelled with in my life!

# Chapter 7

My brother Patrick was still in Pretoria as was my grandmother, great aunt, an aunt and cousins Rob and John, so that was my first stop. Arriving in Pretoria I went to my brother at work, where he hustled me out of the office quickly and down to a café where I waited for him to finish work where he was Articled to a Law firm while studying law through UNISA and was obviously embarrassed by his 'hippy brother'. After a drink with a brief reunion he dropped me off at my Aunt Rosaria, who had not had any notification of my arrival but was, as usual gracious and welcoming but with a stern warning for advance notification next time.

The following evening Patrick took my uncle Robert and I out to dinner. Robert was a staunch Rhodesian Front supporter and was a Squadron Leader in the Rhodesian Air Force. He often travelled to South Africa and Mozambique as an instructor training the South African Air Force pilots in Bush warfare from the air – what this entailed I have no idea. I had a great plate of curried king prawns from Mozambique and while waiting for the dessert a political discussion ensued about Rhodesia. It got heated pretty quickly with my brother trying to keep the peace, Robert stormed out threatening to turn me in to the South African authorities as a communist agitator. However Patrick managed to calm the situation down, but the meal was spoilt and we headed home.

My parents were not expecting me back in Salisbury and I arrived in the evening and headed to their favourite haunt,

The Catholic Club. I spotted my mum who had her back to me, tapped her on the shoulder and said hello. She turned around, haltingly said hello and turned back to her conversation. I interrupted again and asked ' Do you know who I am?'

'Yes, I recognise you as a friend of my son John Ant', she replied.

I was little put off by this reply as the only change that I could think of was that I had grown my hair which was now shoulder length. I continued, 'I am your son John Ant'. I could the see sudden recognition on her face and once again a happy family reunion followed.. My dad bought me a beer, the first time legally with a brief discussion on what we had been doing, as he was now back in Rhodesia permanently, and I updated him on my travels. The next few days were catching with my family, Michael, my sister Margaret who was now married to Mike, while my sister Kathleen who was away teaching in the sticks, at Marula.

I spent a few days at the farm with Margaret and Mike, who was a manager of a farm out past Lion's Den. The owner of the farm he had been managing when I left had died in a light aircraft crash when returning from a weekend of partying at Kariba. The new farm was owned by a family that had a few massive farms in the area. Mike was the same as usual, happy go lucky, hardworking Rhodesian who had no problems with my anti-Rhodesian stance. He was great to see and took me around the farm with him as he worked with his wonderful canine companion, Genoa, his Great Dane. Margaret and I relaxed a bit and played a bit of squash who, much to my dismay, beat me and so I refused to give in and played again and again until I wore her down and won a game!

The next few weeks were spent trying to get work which proved difficult as employers were reluctant to take me on as I had not completed my military training and could therefore be called up at any time, which meant that companies would lose time and money. I headed back to South Africa. Hitching to Pretoria I arrived at Beit Bridge, the border between South Africa and Rhodesia. I was wary about leaving as I was liable for conscription, but I had a new British passport and with my birth place in Zambia I was hopeful to get through. Rhodesian Customs and Immigration was a piece of cake. The South African side proved a problem, I was not allowed in. I cited my brother and other relatives who could not be gotten hold of and I was sent back to Rhodesia, walking across the bridge over the Limpopo River. So often I have crossed this bridge without one look at the surrounding beautiful bush. The Rhodesian Immigration refused me entry. Oh shit. What do I do now? I wandered back over the Limpopo and after a long wait asked an Immigration to please try my brother again, to no avail. Back to Rhodesia, still with all my family there no luck, not getting in. I ended up sleeping on the side of the railway line between the two border posts. Sleeping erratically I was up early, well before the 06:00 opening of the border post. I was the first in and one of the customs officers recognised me informing me he had managed to contact my brother and I was let into South Africa. Hiking to Pretoria was the same as usual and I got to my brother by lunch.

I managed to get a temporary job in a shop's photographic department while a member of staff was off having an operation and would be away from work for about two months and I found accommodation in a hostel. Well the job came to an end; I had saved up a bit of money so I headed off to Swaziland, down to Durban and another trip down the garden route, up through the Karoo and stupidly back to Rhodesia to say farewell to my family as I was heading back to the UK.

Swaziland was a bit of an eye opener for me. The feeling of freedom was everywhere. The people were happy and no sign of racism seemed to exist. I met a guy, also a John, who invited me to stay with him for awhile I agreed. John was a South African who was managing a chain of supermarkets, I forget which. He also was a John Denver fan and played John Denver and only John Denver all the time. It drove me up the wall! I spent the week with him and then headed south to Manzini on Friday afternoon, expecting to be out of Swaziland within a few hours. However this was not to be. I got picked up by a school teacher who was heading home for the weekend. We arrived at his family compound 10 minutes south of Manzini, mid-afternoon. It was a series of rondavels in a circle surrounding a central gathering area. The main building was a small colonial brick house that was well decorated and furnished and it was here that I was shown to a bedroom, followed by an introduction to the many family members. Dinner was a chicken stew eaten in the courtyard and attended by all the family after the matriarch made known that dinner was ready by a shrill ululation. The dinner was good and after seconds I asked the schoolteacher how to refuse another helping politely, simple, leave a little food on the plate! Apparently if you finish everything it is an indication that one was still hungry and requires a further helping. Fortunately the schoolteacher interceded on my behalf and a giggle spread around the compound. A young girl was given the duty of collecting the plates, scraping them off into the animal feed bins and washing up. The older males, including myself retired into a 'smoke hut` This was a hut with little ventilation with a fire in the middle, continually being fed and the smoke was to clean your system through the heat, aid digestion and, somehow or other an aid to your eyes, however mine were streaming and I could hardly see! The last part of the cleansing procedure was a bush of marijuana thrown on the fire to relax the men for the evening. Well stoned we left the hut and returned to the courtyard area where the young kids brought us beer. The males of the family asked if I would like to attend a ceremony involving the King the next day. It sounded great and I so I accepted the invitation. While driving to the stadium the teacher told me that the celebration happens periodically and King Sobhuza chooses new wives from various villages around Swaziland. This, apparently, is a great honour for the village, at that time the King had 70 wives and 210 children. I had no idea whether to comment on whether he was lucky or not! Arriving at the stadium the queue was quite long and it took half an hour to get in and seated. Various forms of entertainment at different areas of the arena were taking place, drumming and dancing, domestic animals being displayed and examined, vendors selling their wares and just below where the King would be seated, potential wives displayed themselves in national dress which was basically skirts and bare tops in blue red and orange combinations. After about an hour of entertainment a chorus of ululations spread through the stadium as King Sobhuza made his grand entrance in traditional dress, basically a red toga type wrap with different adornments of Swazi origin, beads, animal teeth etc. To the beating of drums the potential brides bearing reeds danced past the King one at a time displaying their assets hoping to bring favour to their respective villages. After the dancing parade a bull was brought into the arena and sacrificed while King Sobhuza descended to the slaughter area and washed himself, symbolically in the bulls blood. The bull was then prepared and mounted on a spit for a later meal, in my opinion probably Sunday, the following day. Then came the time for the King to announce his bride or brides and as I do not speak Swazi the school teacher translated that the King was taking no more wives as he was content with his present 70. The stadium went quiet and disappointment from the village elders was discernible from their mutterings. We left soon after with the celebrations set to go on until late Sunday evening. Sunday was spent resting around the compound with chickens prepared by the young female members of the family after which the matriarch of the family roasted them over coals for our lunch. Monday morning arrived and the school teacher dropped me on the main road south at a truck stop just outside Manzini.

The trip down to Cape Town and up through the Karoo was uneventful other than the incredible beauty of the country. Starting with typical African bushland heading to Durban while hugging the coast on one side while the mighty Drakensberg were in the distance. After Durban the road heads straight along the coast to Port Shepstone when it heads inland through the Transkei avoiding the thick impenetrable coast until East London. The road down to Cape Town then meanders through the majestic Drakensberg accompanying us along the coastal road displaying the beauty of The Garden Route in all its glory finally entering Cape Town with Table Mountain flanked by the Twelve Apostles. This is one of the most beautiful routes in the world! Going back up through the Karoo has a different kind of beauty. The grasslands with its hilly landscapes giving way to the flat topped 'Karoo Koppies and dust of semi desert, dry and hot which fades into bushland the closer you get to Johannesburg and then up north over the Great Escarpment before descending into the flatlands of Rhodesia,

I had no problems getting back into Rhodesia, just the luck of the draw I suppose. I hiked to Salisbury once again catching up with my parents at the Catholic club.

Returning home did not go at all well. My father assumed that I had returned to complete my Military Service. This developed into an argument and I was kicked out of the house on my first night home at about 2am. I hitched to my sister and brother-in-law who were farming about 25 miles outside of Salisbury. Although both my sister and brother-in-law were staunch Rhodesians politically neither of them ever held my political beliefs against me. However I was under a lot of pressure: my father would not speak to me and he and my mum were continually fighting, my school friends were all in the army and the majority looked upon me as a traitor and a coward, and due to my friendships with non–white people I was on the police radar and picked up regularly. A few months of this was all I could take and I decided to leave sooner than I intended, I really didn´t know what to do or where to go, I just had to leave. During this time I was associating with PJ, whose sister who was a friend during school days. He and I had a great time together; his family were basically all geniuses. The father a spacial physics professor, his mother a psychiatrist, one sister specializing in some obscure section of medicine, and only just turned 22, the other sister was still away at university and PJ awaiting results to get into university. We spent our time listening to music, between his house and the farm, smoking grass and hanging around the streets of Salisbury.

Eventually with the police keeping an eye on me I got busted. The judge was lenient as I said I was waiting for the next intake in order to do my military service, I was let off with a warning. This incident sped up my departure plans. The night before I was leaving a friend threw a going away party for me, so I packed up and went off to the party. Returning at about 3 am I walked into the lounge where my sister and brother-in–law were entertaining Military Police. After an extremely short verbal exchange I was under arrest for avoiding military service and I was to be taken to Brady barracks, (the military prison), in Bulawayo. I went to my bedroom to collect my rucksack and jumped out the window. I knew the farm better than the MPs. However it was not to be. Outside my window I jumped into the arms of two armed and ready Military Police!

## Chapter 8

I was handcuffed and taken to a prison cell in the RLI barracks outside Salisbury where I was questioned, informed that I was to be transferred to Brady by train the following night and then I had a visit from the Army Chaplain. I was grateful for the anticipated visit as I could explain my circumstances to a sympathetic ear. Once again I was disappointed. The priest, after listening to my grievances, informed me that it was my Christian duty to fight for God against the Godless communists and prevent the spread of the evils of communism. The next day my sister brought me some of my things, tape recorder and music, books and hidden away, my passport. That evening I was taken to the train station with a military escort, handcuffs and leg irons, hobbling along with armed escorts displaying me as a traitor in full public view, while escorting me to a Military carriage on a civilian train, I was then put on a bunk bed and handcuffed and with leg irons in a spread-eagled position for the 12 hour journey to Bulawayo and then taken to Brady Barracks where I was locked up in a jail-like cell, only the outside wall and bars, a thin mattress with a blanket and a bucket for my bodily functions. The section where I was had about 15 cells all with mostly bald, tattooed, violent military convicts. Due to the length of my hair, civvies and general demeanour the convicts kept up a constant rant: 'you are the prettiest thing I have seen in five years' , 'you are going to be f...... by us all in the shower tonight', 'you dirty traitor', 'your death is to be slow', etc., etc. This was constant and the only relief I got was when the prisoners were taken out on work detail. I was not allowed to see anyone, no books – only the cell.

Although not in the military I was under military jurisdiction and informed that I would be there until I voluntarily signed my conscription papers, which would then put me in the army officially. The next three days, were spent between the rantings, feeding in the cell and a daily visit from the Base Commander inquiring whether I would sign the papers or not. The fourth morning I was woken at 4am and along with other new inmates, fortunately mostly minor military offenders, and taken about 20 miles away in a helicopter and dropped off in the bush and told that if we did not make it back to barracks by 8am we would miss breakfast. On the first day it took 5 ½ hours, missed breakfast. We were then kept physically active, digging 6ft x 3ft x6ft ditches, jogging, push ups etc. until lunch time for half an hour and parade ground marching until 5pm, dinner and bed, exhausted as I was I fell asleep. This was the routine for the next 7 days, however I was in time for breakfast by the 3rd day. On the seventh day, 11 days of Military prison had made me realize that this way I would not get out and I signed the papers and was transferred to Llewelyn Barracks to begin my training.

Arriving at Llewelyn, still under escort, I was handed over to the Base Commander who gave me a pep talk about patriotism, duty etc., and then handed me over to the Regimental Police. First stop was the barber where I was shorn, then kitted out and taken to the barracks. I was to have a barracks room to myself as the intake I was to join was only due in five months. After changing into my uniform I was escorted to the Commander once again. Here I was informed that due to the lack of an intake I was going to be given manual labour tasks around the Barracks. As I had an Uncle who was high up in the Military, in the Air Force, I was informed that I would be offered various 'soft options' for my military service. Options like The Army marching band, the Army Chaplaincy etc. and I could think about it until my intake arrived. In the meantime I started gardening. During the first week my routine was set, up at five for a run, breakfast and gardening until 13:00, lunch and then gardening until 16:00, parade ground marching until 18:00 another run and dinner. Return to the barracks to scrub the place clean until lights out at 22:00. Although officially it was lights out, this was actually the time to do my own chores, cleaning clothes, polishing shoes etc.

After 2 weeks of this I was fed up and approached the Commander. As you can expect the Commander blasted me out of his office. However another week went by and 'A' Company arrived at Llewelyn for further intensive training. 'A' Company had already done their basic training and were already fighting and the group who were at the barracks were there for specialized training, some would move on to join the RLI, SAS, Selous Scouts, some to the Grey's Scouts, some would become trackers and some would drop out. The Commander sent me off with this group, to get me out of his hair. The training was to be done in close proximity to operational areas. We set up camp in the Operation Tangent area where ZIPRA, under the command of Joshua Nkomo, was operating. I was not officially training but was handed down from one person to another until I was under a training Sergeant, Sergeant Crundell, who handed me an FN and informed me to follow orders or I would be another casualty of war. This was how my 'tracker' training started. I was with the Rhodesian Regiment 'A' Company for four months. I was put into combat alongside them although due to my 'Political' affiliations I was not permitted to operate as a tracker, (so I had no idea why they were training me in his discipline) as this would give opportunities to leave, as trackers worked alone.

Finally my intake arrived and I was shipped back to Llewelyn. I had now been in the Army 5 months and was still not permitted a pass while all regulars had a pass every six weeks, which was the operational rota. I went through my 3 months basic training which ended just before Christmas. I was called into the Commander's office given a pep talk about how well I was doing and after the Christmas break I would be promoted to Corporal and I was to receive my first pass. At last after 8 months I was allowed out! However the conditions were set. I was to be escorted to my sister's farm and escorted back after Christmas. After arranging to meet a friend who underwent training with me the next day, I was escorted the 500 kilometres to my sister's farm. After the escort left I informed my sister that I had a lot of preparation and would not be staying, I would leave the next morning to return to Llewelyn. She made me take a Christmas cake to have with my friends and dropped me off in Salisbury town where I met my Army friend, Digsby. Digsby took me to Bulawayo from where I hitch-hiked to Plumtree, the Rhodesia – Botswana border town. I went to the only petrol station for a drink and while talking to the petrol attendant, he guessed my course of action, took me to a room out the back and told me to get some sleep and he would return when the petrol station closed at 22:00. True to his word he arrived at 22:00 and escorted me through the bush around the Immigration offices and into Botswana, as we parted I gave him my sister's Christmas cake which he was extremely thankful for. I continued walking West until just before dawn when I climbed a kopje and watched the sunrise over the Kalahari desert. This was the greatest feeling I had ever had and God had not only answered my prayers but also sent his spirit down to me and I felt him flowing through me as I went to sleep. A truly great Christmas, one of the best ever! Rising at sunset I played Jimi Hendrix, Hendrix in the West, on my portable tape recorder with such a feeling of freedom that I had never experienced and never have since! I changed out of my army kit and into civvies, as I had not packed socks I kept my army socks and boots.

I spent 3 glorious days walking through the Kalahari semi-desert region towards Francistown, approximately 150 km into Botswana. I had taken enough rations for 7 days but water was a problem and I had to fill up my canteen whenever I could, even if it was full when I found water I would hang around drink and then fill it up again. During this time I was entirely on my own, walking at night and resting during the day, I had never felt so happy and protected. After a night's walk I spotted a village not long before dawn and so I decided to call it a night and retreated a bit and settled down. However a short time later one of the villagers approached, told me that he had witnessed my arrival and had come to warn me of a snake pit not 20 metres from where I was resting. I thanked him and moved on. Mid-afternoon, while I was snoozing I suddenly found myself surrounded by Botswana Para Military forces. I was handcuffed and placed under arrest and taken into Francistown Prison.

On arrival at the prison I was searched and beaten and then led to the cells and locked up. The cell consisted of 15 other prisoners, a thin mat for a mattress on the floor and a metal bucket by the door for our bodily functions. I was the only white person in the cell and with the upbringing I had had it instilled an irrational fear and on that first night I got no sleep. The cell doors were opened at 6am and we were let out into a rectangular courtyard surrounded by cells and with a kitchen in the one corner where we queued up for breakfast, sadza, (maize meal), with milk and sugar. After breakfast most of the prisoners were taken out to work and this left about a dozen or so of us in the courtyard. They were either sick, too old for physical labour or awaiting trial. One of the other prisoners was a white mercenary from the USA who had been fighting in Rhodesia and was holidaying in Botswana when he was picked up by the Police as a known mercenary. He had been in the prison for about two weeks and had managed to contact the American Embassy and was waiting for them to get him out. The day was pretty dull with lunch at 12:00, sadza and meat and dinner at 18:00 with sadza and gravy. Straight after dinner we were locked in the cells for the night. A couple of hours later I was taken from the cells to an interrogation room where the Prison

Warden was seated with a man dressed in civilian clothes and one of the prison guards standing by the door which was closed after me. I was told to sit down and the interrogation began. As the Rhodesian Army had taken my passport away I had no form of ID and when I left Rhodesia was not at war with Botswana. However, during the interrogation I learnt that Rhodesian Forces had infiltrated into Botswana a few days beforehand and had blown up the UANC offices in Francistown and I was suspected to be one of the infiltrators. This was not good for me, I still had my Army issue boots and I had forgotten to dispose of my dog tags.

The interrogators were not too physically violent being content to just the odd beating at random through the night. During the sessions they would drink whisky and a Browning Hi Power 9mm revolver was placed on the table between us. The guy in civvies picked up the revolver pointed it at me and shot various times into the wall behind me. Just before dawn I was escorted outside, tied to a pole, a squad of nine marched out took aim and fired. The bullets thudded into the wall behind me. I believed that I was going to die. I prayed almost all the time. Over the next few weeks I was kept in solitary with the night time sessions constantly looking for answers that I did not have. Fortunately the 'Firing Squad' did not happen again but the cell shootings happened several times a night. I did not think that I would get out of there alive. Suddenly one morning I was let out back into the courtyard, they must have believed my story! My prayers had been answered!! Thank you Lord!

I put in a request to see the Warden which happened a few days later when I asked if I could contact the British Embassy. My request was denied. A week or so later I was escorted to an office where I was told I was to be interviewed by the press and that if any 'bad publicity' was mentioned I would never get out of prison. This was followed by visits by various members of the press. Articles stated extremes referring to me as a 'mercenary', captured 'Rhodesian Special Forces', 'spy', 'deserter' etc. The result of this was mostly good – it forced the British Embassy to come and listen to me, but with no papers it would take a while to get me out. The negative side of the publicity was that it informed the Rhodesian forces where I was. I was visited by agents of the Rhodesian Forces who informed me that if I went back to Rhodesia voluntarily I would receive minimum punishment and return to duty, but if I refused they would break me out and take me back to a Court Martial for desertion which could result in the death penalty. Once again, after what I had considered a miracle, my world was turned upside down! I tried to contact the Embassy once again, with no response. Every day I was on edge praying for a solution when out of the blue I was transferred to Gaborone Prison, 500 miles south. Gaborone Prison was a prison for hard core criminals and my reception was a frightening one, death threats for the 'Rhodesian soldier' were common and the prison authorities took them seriously and put me in a solitary cell for my protection. On my first day I was let out to the exercise yard where there were a few other people, one of them a white middle aged guy. He was quite friendly and we started chatting. After giving my name, he asked who my dad was. Lo and behold, he knew my father. My dad had been investigating fraud within Barlows in Francistown, and as he was a brilliant accountant he had found the fraudster and I was in the same prison as him! Fortunately he did not hold grudges and praised my dad as a great accountant and he had underestimated him and hence got caught. However we became friendly and as he was rich, through his fraud, he had 'favours' given to him by the guards, which meant I ate well with him providing the meals. I remained there for about 10 days when the British Embassy picked me up and delivered me to the airport and put me on a flight to the UK. During the flight I was attended well by the cabin crew even though they were informed by the British Embassy to keep an eye on me. However the flight was full and there was not a seat for me, so I was put on one of the Air Hostess seats, a small uncomfortable fold away seat. The Embassy had taken all my money, which the Botswana Prison authorities had returned to me, and informed me that it was the first payment towards my repatriation costs. Furthermore a staff member from the Department of Social Security would be at Gatwick to help me settle down, my temporary passport would be withdrawn and I would not be issued with a new one until I had paid off the outstanding debt. This was all fine, I was overjoyed to have the previous year of my life coming to a close.

We arrived at Gatwick at 6AM on a Sunday morning in February 1977, with a light layer of snow on the ground and the welcome orange hue from the lights of European civilisation. I felt elated and prayed in thanks for coming through the last part of my life. Once clearing Customs and Immigration, who took my passport, I proceeded to the Meeting point to meet the Social Services Officer. After about an hour I gave up and decided to hitch-hike to my Uncle at High Wycombe in North London. I didn´t know his address but he was the owner of a Petrol Station and I knew where that was. I set out with only the clothes on my back, a thin summer cotton shirt, jeans and my army boots and socks while carrying a bag with books and toothbrush, soap etc. Although it was freezing I did not feel the cold immediately. The journey to High Wycombe took almost all day with some lifts and a lot of walking I arrived, frozen, at the petrol station around 7pm and managed to get hold of my uncle who came and picked me up. When I arrived at the house my aunt and 4 cousins greeted me and after warming up with tea and food, a condensed version of the last year came pouring out, and then silence. The family disappeared and my Uncle returned a few minutes later and we went out to the pub for a drink. During our chat at the pub I was told that as a deserter I was a disgrace to the family and not welcome in his house. I was permitted to stay the night and the following day I was given GBP10 and dropped off at the Tube station. I later discovered that this was not his decision but my aunt Shelagh.

I made my way down to Shepherd's Bush in London, where I hoped some friends from Rhodesia were staying. I had a good memory in those days!! I arrived mid-morning and as luck would have it, the sister of one of my friends was at the bedsit and informed me they were next door. I met up with Mike and Nikki who had been expecting me a year earlier. Again I repeated the condensed version of the last year and then for the first time in what seemed a lifetime I relaxed and chatted with friends and finally slept like a baby!

The next day I proceeded to the Social Services Office, and again told a really condensed version of what had happened and then I was left in the booth for about an hour. When the lady returned she informed me that there was no record of me anywhere, I had no ID or Passport and that she would follow it up and contact me when she knows something. I returned to Mike and Nikki, stayed a few days and left for Sussex where I had more friends and family. When I knocked on the door of uncle Hemery's, (really my second cousin once removed), house, I was greeted by my aunt who turned me away. I proceeded to St Francis Hospital, where I had worked during my last sojourn in the UK, and looked up Staffy, who as luck would have it, had a spare room in a communal house. I met him after work and went to what was to be my home for the next three months. The other residents were a couple with a 2 year girl, and from that day on and for many years the experiences of the last year were locked inside of me, only telling people that I had dodged the Rhodesian Army and did not want to return.

The next three months are still a blur. I retreated into myself, only leaving the house to sign on, which came through after about 6 weeks, and getting food. The rest of the time I spent in the bedroom and occasionally in the lounge. I still do not really know what happened during that time, other than reliving the army and the path I had chosen to escape from it were my only thoughts and memories. Visitors came and went and people stopped talking to me, other than Staffy and Roger. One day out of the blue, Brian, a South African who I had seen occasionally at the house, dropped around and I told him Staffy and Roger were out, but he insisted on coming in. We sat in the lounge and he opened a bottle of Tequila which we finished between us and I managed to scramble upstairs to my bed before passing out. The next day I awoke to a clarity I had not had for I don't know how long. I left the house, found a job back at the hospital and found new lodgings with a single mum, Celia, renting out a room to make ends meet and started my re-integration into society. Years later I learnt that Roger was about to inform Social Services that I was in need of psychiatric treatment, probably due to war experiences. However I settled into a comfortable routine and integration was slow.

# Chapter 9

The next few years were spent on education, not only formal education but I read a lot, often as much as 5 to 6 books a week! I also started work and probably the most important, I started to learn about life. My upbringing in Rhodesia had been sheltered and manipulated, something that often happens in wartime. "The Idler" magazine from 11/11/1758 says "...among the calamities of war may be jointly numbered the diminution of the love of truth, by the falsehoods which interest dictates and credulity encourages." Or in later times simply stated as ʺThe first casualty when war comes is truth.ʺ by Senator Johnson in 1918. This was certainly true when your upbringing is in a war environment. The result of this is that I did not believe anybody in authority and started my own evaluation of society.

Mike and Nikki and another person I met, Kevin, got together started to squat in a house some friends of his had just vacated. During our first week in the house we were raided by the police. The front door was smashed in, what seemed like dozens of police stormed into various rooms and kept us separated while they searched the premises. Once this was complete we were questioned, ID's taken etc. I, unfortunately had taken to gardening and had a little marijuana plant in my bedroom. The police then apologized and left, taking me to the police station to be booked. While there I discovered that they were looking for the previous tenants who were drug addicts and suppliers of heroin.

Through the press we subsequently learnt the previous occupants were brothers, 3 of 8, and one had died of an overdose and the other 2 buried him in the back garden. They were sent to jail for 10 years. This was my introduction to the drug culture. It fascinated me and I started to hang out and made friends with many people involved with them. These people were anything from party pot smokers through to addicts. Through my friendship with them I learnt that they too were disillusioned with society and as they were in a similar frame of mind as me they became my unwitting tutors. The drug addicts I met were often from 'good' homes and were quite intelligent when it came to politics, society and the church. I learnt a lot about the church and the corruption within it.

I got a job back at St Francis, the mental institution where I had been working previously. This time as a porter. I gained quite a lot of experience there, spending a bit of time in various departments. First as a general porter, cleaning the corridors and other public areas, then onto a ward with the criminally insane, then onto the children's section and finally into the surgery. I enjoyed the children's section the most. They were not really insane kids in my opinion, just a bit deviant. I kept the place clean put the meals out for self-service and cleaned up after them. This left a lot of time on my hands and I started talking to them and hearing about their lives. The kids had a way of sneaking out at night (there were bars on the window and everything was alarmed but they never told me how they managed it) and would pop over to the pub across the road. The girls, who were around 14 or so and looked mature for their age, would go into the pub chat up the men, con money out of them buy alcohol and bring it out for all of them to share. These adventures often found them in trouble with the medical staff but they refused to say how they got out.

I used to play games with them during my slow times and one of the games was table football, fast becoming a lost art! These game times led to them accepting me and talking to me about themselves, which in turn led to the staff getting pissed off with me, as the kids would not speak about themselves to anyone in authority and requesting that I get transferred out. This is when I got transferred to the surgery. Initially I enjoyed myself there, it was only for operations on the brain and my job was to clean and sterilize everything, after which the head nurse would inspect and re-sterilize, which, after all was her job. I never figured out why she got me to do it in the first place. Watching an operation on the brain was not the same then as it is now, with monitors and cameras, etc. It was four people all trying to see what is going on with the surgeon, the only one who really could. I soon got bored there and resigned from the hospital.

Meanwhile my social life was quite active. I was meeting all sorts of people, hippies, bikers, musicians, loafers and hard workers. One thing they all had in common was drugs. Few were addicts with heroin and physeptone being the addicts' drug of choice. Heroin we all know about but very few people realize the effects and the power of the drug and how easy it is to get lost in it. Physeptone, not really the drug of choice but the most easily available and one of the biggest mistakes made by the National Health system in the UK. Physeptone was a drug used to wean heroin addicts off drugs, however it turned out to be more addictive and certainly more easily available and cheaper. Addicts would submit themselves to psychiatric observation for a month at the end of which the psychiatrist would give the addict a weekly prescription which they would get from a pharmacy twice a week. This system was deeply flawed as people would go through assessment, get their scripts and sell the drugs they didn't use. Users got more and more addicted, pharmacies increasingly became targets for break-ins and a mini drug economy evolved (this was before the huge smuggling rings came into being in the UK).

The drug scene was a more personalized one, with addicts doing most of the buying and selling, including addicts who 'had control' of their addiction - people who could work, socialize, do sports etc. This latter category were people who travelled regularly to various Asian countries, India, Lebanon, Morocco, Thailand, Afghanistan, Pakistan, etc. and buy varying amounts of drugs that a single person could safely carry. Hence with a stream of individuals travelling out east to score heroin and hash the supply line to the UK was secure. During this period of time my drug of choice was hash, due to the lack of good grass and occasionally, psilocybin (magic mushrooms). I also rarely took speed and tried cocaine which was really expensive and gave about a 10 minute high – a waste of money. I never went onto any of the hard drugs. Kevin, our housemate, had a money making scheme: he had himself assessed as an addict in order to get the script and sell the physeptone. Three months after he came out of the assessment he died of an overdose, his mum was the administrator of the hospital but due to patient confidentially, knew nothing of her son's situation until it was too late. Birdie, an acquaintance, was riding a motorbike while high on physeptone, died through an accident, James died through an OD, Kate OD'd, and so the list goes on. In three years I saw at least a dozen people die from or through drugs. Brett a regular traveller to Thailand, also an addict, set up an underage prostitution brothel in his mum's (a wealthy gentlewoman) caravan in the garden who knew nothing about it until Brett was arrested. Drugs is not something to mess about with and it was not long after this that I gave up cigarettes and hash etc.

I was enjoying reading and social studies as well as my social life and I signed on the dole and went through a period of working for short periods of time. I had jobs that included conveyer belt unloader, drilling holes into little blocks of metal, making pallets, delivering pallets, DHSS admin, until I was eventually told by the Job Centre that I was unemployable, I took pride in that, as I knew it was rubbish and just another example of the failing social system, a system that does not want to help its people but just get them out of the way, I continued to get jobs anyway.

It was during this period that I met and fell for the woman who was to become my first heartbreak, Fiona. I met her at the Kings Head in Cuckfield one night and we got on like a house on fire, a chatty, confident and outgoing woman. She had noticed me in Sainsburys where I did shopping and she had, apparently, tried to get my attention by giving me free food and discounts which I never noticed. I was enamoured with her and we became a couple. Fiona had her head screwed on and knew what she wanted. She was writing 'A' level, working weekends at Sainsburys and had a cleaning job up the road from where she lived. Her mum had died when she was quite young and the first time I entered her house I was surprised at how sparse it was, no decorations, not even family photos, perfectly clean and tidy, and I mean perfectly. She also ran the household which included looking after her younger brother, Peter, who was about 12 or so. She didn't mention her dad much except that he travelled a lot, until one day I met him unexpectedly. Fiona had invited me over and not long after I arrived her dad walked through the door, arriving back early from a trip. We spent the next hour talking while Fiona went off to her cleaning job. I was amazed at how well versed he was in Rhodesian and South African politics, he even knew my granddad! He was a tall and powerfully built man slightly balding and was a wealth of knowledge and very secretive while prying into my affairs, he actually scared me. I discovered later that he worked for MI6, I told you he was scary! Fiona and I had a brief and intense relationship and she broke it off when I discovered she was having an affair with another man. I found out about the affair, confronted her and she said it was only sex and no emotion involved, which was not alright with me and I told her to break up with him and she just called me immature and broke up with me. Oh well, first heartbreak.

I also met Mary. She and I became fast friends, never anything sexual, my attraction to her was her joy of life, concern for others and her ability to see people for what they are and accept them. Mary had been abused by a stepfather and her mother never believed her. I met Mary when she was 17 and just recovering from her abusive past, if one ever does, and to live with her trauma. We became really good friends, went on long walks and chatted, went to the pub , chatted and drank, sitting up all hours of the night listening to music, going to concerts, visiting various places including a tour of London and we just enjoyed each other's company. We became constant companions and friends. She was intelligent, level headed and had an artistic bent. She eventually did a course in stained glass and opened her own studio. Although Mary smoked hash and enjoyed a pint or two we had a lot of conversations around life and politics and I started to see beyond my own blindness towards society and started to delve deeper into politics, while still enjoying the mindless hedonism surrounding me!

I also met James, a weird guy who was a Psychologist as well as being a Mycologist. We also talked a lot and got on really well. James would bugger off to Wales (he was Welsh) every spring and summer to pick psilocybin mushrooms and I took them for the first time. Arriving back from Wales he came straight round to us, took out his collection of mushrooms and started sorting them. Mike and I joined in and learning the ropes. James also told us to eat the freshest ones which we started to do while sorting. Soon the effects started to take place and a coy grin spread across James's face. I asked how many we should take , to which he answered 15 to 20. By this stage both Mike and I had consumed well over a hundred and soon enough we were on an intense psychedelic trip! James also introduced me to a carer working at the same autistic child home, a girl called Sam. She had frizzy afro style hair, another intelligent being and soon James, Sam and I were discussing life, the universe and everything on a regular basis. Sam and I started going out. However it was soon apparent that our attraction was intellectual and not sexual and one evening when Sam had gone to a concert in Brighton with some of her mates I decided to break up with her. In the early hours of the morning I heard knocking at the door, so I got up and let Sam in. She said that although she was aware that we were about to break up could she just spend the night here. I saw she was distressed and obviously agreed. A few minutes later she broke down and confided that on the way back from the concert her mates had stopped at Ditchling beacon, raped her and left her stranded. She walked hours to get to me. Although I was aware of the horrors of violent rape, this was the first time that I had been the first contact for a person I was close to. I didn't know what to say or do. Slowly the details came out and the questions I asked were about her and what she wanted to do, but I felt helpless and useless. Eventually we fell asleep after Sam had had a cold bath, why cold I don't know, and we slept sporadically for 18 to 20 hours. When Sam finally got up she just told me that she didn't want to do anything about it, no police, no friends, social workers, nobody. Although I disagreed with her, it was her choice and I have honoured it until now.

Not long after this Nikki's sister and her boyfriend arrived from their travels around Europe and the Middle East and with nowhere to go they moved in with us, making a rather cramped house. However soon enough Paul and Sue found a house in Cuckfield belonging to a Polish Countess, no less, and we moved in. Six of us took up our new residence, two couples and two singles, Paul and Sue, Mike and Nikki, myself and a girl named Trixie. Trixie had been living in the squat before us so we asked her out of courtesy to join us, explaining that we wanted to live like a family unit, cooking and eating together, chores together etc. This proved the wrong move. Mike's brother, Do, had arrived in the UK a few months previously and had been living up north and decided to move down south and so he moved into the squat. Trixie proved to be incompatible to the arrangements in the new house. Cooking on her own and leaving a mess in the kitchen, refusing to help clean the house etc., etc. Paul and Sue went on holiday to South Africa and Rhodesia and a big argument developed between Trixie and myself. We fought for days and eventually I said I was kicking her out, obviously she refused stating that she wanted to speak to Paul first, well he arrived back and backed my decision and off she went swearing and cursing to her mum's house. After that the house settled into a peaceful routine and soon Paul and Sue announced that they were getting married. Parents and family arrived for the wedding and chaos ensued, including me taking the blame for Paul and Mike's hash, as I was the only one without family present. This turned out to be a bad move as Sue and Nikki's dad, who became a regular feature in my life due to the friendship, blamed me for years for being their drug dealer and addict.

Soon enough the lease was up, Paul and Sue moved to a Tied cottage in Bolney, Mike and Nikki to a Tied cottage between Haywards Heath and Cuckfield in Copyhold Lane, and I moved, firstly into a tent on the outskirts of Haywards Heath and then into a room offered by a workmate when winter was approaching. Paul and Sue soon had a baby, Nick, and not long after moved to Johannesburg.

I had studied my environment enough, I had studied society and history enough, I had discussed the world enough, the decadence of Western Society disgusted me, Politics was corrupt, the Police were the tool of corruption, Civil Servants were lackeys and the Church was corrupt and yet it was still a reasonably peaceful world. With the beginnings of international terrorism, the ending of the wave of independence was close and spreading hope throughout the world, people could still hitch-hike anywhere in the world (except Russia, China and a few other places), hell, Buhtan had only started letting tourists in a few years earlier after building hotels and infrastructure! An independent Zimbabwe was not far off with the South African Anti-Apartheid system in South Africa becoming a bigger and bigger target. The hippies had opened western society's mind to freedom, sex, political corruption drugs music etc. The world was opening up I and I wanted to see it. I wanted to travel again, Africa was off the books for now, it was home and I would return, the States was too vast at the moment, Europe is a museum I had already visited, Canada was too cold. So I started wandering, directionless and I took the first step, a ferry to Holland.

# Chapter 10

As I didn't want to stay in Europe I started hitching out to Germany, got a lift with a predatory gay man in a Porsche who refused to let me out of the car, I had to leg it when he stopped for petrol. I continued through Germany, Switzerland, Italy and Greece, virtually nonstop. I slowed down when I got into Istanbul. I rested up and appreciated the change in culture, I continued to retrace my steps of my previous travels, down to the tranquillity of Bodrum. I spent a week there and then moved on to Iraq. Saddam, although not yet the elected leader, was the de facto leader and the people had a totally different attitude from my visit five years previously. I took a bus straight through to Iran. Ayatollah Khomeini, not quite the Supreme Leader but still the Leader after the revolution, was not allowing certain foreigners in the country but was still issuing Transit Visas, so from Shalomchcc to Sarakhs was three days of train talking to other travellers, avoiding the guards and reading.

Arriving in Afghanistan, was peaceful and the people were friendly and helpful. I proceeded to Kabul and then onto Khost were I rented a room and intended to stay for Christmas. I had been thinking of my family quite a lot and sent letters to parents, brothers and sisters to let them know I was to be based here until January, and I could be reached through the local Post Office. I settled into the area well and was enjoying the solitude and the locals who were very laid back (even though a civil war was dominating the north) and who basically worked for a Tribal Leader whose main export was Heroin and Hashish, but I was left in peace to enjoy the beautiful valley and its surrounding mountains.

I spent most of my time walking, thinking and reading the Bible. This time the Bible was not just History and Philosophy but the Spirit of Christ (not the Holy Spirit) started to enlighten me. In my early years Religion was part of my upbringing, during my teenage years I started to explore Religion to get away from my family's religious control, my 'Educational Years' was a time of rejection of presented alternatives, but all along I kept my beliefs, but why? That was what I was finding out now. Often in the evenings I would chat with the locals about religion and their knowledge of the Old Testament was better than mine but on The Koran and The New Testament we differed greatly but no animosity ever entered the discussions. I discovered that I wanted to be a Christian because I now believed through my communication with the Bible and the Power of God and my belief strengthened although I still could not reconcile with The Church.

A week or so before Xmas I got notice of a package at the Post Office. I immediately went there with hopes of communication from my family. On arrival the Post Master informed me that he did not know where I was and that he had sent it back that morning. After a long and drawn out process, there was a phone call I was informed that I could pick it up at the main Post Office in Kabul. So I went home and packed things for a few days and took the evening bus to Kabul. On arrival I found a Yata, (Hostel), ate and went to bed. The following day I was up early and made my way down to the Post Office. I was early and had breakfast at a local cafe and then proceeded to the Post Office and picked up a small parcel. I then returned to the cafe had cup of 'tea' while I opened the parcel. Two letters, one from a friend Don, informing me he was heading this way and one from my mum, along with a belated 21st birthday present, a gold signet ring with the my initials engraved on it! I was happy to learn that not all my family had rejected me! I walked back to the Yata and collected my things for my return trip to Khost when all hell broke loose. People running, some curious and peeping around corners, out of windows, slightly ajar doors, cars hooting and trying to hurry in the chaotic streets. Then they came, Russian tanks and troops, instructions screaming out of a bullhorn and foreigners being rounded up, me included. We were taken to the town hall where we were guarded for nearly 24 hours and then herded onto busses to Pakistan. The rest of my belongings, basically some clothes and books were lost. The bus dropped us at the Pakistan border and we caught another bus to Islamabad. For about six months I wandered around the Indian subcontinent, not really stopping anywhere, a day here, a day there, no more than a week anywhere. Generally I found the travels great but I did not think about much at all.My time of travel and contemplation came to an end and I slowly moved towards Crete which meant a flight from Karachi to Istanbul due to the growing problems in Iran. Arriving in Istanbul I met a German family, Ralf, his wife, a daughter about 7 or 8 and a baby a few months old. We were all staying in a youth Hostel near the old part of

Istanbul and a few blocks from the Marmara sea. Ralf had learnt his English from listening to Bob Dylan, his wife spoke no English but his elder daughter was a marvel at languages. Through their travels, and Ralf had been travelling for over 15 years with both daughters born on the road. The daughter spoke 9 languages, including Hindi, Arabic, Greek, English and, obviously, German. While sitting on our beds in the dormitory after a street food dinner we were discussing our various travels when a commotion of loud voices and heavy footsteps rushing upstairs interrupted our conversation, Ralf jumped up and ran to the door, shouted something to his wife who grabbed a packet out of their bags threw it to Ralf who disappeared out the window and the last I saw of him he was skipping across the haphazard rooftops of Istanbul while virtually simultaneously a dozen police crashed into the room shouting and grabbing anyone who moved. The bustle calmed down and we were all separated while the police searched our belongings one at a time. It was a drug bust, and Ralf had been carrying. Nobody else was but as Turkey had the death penalty for drugs, even hash, understandably everyone was nervous with the reputation of corruption among the Turkish police, (Midnight Express had been released about a year earlier). It took about an hour but we were all left to get on with our evening. I tried to talk to Ralf's wife but she just took her kids and prepared them for bed.

I left the next day and found myself sleeping at the port of Pireas, waiting for the morning and the one and only, ferry to Crete. Around midday I eventually found a room in a farm cottage outside Kalamaki near Tympaki. It was a large but basic room, I suppose like an old bedsit type, with a double bed, a single electric light, a square 4 seater table and a fireplace for both warmth and cooking. With autumn in full swing and the days shortening I didn't want to sit around doing nothing as I was running out of money but at this time Greece was not a member of the EU so finding work wasn't easy. I met an American couple renting a cottage nearby and they suggested catching snails. French lorries would arrive at around 7am every day and pay cash by weight for the snails. So I entered the snail catching industry and made enough money for my day to day expenses and as I was getting up early I could enjoy the autumn days which were bright and sunny, mostly, with occasional thunderstorms.

A couple weeks after my arrival I noticed a blue van parked at the rear of my room which had a 2 bedroomed granny flat and I guessed it had been rented out. A few hours later while sitting and reading there was a knock at the door and in walked Ralf and we were both surprised to say the least. We started talking about how and why we came to Crete. I discovered that this was his wintering sojourn and he had been doing it for years, first in the room I was occupying and then as his family grew moved into the flat. He was well known in the area and generally took work to occupy himself. He had a seasonal job every year that required 4 people and offered me a position. The money was really good, more than I was earning a week with the snails and only three hours a day – loading cucumbers onto refrigerated lorries headed to Germany. So started my brief career as a cucumber loader! The pay from the company itself was not good but the lorries came on the daily ferry that arrived at about 9am and returned at 2pm to Pireas. Hence 5 hours to get to the mid southern part of the island, fill up and return to Heraclion. This led to tips from the drivers and the quicker we worked the bigger the tip and this is what gave us our main income. The local Greeks did not like the pressure and the German drivers were happy doing business with their own. The lorries had a capacity of 31,000kg and a length of 14 metres. The Greek company employees would bring the pallets to the loading bay, three of us would run the length of the lorry with 4 boxes of 7 kg each and stack them in a specific pattern while the fourth person would feed the three stackers. I was the feeder lifting 31,000kg in three hours! It was the most gruelling work I had had to date and would take at least an hour to recover while eating lunch and having a few beers. This went on for about a month before the season ran out and I had to move on to other work.

The other jobs I had on Crete included clearing rocks out of a field and burying them - a local land owner gave me the work and would bring me lunch with a bottle of wine and then expected me to get back to work in the afternoon! Needless to say I got more work done in the morning than the afternoon! Olive picking and olive pressing were other jobs and then I had to commute to the north of the island for my final job on Crete – orange picking. Ralf and I became quite chatty although he kept his family at a distance. We occasionally had communal meals and sat around drinking and he smoked hash which I had given up by this stage.

Through our conversations I confirmed that he was a drug smuggler. He would buy hash and heroin in Afghanistan and

Pakistan (his Afghanistan route being disrupted by the Russians) buying his goods in the north of Pakistan he would drive to Quetta in mid Pakistan where he would get on a train to Zahedan in Iran while his wife and kids drove there. The train would stop about 10 kilometres from the border, the drugs loaded onto dozens of trail bikes which would be ridden through the desert border area while the train continued through Customs and Immigration and stop again to collect the drugs from the bikers who would then get paid. Ralf would then meet up with his wife and kids, drive through to Turkey where he had a regular contact at the border and continue into Greece for the winter, then continue up to Germany in the spring.

The people of Crete were open and trusting, the village supermarket, pub and gathering centre was on the local square outside a general store as it had the only public TV in the village, owned by a lady, Maria (I felt that all the elderly Greek women were called Maria).

Maria's daily fresh deliveries always arrived in the early hours of the morning, before she opened and if anyone wanted something they could take it and leave the money in a tin left for that purpose. One day her produce and milk was stolen and we, the foreigners, came under suspicion. As Ralf was well known to the villagers they ask him for help. We got together with some other tourists and set out to find the culprit, who we had caught before midday, an Englishman, high on a natural local drug, datura, which is a psychoactive plant related to the Mexican genus. We hauled him up to the village where he was handed over to the locals who made him pay for what he took and then ran him out of the village with the threat of the police if he returned.

One day Ralf returned from the village saying that Zimbabwe-Rhodesia was getting independence. I had been off the grid for so long that I had totally missed the Zimbabwe – Rhodesia period. I hurried up to Maria's place to watch the news, settlement talks for an independent Zimbabwe were underway and I realized that a real possibility for Independence was opening up and decided to go home. Three days later I was on a bus to London. This was my first sojourn in London, although I had visited many times. I stayed with friends Sarah and Rick in Bethnal Green and got a job as a forklift driver at a local warehouse. Sarah was a great cook and one evening cooked a special meal for us and some guests. She would not tell us what it was and so we enjoyed a lovely three course meal with the main dish being fried and battered chicken legs which did not taste quite like chicken but were really tasty. Only after the meal Sarah informed us that we had just eaten frogs legs! Sorry people, not my choice of a meal although it was really good, it would be my one and only time as it is more the thought than anything else that puts me off. I enjoyed my time in London going to concerts, (I saw Pink Floyd playing The Wall), reading, getting to know the London markets, pubs, museums, even joining in on a protest march with students and working. However my primary aim was to save money and head home to Zimbabwe.

# Chapter 11

Before moving on I would like to address me, my frame of mind and how I had changed, grown, shrunk or whatever during the intervening years.

I had observed different societies and individuals around a good part of the world, a few countries I had lived in, a few I passed through. I had studied, I had varied work experience, but how had I developed? I have always been an optimist and mostly critical of authority. However I had gone through rejecting my Catholic upbringing, foraging through Buddhism, read the Koran and the Bhagavad Gita, chatted with Hindis and Muslims and returned to my Christian roots, although still apprehensive of the church. My conclusion was that God manifested to man as man wants to see God. In other words we all have the same benevolent God just different ways to worship. I had experienced and become fascinated by the drug culture, which I believe that anyone who has not been involved in it can understand and help its addicts. This is shown by example through Alcoholics Anonymous, so why can't society do the same with drug addicts instead of victimizing them? Authority, be it in politics, Police, church or the schoolroom is corrupt, although I learnt that not everyone in positions of authority is corrupt.

I became a true follower of the 'Hippie Revolution' and I believe that the freedoms we experience are a direct result of those relativity few people who didn't really know what they were doing. Obviously the hippie movement had some leaders, Abbie Hoffman, Timothy Leary, Allen Ginsburg, Ken Kesey, Jack Kerouc, etc. The hippies just lived their lives as they saw fit; men grew their hair, pre-marital sex was no longer taboo, great music, Grateful Dead, Janis Joplin, Jimi Hendrix, The Doors, Jefferson Airplane, etc. came out with psychedelic music, Bob Dylan, Joan Baez, Nina Simone, Country Joe, etc. were the leaders of protest music, the guitar became a lead instrument in its own right. Pink Floyd, The Who, Led Zepplin, Credence Clearwarter Revival, Steppenwolf, etc. wrote music, not pop songs, some tracks going on for 10 minutes or more and what did all these groups have in common: telling people to think for themselves and of course, fighting the record companies for their expression of music. Music has played a massive part in my life and through the great music I started to follow the musicians themselves, not only the ones who died through drug overdoses or the narcissists but people who were helping society and fighting the tyranny of government. For instance Frank Zappa, known by many for his guitar was not just a great musician but a great composer. His music was not stuck on one genre but he wrote and played rock, pop, jazz, jazz fusion, orchestral, classical modernism, African American rhythm and blues and doo-wop, writing classical compositions while still in high school. His iconoclastic views parodied politics, people, religion, sex, pop culture, men, women, mainstream education, etc. He was a fervent believer in freedom of speech, political participation, anti-communist , anti- religion and a capitalist, also being anti-censorship. He was anti-drugs, although a heavy tobacco smoker but advocated for legalization.

The USA government tried to introduce censorship and age restrictions to music, Frank Zappa was one of the few musicians, along with John Denver who attended Senate hearings in defence of artists' rights to freedom of expression. I will return to this subject later.

Zappa is just one of the musicians who have had an influence on me. Others include Alice Cooper, The Tubes, Pink Floyd, David Bowie, Jefferson Airplane, Jimi Hendrix, Meat Loaf, , not just for their musical ability but also for their visual stimulus, while great groups like, Steely Dan, Procol Harum, Audience, It's a Beautiful Day, Little Feat, Allman Brothers, Steve Miller, offer brilliant compositions and great lyrics that are not just rehashed love songs. Groups like Led Zeppelin and Deep Purple introduce 'Heavy Rock' in great style and led the way for heavy metal. Roy Harper, John Martyn, Joni Mitchell, Ry Cooder, Free, oh, the list of great musicians goes on and on and what they all have in common is that they were great innovators who led the way in not just music, but the liberalization of our society.

Books were also an integral part of the 'Hippie Revolution'. For me, reading and music went hand in hand and many books of the sixties and seventies contributed to the enlightenment of the age we now live in. Reading, along with the classics (Chaucer, Shakespeare, Dickens, Austen, Tolstoy, Hemmingway, Dostoevsky, Orwell, Melville Joyce, Wilde, Tolkien, Hardy and so the list goes on and on), brought me to love science fiction and science fantasy, (Asimov, Bradbury, Dick, Clarke, Heinlein ,Frank Herbert, etc.). These genres really helped me get a grip on my view of society but the books that introduced me to the modern world and the society in which we live, were the books that were skimming the edges of society often entering the illegal. Abbie Hoffman was tried for conspiracy and inciting a riot for organizing protests, and generally was a thorn in the side of various government organizations including the FBI and the CIA. His book 'Revolution for the Hell of it' landed him a five year sentence but the content was a chronicle of his political activism with a strong anti-war theme. Abbie Hoffman was also into LSD and the book details an attempted levitation of the Pentagon by 50,000 anti-war protesters. Although a little on the crazy side, Abbie Hoffman managed to reach millions of people and was one of the leaders that 'woke society up'.

Timothy Leary was a psychologist who loved psychedelic drugs and proclaimed 'the hero of American consciousness' and a 'neuronaut'. Leary was fond of catchphrases like, turn on, tune in, drop out'. He worked on various psychedelic drug trials including the Psilocybin Project and the Concord Prison Experiments. Leary was fired from Harvard University due to the experiments. He believed that psychedelic drugs were "for serious purposes, such as spiritual growth, pursuit of knowledge, or their own personal development" and testified to this in the 1966 Senate subcommittee, after which LSD was banned. When asked about the dangers of LSD he replied "Sir, the motor car is dangerous if used improperly... Human stupidity and ignorance is the only danger human beings face in this world." Also in 1966 he was found with a small personal amount of marijuana while crossing into Mexico and was sentenced to 30 years in prison, he appealed the case. The song 'Come Together' was written by John Lennon for Leary's candidacy as Governor of California on the day his conviction was overturned by the Supreme Court. He was bust again with 2 roaches,( hash joint butts), and sentenced to 20 years, 10 for the roaches an 10 for a previous possession charge. Leary and his wife bust out of prison and were smuggled out of the USA by the Weathermen. Eventually being caught in Afganistan, returned to the States and stood trial for offences totalling a possible 95 years, he went to jail and was released in 1976 after making a deal with the FBI. No one was charged or convicted through his information. He continued to have a following including many famous people, Michael Horiwitz, (the father of Winona Ryder and his god-daughter). Timothy Leary died in 1996 but lives on in many songs and film references as well as books.

The last thing I would like to mention before moving on is conspiracies. Yes I was also introduced to Conspiracy theories,with JF Kennedy being the first and most obvious. However this led me on to reading many books and fact checking through 'reliable' history. I looked at the Freemasons and the Knights Templars as well as some of the more modern ones. However the one that caught my eye in a big way was the Illuminati, especially the Illuminatus Trilogy by Robert Anton Wilson and Robert Shea. The book was released in 1975 and contained the authors' version of conspiracies, history and science fiction and written as a satire. To further add to the conspiracies when the book was released in the UK rumours abounded about the book. The USA publishers refused to publish it and so the UK, with a greater freedom of press, published it. The co-author Robert Shea who conducted the research into the Illumanati died in a mysterious accident while trying to publish the book in the UK. Robert Anton Wilson had gone into hiding etc., etc. Without the means to easily check these facts it contributed to the belief in the truth that lies behind the book. Of course these rumours were eventually quashed, especially after Robert Shea was alive and well while carrying on his life as normal in the USA. I never really found out whether this was an advertising gimmick or just a conspirer who read the book spreading the theories through his conspiracy network. Either way the book is a great read and as it is written as fiction it leaves you wondering what is true and what isn't.

I read many other counter culture book authors like Herman Hesse, Kurt Vonnegurt, Joseph Heller, Ken Kesey, Jack Kerouc, Hunter S Thompson, Carlos Castenada, etc. As you can imagine all this absorption in a short period left me with a lot to sort through as not only was the political world reshaping but so was my mind. Onto Zimbabwe!

# Chapter 12

About 18 months after Zimbabwe got independence I arrived home. The first thing on my list was to catch up with family and friends and to this end I visited my sisters on their respective farms, soaking up the spectacular land, the beautiful sunsets, the tranquillity that only Africans can understand. I also visited some of the infinitely alluring landmarks of Zimbabwe, Hwange, Victoria Falls, and Kariba. Back in Harare I started to look around for some old friends, various of whom had also returned, but sadly some I could not trace, and so the first few months were almost like a continual party, catching up with who had been where and done what.

I was also introduced to a new group of people: blacks returning to Zimbabwe after exile and a new middle class in the country. I felt vastly encouraged by what I was seeing in Zimbabwe. Almost everyone was looking forward to a bright future, except, of course a few die hard Rhodesians. I also got my first permanent job since my studies finished and worked with the biggest photographic company in Zimbabwe, which launched my career. For me this was perfect for my return home as I was travelling around the country doing a variety of jobs from weddings, pack shots, farm portraits etc. and this brought me back into contact with the country and the people. The whole country was happy and racism had taken a back seat. The economy was booming and it was expected that the National debt would be paid off in under 10 years, this is after a 30 years of the protest, including 'the troubles' leading up to the guerrilla war. Some of the politics was still being ironed out and then the first elections since independence were approaching.

People were saying that the independence vote was one for Independence and only Mugabe could have brought it about, whereas this vote was for the future of the country and the result showed that Mugabe, although he won the elections was not as popular with the people as previously thought. He started his campaign of terror. First slaughtering his main opposition Joshua Nkomo's followers, the Ndebele tribe, murdering over 30,000 innocent people and the world stood by and watched.

My social life was great and I moved in with a friend, Spike, who I had met in the UK and was a friend of Mike's. I also met Everistis. He was a Commander in ZANLA in the North East districts and was instrumental in getting Mugabe out of Rhodesia on release from his imprisonment. We talked a lot about the war but with no judgment on either side. Rhodesia was defending its position, Zimbabwe was fighting for Independence, Zimbabwe won and now there was no need for retribution, we could all live together. Long before the Zimbabwe troubles started Everistis started to dislike Mugabe and was saying he was not the man he thought he was, he did not elaborate but was losing confidence in the political system.

I got a girlfriend, Sarah, who was Sue and Nikki's sister. Their family was a family of four daughters and no sons, hence the father, David, was very protective of his daughters. An episode in the UK when Mike had told David that his hash was actually mine was now coming to bite me in the bum.

While I was just a friend of Nikki and Sue I was tolerated, but when I started going out with Sarah, David declared war on me. I was banned from the house, my phone calls were disconnected (we didn't have mobiles or cell phones in those days) and I was generally blocked at every move. Our relationship was strained but surviving. Meanwhile Spike got himself a girlfriend. One day he was cutting his nails and toenails in the lounge and when he completed the task he gathered the cuttings, and searched for possible missing clippings, gathered them together, took them outside and burnt them. I enquired about this curious behaviour to be informed that he was probably breaking up with his girlfriend when she came over later. This information didn't really answer my question as he was a bit of a womanizer and breaking up was common for him so I pressed the question. Well unbeknownst to me his girlfriend was a witch and he was worried about retribution!

I lost my job, just not enough work and I was told that I could still do weddings and other events on an ad hoc basis. Looking for work proved difficult, the law was proportional employment by race - experience or qualifications were of no consequence. I moved back in to my parents as I could no longer pay rent. We had a monkey at this stage, a cute little vervet with a desire for whiskey. My mother would have a glass of whiskey in the evening and Cheeky, the vervet, would pounce on it instantly. He was still quite young and needed company almost all the time and would sleep on the pillow. During the day he would roam around the garden, about an acre, but always come in the house to sleep and socialize. One day he disappeared. I combed the neighbourhood, searched in gardens, empty plots, everywhere. He was just gone. I got home one evening when the gardener came and showed me something, Cheeky's head. I was angry, pissed off and ready to murder! I asked if he knew who had done this, he said no , but it is part of a Sangoma's, (basically a witchdoctor), ritual and if I tried to find out who did it, I would be cursed and anyway witchdoctors are legal in Zimbabwe so no legal retribution would be forthcoming. I was just pissed off.

I, unfortunately, suffer from a form of dermatitis which western medicine has not been able to control. Every now and then I would travel out to my sister's farm to visit a witchdoctor, who would give me a bag of herbs to mix with hair oil which I would put on the affected parts for half an hour before having a hot bath. Part of the ceremony was to catch a chameleon and symbolically move the chameleon over my body. This part of the ceremony I passed over as I knew the herbs in the oil worked. However my mum had a gardener who was a great believer in witchdoctors and insisted that I do the ceremony as instructed, so in order to pacify him I agreed and asked him to find me a chameleon in the garden. A little taken aback he agreed and left, returning about half an hour later with a 3 metre branch with a chameleon perched at the end. I had forgotten that the chameleon is a mythic creature to the Shonas and they are afraid of them!! I took the chameleon off the branch, they are fierce looking creatures when scared, and put it in a drawer while I had my bath and then took the chameleon out while the gardener witnessed me releasing it again and he was extremely happy that I had fulfilled the witchdoctor's wishes and was quite relieved that the chameleon was now back in its environment.

Finding work was impossible and the country was declining rapidly I decided to leave and immigrated to Johannesburg, South Africa. Again I got a good job in the photographic field in a large chain, Game, as the Photographic Department Assistant Manager and moved in next door to some long-time friends Paul and Sue who now had 2 children, Nicholas, who was born in the UK, and Tessa. The accommodation was easy to get as Sue was the supervisor of the flats, while Paul was working in a small printing company. I soon got promoted at work and was running the Photographic Division of one of the biggest companies in South Africa. Along with this went approximately 300 employees, most of whom were Black, Indian and Coloured, this once again threw me into a political arena I did not want and was not prepared for.

Although South Africa was a lot more peaceful than Zimbabwe, press censorship was paramount and an undercurrent of violence permeated the society. To clarify, the people in the street were great. irrelevant of sex, colour or religion but throughout South Africa violence was escalating against the government and then spread into suburban areas and shopping centres. Bombings in towns were becoming more frequent as were attacks on farms, power stations, etc. However life carried on as normal, the music concerts and festivals were great and held to mixed audiences although the culture of music limited the mix of the races. Hillbrow was the centre of youth culture where at places like Hilbrow Records one could obtain any album, legal or not, night clubs were active and politics was ignored by the white minority youth who were in favour of a free South Africa but too lethargic to do anything about it other than to have black friends who they would meet at concerts and night clubs; basically ambivalent. On the other hand there were a handful of white South Africans who did stand up and fight for the blacks but they were few and far between. As in Rhodesia the white South African males were brought up to believe in the state, the fight against the communist aggressor and doing their duty through conscription.

However the Apartheid system was starting to crack even if few people realized it. I had many conversations where people refused to accept that change was on its way even when you could see it in enclaves all around South Africa. Sun City was within Bophuthatswana, a Bantustan, where mixed marriages were accepted as well as gambling, inter racial sex etc. and was aimed at the middle and upper class whites in South Africa to come and spend their money in a multi-racial haven, nick named, appropriately, Sin City. This was with the blessing of the South African Apartheid government. A similar situation transpired in the Transkei, an 'Independent' homeland, although a bit far away for the success that Sun City had.

Well, back to my work. I enjoyed it but it really showed me that criminality exists on all levels of society. During the first year or so at Game in Johannesburg we went through four Managing Directors. I may have the order incorrect but they were fired for the following reasons; incompetence – the first few months after opening the shop was in a total mess, stock not arriving, aisles in a state of chaos and impassable, doors not opening on time, signage not kept up to date, etc. The next manager was fired for theft in collusion with the Security Manager. They would pop down to the shop on Saturday afternoon or Sundays when the shop was closed and load up a bakkie with goods including fridges, stoves, washing machines, stereo systems etc., yes, the big stuff. Not long after he was fired I saw him working in a Fish and Chip shop. The next manager, seemed to, finally get things under control but he had zero communication ability. I enjoyed working at Game as there were many really nice people and they formed a good part of my social life. I soon got promoted and was running a sizeable chunk of the store, the photographic, audio and video as well as the whites departments.

The store, due to its size, had to have strict security measures, and upon finishing for the day staff passed through a security point where staff and/ or their belongings were inspected. One day a commotion was happening near the exit when a rather large lady was being conducted into the 'search room'. She was given a strip search whereupon two kilos of Quality Street chocolates were found stuffed up her fanny, while some poor security guard had to fish around in there to get them all out, soggy or not!

I had a Kawasaki Z750 at this time and along with some mates we would go on various good rides. One popular ride was the breakfast run on Sunday mornings to Hartebeesport

Dam, I cannot remember the name but it may have been the Flying Saucer Cafe, or nicknamed thus. It was not a run where bikers gather at a starting point as in this part of South Africa has two major cities, Johannesburg and Pretoria, but also many smaller ones, Rustenburg, Randburg, Centurion, Halfway House, Roodepoort, etc. The ride could be anything from an hour to three depending on the route and activities you stopped at on the way. At one point bikers would gather on an old but good tarmac road for drag racing, another point for wheelies, doughnuts and general mayhem and also many beauty spots to stop and admire. There were just many bikers on the road and the closer you got to the dam, the more there were. While arriving at the café, hundreds of bikes would be there all shapes and sizes, modified, home built, straight out the box, decals and painting in amazing designs, all there just for breakfast and the ride. By about 13:00 the bikes were dwindling as people were heading back, usually along the most direct route.

Cycling and motorcycling have opened my eyes to the selfishness of motorists and a great comeuppance happened while riding to a motor bike meeting in Natal as three bikes were riding behind each other and not abreast, just enjoying the ride when a Chevy Camaro came hurtling past in between the third and second riders, forcing the rider off the road and nearly causing an accident. After a car had passed on the other side of the road the Camaro did the same thing nearly knocking the second rider off his bike, as he did it the third time, Peter the lead rider took out a Magnum 44 and put a bullet straight into the Camaro engine block which ground to a halt while the three bikers just cruised on. Cyclist are the worst, they have no respect for anyone else on the road, they do what they want and treat public roads as their private property. They really need to learn road courtesy and stick to the law of the road. Meanwhile back at work...

# Chapter 13

The workers were restless and a general strike was brewing. I tried to inform my employers of the upcoming strike and knew that this one was going to be critical and violent. My bosses had no ears for me and called me paranoid. I requested a two weeks due leave starting the weekend before I knew the strike was starting. I spent a glorious holiday exploring the Namib Desert on my motorbike.

Namibia is a great place with nature at its unfettered best. The first place I wanted to visit was Hotazel, it was still in South Africa but on the weather reports it was the hottest place in South Africa and I just liked the name. It was a reasonably short ride, about 600 km on virtually deserted good tarmac road, and I got there in under 4 hours. Not much to be seen, but a bar, general store, petrol station, a post office and a park. It was a small hub for two mines in the area. After a lazy lunch in the midday heat, happy that I was there in winter with temperatures at about 37*C, I set off for the Transfrontier Park , a game reserve that spans the border between Namibia and South Africa. However the road soon turned into a thickly sanded dirt road making my 750cc road bike a bit heavy and was sliding and ploughing through the sand so I turned back to the main road and headed back to Uppington and continued through to Karasburg where I spent the night. The following day I made the short ride along a rocky road with Fish River Canyon being my destination. Approaching a few stone buildings in the distance I decided to rest and water up but as I approached I saw a gap opening up and slowly the majesty of Fish River Canyon came into view while the stone buildings turned out to be deserted stone huts for sleeping and a braai area with an all-encompassing panoramic view of a horse shoe shaped section of the Fish River Canyon. I rested during the afternoon and the following day found a path leading down to the canyon itself. It was a gruelling hike but swimming in the cool waters of the river and spending the better part of the day wandering around this pocket of lush green in the heart of the desert while a few different species of buck were meandering around their feeding grounds and the obvious bounty of the smaller of God's creatures, lizards, dassies, etc. were darting around whilst, birds were gracing the skies, black eagles were on the hunt for their daily sustenance. All too soon I had to head back up the exhausting path to the encampment. The day had been long and tiring and so I just opened a can of beans for dinner and climbed into my sleeping bag and fell asleep between my bike and the campfire.

After a hearty breakfast of fried egg and bacon I set off for my next destination, Luderitz. A short way back along the rocky road there was a junction, a short cut to the Lüderitz – Keetmanshoop main road, it was not a long way but again the road was rock and sand so going was slow and the approximately 175km took be the better part of the day, so I found a small hotel to spend the night and freshen up. Dinner was great and filling and the local farmers came in for a drink and a jolly evening was had by all. The next day I headed out to Lüderitz, passing a sign warning that anyone stopping along the route through the diamond area would be arrested. The road was not too bad and so I made good time until a sand storm hit. The farmers in the pub had warned me about them stating they could strip a vehicle of its paint in under 10 minutes! Well I stopped and covered the windward side of my bike with panniers, tent, sleeping bag and anything else I could find. The sandstorm was a quick one and only delayed me about an hour. While I was reloading my bike I saw a mob of wild horses congregating not far from the road. I admired their nobility for a while and then continued my chore and headed off to Lüderitz. Upon arrival I was stopped at a roadblock and asked why I had broken my journey and searched for diamonds, once again unpacking and repacking my bike. I eventually made it into a chalet on the outskirts of this small town which had two main industries, De Beers for diamonds and fishing. Lüderitz was originally a fishing village until diamonds were found. For those of you not aware of the Diamond coast, it is an area of 26,000sq/km along the Namibian coast and extends about 100km inland and 320km along the coast.

The story goes that in 1908 while constructing a railway line one of the German workers saw something glittering in the sand and directed one of his workers to pick it up. It was a diamond and hence, a beautiful town was founded, Kolmanskop. The town was extremely rich with its architecture reflecting German towns, it hosted the first x-ray centre in the southern hemisphere and the first Tram in Africa! The affluent town had all the amenities, hospital, power station, school, etc. However when diamonds started to run out and the area around the Orange river opened up with people just picking up diamonds in the sand, Kolmanskop was deserted as the inhabitants moved south to easier pickings. I visited the town accompanied by a De Beers guide, but at that time Kolmanskop fell under the general rules of the Diamond Coast, no photography, so the only visual media I was allowed was to buy some postcards.

I also discovered sand roses while walking along the beach near the lighthouse. The lighthouse keeper saw me roaming the beach and we started talking. He showed me where the sand roses are formed on the underside of compacted beach sand due to evaporation around some crystals. He also showed me how to, and helped me to, dig up some before inviting me to the lighthouse for a drink and dinner. During the discussion I told him about the sand storm and the horses I had seen on the road. He immediately asked if I had taken photos of them and he was disappointed with my negative reply and then explained that horses belonging to the German Army during World War 1 had been released into the desert after the war and had not been seen since the 1930's and was generally believed that they had died out. I was the only person to see them in 50 years! What an idiot I was.

After a lazy few days around Lüderitz and exploring the area including a private guided tour of Sperrgebiet, organized by the lighthouse keeper, I set off for my next destination, the Hoba meteorite near Grootfontien. I left early and instead of going straight to Keetmanshoop and the national road up to Winkhoek, I was told of a slower, more direct but panoramic route that crossed part of the desert and I decided to take this route. It was only about 200km to the next mining town, Helmeringhausen, but was advised to take it slowly as the road is sandy and rocky probably taking up to six hours. I was also warned that if something happens it could be 2 or 3 days until another vehicle would be on that road. However it sounded great and I took it.

The road was rough, sandy and rocky and I could not do more than 50 - 60 km per hour but the ride was splendid. After reaching the turn off to Helmeringhausen the landscape changed to a mixture of sparse grass lands leading to massive dunes on one side and distant mountains on the other. Around 06:30 the sun rose over a kopje in the distance bringing beautiful sandy rose waves of streaky light stretching through the cloudless sky. I stopped to take a picture and admire God's canvas before remounting and moving. The road was tough going with soaring heat and round about 10:00 I again stopped for a brief rest, some water, remove my helmet and coat which had been needed when setting off in the morning, it had been bloody cold. I had been riding for about 5 hours when I rode down a dip as the first vehicle I had seen since leaving Luderitz came into view over the horizon from the other side of the dip. As we approached I noticed that it was a police Land Rover and we stopped to chat as we passed. The policeman enquired about the state of the road, as one of his duties was to check for problems along the route. After chatting for a while he informed me that unfortunately he would have to issue me a fine for riding without a helmet! I was flabbergasted! All around was sand and he was the only person and car I had seen all day. I pointed this out to him and he just replied that the law was the law and I could pay the fine at any police station along the route. Pissed off I continued my journey.

A short time later I arrived in Helmeringhausen which appeared a smaller version of Hotazel but at least it had a pub and a room. I cleaned up and went downstairs for a beer and great big plank steak for dinner. Locals from the area drifted in, mostly mining families and local service business workers. I got chatting to a chap who was a tourist guide for the area and he brought photos of his specialty, dune rolling. I had never heard of it but looked fun. I went out the next morning with him. We went out in two Land Rovers, one to the top of the dune, which requires driving skills beyond my imagination, while the other made its way to the bottom. We were sitting in the rear of the Land Rover which had customized seats and strapped in with pretty tight seat belts. At the highest point of the dune he slid the vehicle over the top and rolled and rolled, which carried on over and over until we reached the bottom! Best Fairground ride I have ever had!!

I returned to the room and left for Windhoek at about midday. The road continued to be rough and rocky while traversing the Tiras Mountains until three hours later I completed 140km arriving in Maltahoho. I decided to continue through to Mariental, which was the main North - South road taking me to Windhoek and beyond. To my delight and good fortune the road soon turned into tarmac and I completed the trip a little after sunset. Again I took a room and freshened up, had a beer, dinner and went to bed early as I wanted to be on the road before sun up.

Rising early I left as planned and once again stopped on the road to watch the sunrise. Windhoek was about 270 km and sitting at 185 to 200kmph I anticipated about an hour and a half ride and I wanted to be well north of Windhoek by sunset as I am not fond of cities. However about 10 minutes from Windhoek my bike started playing up. Stuttering, farting, grinding and generally bad behaviour, the last 10 minutes actually took forty-five minutes while finding a mechanic took another hour. The bike had been put through a lot on the sand and rocky roads. Sand had taken up residence in every conceivable nook and cranny, the chain looked like miniature moon rocks had taken up residence and the back tyre was virtually threadbare. Luckily it was still quite early and the mechanic could get it done by closing. So I spent the day wandering around Windhoek and looked around my old haunts from the early seventies to see if anyone I knew was around but no luck. I returned to the garage just before closing, picked up my bike, enquired about a camping site on the Grootfontein road and set out. The bike felt good, a clean-up, full service, new tyre and new chain put some life back into her and I opened her up sitting at 210 to 230 for a good half hour until I came to a nice quiet camping site just off the main road. The camp site was tranquil with only the staff wandering around and, with the glorious sunset only an African can feel in their bones, just over with a red dusk spreading over the land, I approached a staff member for wood or coal in order to braai my dinner, instead an invitation to join them was forthcoming and so it was that I joined the locals for sadza and my first and only taste of snake meat. I don't say only because it was not tasty, because it really was, but for me it is just the thought of eating snake, like frog legs, that puts me off.

After dinner I went back to my tent and grabbed my sleeping bag and went to sleep under the stars. The stars under an African sky are plentiful, bright and really make you feel humble but under a desert sky the stars seem to outnumber the gaps between them and the brilliance of the night is like hundreds of thousands of glittering diamonds lighting your way through the universe. A truly spectacular sight! I got up late, made breakfast and set off for Grootfontein just before 10:00, arriving about two and a half hours later, had a Wimpy lunch and headed out to Hoba meteorite. It was in the ground with nothing around it other than the excavated hole, being about 3 metres squared and 1 metre in depth, it was a dark metallic grey with a tiny right angle chip of silver, maybe an inch by an inch, which seemed to have been cut off from it. Locals tell the story that when professionals (I assume scientists) came to move it, they couldn't and so cut a small piece about an inch cube which was too heavy for a man to lift and so had to be machine lifted and taken to the lab in that manner, the meteorite is estimated to weigh 60 tonnes.

I set out for The Etosha National Park and arrived at Namutoni about an hour later after stopping off to view what is considered a beauty spot where the vast natural underground water system surfaced forming a small lush area. Being on a motorbike I had to join a tour which would take me into the park to Halali Camp. While I was waiting I chatted with some of the locals and workers around Namutoni, a German Fort built in 1896. I enquired as to the origins of the fort. One of the locals told a story about the fort. An army captain, Captain Anthony was the original inhabitant having built a small house for himself and his family. He grew to love the area and the vast wildlife. He would regularly go out for days at a time, game spotting and shooting, not for trophies but for his family and the locals. One day he left on a walk about which he anticipated to be about a week. Ten days later some of the porters arrived back without Anthony. The explanation to his wife was that while out hunting he was attacked and killed by lions: no more Tony = Namutoni!! The truth of this tale I have never been able to confirm.

Another piece of luck happened while waiting for the tour bus, two guys about my age arrived in a car, had booked a chalet for three but one of their mates had dropped out at the last minute and asked if I would like to take his place. Of course and thanks very much! Arriving at the camp as it was getting dark we checked in and then went to have a beer overlooking the watering hole. It was fantastic to see various animals, elephant, lion, various antelope come right up and drink almost right under you. Game viewing is great as are the animals and Etosha has many, but not only does it have animals it has various geological features that alone are worth the visit. The great expanse of the salt pan is 4,800 square km being 120 km long in a natural park, 22,270 sq km, a massive park, but only the second largest in Namibia! To give a comparison of size, Wales in the United Kingdom is 20,768 sq km. The salt pan was dry and all you could see was white ground stretching miles north, east and west with little specs of animals in the distant while ostriches and antelope grazed along the rim. Five days of great game viewing with a one day trip to the Petrified Forest just out of the park near Khorixas.

Soon enough it was time to leave Etosha and head on to my next destination, the ghost trees in Dead Vlei. I stayed the night camping under the stars just south of Okaputo, where I went for a beer and a meal in town as the camping site had no such facilities. I started chatting with one of the local farmers who was asking me about my trip, etc. Then we moved on to work and I informed him of the date I was due back at work at which point he burst out laughing stating that it was the day after tomorrow! I had lost all track of time and realized that I would have to make the trip to the ghost trees another time. I went back to the campsite, brought out the map and planned my trip home. The shortest route home would have been through Botswana but that was mostly a dirt road, so the trek would have to be along the main roads, about 2,000km, I was in for a hard ride. I left at 06:00 and arrived home about 21:00 only stopping for short rests when I filled up with petrol.

On arrival at work I was informed that I was asked to go and see the Managing Director by a new employee. Entering his office I was immediately told that my foreknowledge of the strike must mean that I had inside information about the ANC, I was dismissed from my employment, accused of being a political agitator and informed that I had been reported to the authorities. I later found that all he had told me was a load of crock and that he wanted my position for his nephew. However this left me without work, which I quickly rectified by getting a job with Stan's, a photographic chain throughout South Africa. This did not last long only a few months before we had a mutual agreement due to a personality clash with Stan, the owner. I then got employment as the head of the photographic department in the Sandton City Hyperama, where one of their staff had been overlooked for promotion and was very aggressive towards me. However I managed the department well and arranged 'Product Knowledge' sessions with suppliers in order for my staff to keep up to date with the market. These usually involved snacks and drinks, a presentation of various products, question and answer section and finish off with the staff examining the product themselves. On one occasion I asked a friend of mine, Joe, who was the electronics engineer at Mitsubishi to do a product session for us, as at this time Mitsubishi was not doing them but a few weeks later Joe had pulled the strings and a session was arranged I have always thought that Mitsubishi electronics were great and I valued Joe, his electronic knowledge and his friendship. The session went well and during the question and answer section I was questioning the difference between other leading products and the innovations of Mitsubishi, Joe enjoyed the chance to disseminate his knowledge as he could show the advantages of his product Rand for Rand. However on Monday morning I was called into the General Manager's office and, alas, once again given a months' notice, having to leave the premises immediately for tarnishing the Hyperama's name by asking inappropriate questions and causing a rift with one of our suppliers. I tried to explain that the only Mitsubishi member of staff present was a friend, Joe and he and I had appealed to their management in order to arrange the session, all to no avail. I proceeded to my workplace and cleared out my space while my aggressive colleague looked on with a beam on his face, he had finally got the position he thought he deserved. A week later when I went in to get my severance pay I learnt that my cheerful colleague had resigned, as once again, a new manager had been recruited from the outside. I also presented a letter from Mitsubishi, Joe, stating that I had done nothing to tarnish the name of the company and had been thorough in my attitude and questioning to the benefit of Hyperama staff. I had not thought of a wrongful dismissal suite but the general manager asked if I was going to pursue and offered me six months to forget it. I accepted and left with, in total 8 months' pay.

I then got a job as a night shift supervisor at the Kodak labs in Doornfontien, almost central Jo'burg. It was a good job, I would start at 20:00 and finish at 05:00. I had to monitor the paper processing machines, chemical and photo quality control. The nights were really busy averaging between 8,000 and 14,000 photographs per night. Unfortunately the round trip to work was over 100km and after six months I resigned and decided to visit friends and family in Zimbabwe. I only spent a week there catching up and headed home, approximately a 14 hour ride. Leaving early, the ride to BeitBridge was quite quick, doing the 600 odd kilometres in about five hours, but once in South Africa the Police are really vigilant, punishing all traffic infractions without mercy! I stuck to the speed limit all the way until I hit the dual carriageway just before Pretoria and I opened up, sitting at between 180 – 200 Kmph until I slowed down to join the Jo'burg ring road taking me to Randburg. I noticed a Police Car, siren blearing, coming up fast behind me, so I pulled over. The policeman hurried out of his car, swearing at the top of his voice, grabbed my keys out of the bike and threw them onto the side of the road. 'Do you know how fast you were going?' he inquired.

It was a 120 zone so I said 'about 150. I'm really sorry sir but I have had a long ride from Zimbabwe and when I saw the turnoff and I was excited to get home and opened up a little'. '150, just opened up' he screamed, still angry, 'I clocked you at 210 near Roodeplaat and I have be chasing you for over 50 km!' I apologized, took my R800 speeding fine (in those days about half a month's salary), found my keys and finished my trip.

R800 was too much to pay so I decided to contest poverty in the Magistrates' Court in Randburg. As luck would have the Magistrate was a biker and reduced my fine to R50! Talk about luck.

# Chapter 14

After a few weeks of job hunting without success I decided to go back to the UK and then spread out with a bit more travel. Looking at my finances I realized I didn't have enough money to do what I wanted, I made the first of the three worst decisions of my life. With a friend we decided to take some grass into the UK to sell. My friend, who shall remain nameless, organized a pickup of a sack of grass which I collected down in Zululand. I packed it in a tea-chest with household items to make it look like I was emigrating to the UK. I sent it to an address of a house that I was going to rent with another couple of friends but at the moment it was undergoing renovations so the goods would arrive to an empty house under construction. Off I went to the UK. A few weeks later the tea-chest arrived, no problems and in the meantime I organized the help of another friend, Mick I called him and we unpacked the grass, I was not smoking but Mick and others around me were. We weighed the grass which was about 12 kilos. We were going to sell it at the going price, £1.00 per gram which should bring in about £12,000 before expenses etc. We decided to weigh up a kilo at a time and after selling 2 kilos I decided to start my travels. My arrangement with Mick was that 50% belonged to my friend back in SA and the other 50% would be split between him and myself, selling expenses, which was basically petrol, came out of his 25%. With all the agreements made I trotted off to Iceland with another mate Mac.

We arrived in autumn at about 21:00 by the time we were through Customs & Immigration. We got on the bus while watching the sunset on the way into town, Arriving in Reykjavik, we were pointed in the direction of a Hostel, checked in and got to our room in time to watch the sunrise! No, it did not take that long! It was autumn, the days were still long and getting used to the days took a while as we lost track of time. The next morning we walked around the streets awestruck by the city. Many buildings were made of wood, including a multi storied car park! The city is surrounded by sea with various islands close to the shore while mountains appeared as a beautiful backdrop in the distance. We discovered that there was only one road around the island, on the coast and the busses did the circuitous trip leaving at various times during the day. Iceland is reasonably small but full of beautiful scenery. We took the bus to Helgafellssveit, a little village north of Reykjavik. The trip took about 3 hours through grasslands dotted with black sheep with a few hills interrupting the green pastures while the mountains had a continuous presence in the east. Passing a few villages along the way we arrived at our destination with a bit of a shock, there couldn't have been more than dozen houses and a few shops. While picking up some supplies for the evening we enquired as to where we could camp. With the directions given along with the information that there were no camping sites around and we would have to clean up afterwards we set out on what turned out to be about a half hour trek along a dirt road to a lake next to which we pitched our tents, cooked supper on a camping gas stove and wandered along the lake shore. One thing that had struck me was that there seemed to be no trees, plenty of moss and other small plants, but no trees.

Although the days were warm it got chilly at night and we slept with clothes on in our sleeping bags. As it got dark, with silence all around I lay awake straining to hear the sounds surrounding us, yet all I could hear was the gentle lapping of water when I noticed a light gently moving outside. I left the tent to be struck by green light waving around the sky. The beauty was phenomenal and after an awestruck minute or two I dove into my tent to grab my camera in order to capture the dancing of the Aurora Borealis and of course I woke Mac up to witness nature at its best! We hung around another few day days exploring the area before moving on. Rising early we caught the 08:00 bus out and spent the day gazing out of the window at the multitude of fjords, pastures, and sheep with the odd farmhouse scattered here and there before arriving at Akureyri.

Akureyri is at the end of a fjord, lying between two of the highest points in Iceland; it is also a fertile area. Being one of the oldest and largest settlements, the architecture is along similar lines to Reykjavik but due to the long fjord has a calm harbour with a history dating back to the 9th century. However my interest in towns is limited so we only spent one day and two nights there. Taking the bus to Reykjadalur, a hot spring nicknamed Steam Valley, is a stretch of land with steam dissipating into the atmosphere with stretches of land cracked open appearing as if the island was going to tear apart. We entered a cave with two entrances about 50 metres apart and the first thing we noticed was a warning sign against touching the water which was like a mirror with steam vapour gently hugging the surface. The ground in the area was warm, mossy, and wet while in the distance I noticed a factory. Back at the campsite there was a hot pool with both locals and a few tourists relaxing. I enquired about the factory and learnt, to my amazement, that the commercial and urban heating system all came from the hot springs and piped into homes etc!. The following day was spent on a bus to Hoffell, at the bottom of Vatnajokulspjodgardur National Park, the largest glacier on Iceland. The first thing that I noticed was vast swathes of black ice!

After setting up camp for the night we went to bed rather early as the following day we would be climbing up to the glacier. Rising early we left by 07:00 and set out on what started as a gentle climb and got steeper the higher we went. The path was clearly marked and easy to follow, with, as previously noticed, few trees and those that were there only small trees about man height. When I asked a local about the trees, or lack of, I was told "if you see three trees together in Iceland, you have a forest". But seriously, I was surprised to learn that when the Vikings arrived Iceland was full of forests but Iceland was warmer then and everything, in those days, was made of wood, along with the deforestation came cold weather, sheep farming and lava from volcanic eruptions and hence the trees disappeared. It took about three hours to reach the demarcation line between solid earth and ice. Looking over and up along the glacier you can see peaks and troughs along the waves of black tipped ice. The power of nature once again forces your contemplation as you can see the force with which the ice has flattened, covered and destroyed the mountains in its path. The glacier seems to have two tongues surrounding the mountain and will eventually flatten the spot where we were standing. Turning around, looking away from the glacier, a vast flood plain exists, stretching to the distant sea with melted water rushing out from dozens of open lips of the glacier forming a myriad of glistening snakes gently making their way to the sea. Mac and I decided to take a short trek on the ice, unsuccessfully, as we were not properly equipped and even trying to reach one small ice peak, maybe 20 metres high, ended quickly with me on my butt! Returning to land and admiring the view on a walkabout it soon came time to return to camp, arriving, totally knackered, in the early evening, bought a meal in the local shop and went to bed.

The next day we heard about a mountain called Eystrahorn about 50km south, so we decided to head there, getting a lift with a local.  Again nature was showing me her power. A solid mountain of rock, maybe 800 metres high and yet mother nature had chipped away at her over the centuries forming  massive scree slopes of stone and rock spreading across a vast area. Determined to reach the top of the scree at the bottom of the cliff face we set off for what was possibly the hardest walk of my life, the scree was loose and it seemed  that every step you took upwards resulted in two down! However this was not the case as we reached our destination after a good few hours. The massive scale of the mountain can only be appreciated when you are there as the photos I took did it no justice. We made our way down, being a lot easier as now one step resulted in about three with the sliding, but still a difficult walk. Once at the bottom we managed to get another lift to the campsite, where we sat around with other campers cooking, swapping stories and playing guitars until darkness fell and we retired for the night.

The following day we caught a bus and asked the driver where our next stop should be. About an hour into the drive he stopped the bus and pointed out a direction and told us that in the direction indicated was a good walk, so we set off. The land was generally flat with hundreds of little round hills about 4 or 5 five metres round and a couple of metres high, but smooth, almost like a mini mountain range. We met some other people along the route and walked together for a while, we came across a little lake and a river flowing out of it and Mac and I decided that was the spot for us. We pitched our tents and stripped down to sunbathe as it was a hot day and we just lay in the sun watching the little icebergs float on down the river. I have never been one for sunbathing and as I was boiling hot I decided to go for a swim. My foot entered the water and with a scream I jumped right out! The bloody water was freezing. I guess the icebergs should have given it away but it was a really hot day! Anyway the rest of the day was spent exploring during which we found a little bright green house. It was facing south and had a nice green lawn covering it with a door and a window in the front and as we walked around there was no other light source, just a few of, what I would assume, were ventilation holes. Such a curious little house. After cooking dinner we turned in for the night waking early to the sound of birds twittering around the tents. Leaving the tents did not scare the birds off and they remained our companions while we ate breakfast but they flew off when we started to pack up for our last bus ride into Reykjavik whereupon we went straight into a hotel, checked in and then met in the bar, where I was shocked at the price of a beer, £5.00!!! This at a time when a pint in England was about £0.72. Although I had expected it to be a bit more expensive as beer was illegal in Iceland and only sold at international hotels. Our last night in Iceland was uneventful and contemplative.

Arriving back in Sussex I went to stay with a friend, Pat. Pat is a difficult character and although we have a lot in common, he is extroverted while I am introverted. I met him while staying with Roger and Staffy years before. Pat is drug dealer and a shoplifter, but let me clarify. He would only sell hash to his friends and occasionally amphetamine and coke on request. He was not a big time dealer and basically sold the drugs in order to finance his own habits, he was by no means an addict. Pat had a succession of beautiful women and I mean beautiful, but didn't treat them well. Never violent but just not nice. At this time he was going out with a beautiful Peruvian lady who was a secretary at the Embassy in London and would travel down to Sussex at weekends. We had a congenial relationship and generally got on well. However Mick and the grass had hit a stumbling block and he had been doing nothing but smoking it with his mates while I was away. It was considered too stalky to sell in its current state. People liked it but due to the stalks they would not buy it in that state. So we set about cleaning it, removing the stalks and seeds. This reduced the end product from 10kg, as I had got rid of a couple before going to Iceland, to 4.5kg as Mick had smoked the rest. This should give us a total of £4.5 grand plus the £2 grand I took to Iceland would be £6.5 grand. This was decided to be £2 grand each plus £500 for expenses. Therefore as I had no more income and it was getting expensive to live in the UK I made an agreement with Mick to keep all the expenses and just send me the £2,000 when it was sold.

I bought a ticket to Jo'burg but not before somebody requested that I send some to him, a guy called Tony. We discussed how and where but I was in doubt and said maybe. Before jumping on the plane I spent the rest of my cash on photographic equipment which was my aim from the beginning.

## Chapter 15

I am taking break to rant about a subject that has been plaguing me for at least half my life. While walking the dog this morning I was listening to one of my favourite albums, Sunfighter by Grace Slick and Paul Kantner (from Jefferson Airplane / Starship fame). The track Silverspoon came on, a song Grace Slick wrote due to their vegetarian neighbours in Bolinas, California pressurizing them to become vegetarian. Her response was 'Silver Spoon', a song basically advocating to eat what you want.

"Throw down all your
Silver spoons - eat
All of the raw meat
With your hands
Pick it up piece by piece
Pick it up piece by piece
Pick it up piece by piece
Where are the bodies
For dinner?
I want my food!"
"I say you
Ought to eat what
You will - shove it
In your mouth any way
that you can."

It carries on in this way even asking the question as to whether you would eat human if you were starving to death - a question that has been asked through the ages. It is a great song with great music! I do not agree with the sentiment of pescatarians, vegetarians and vegans pushing their agenda down our throats. Don't get me wrong, if you don't want to eat animal products, that's fine, but let me eat what I will. I lived with vegetarians for a number of years and had great meals as cooking was done on a Rota and I learnt some great vegetarian recipes, but I still went out to eat my meat at least once a day.

After doing research into vegetarianism and veganism I found two flaws with the majority of the scientist promoting not eating meat. Firstly the benefits of meat are only mentioned in passing. Secondly the benefits of not eating meat are generally compared between good and healthy vegetarian foodstuff and bad, fast food meat diets. This will obviously give a biased result, which only now is beginning to be redressed.

Check out the Vegetarian Society page, vegsog.org and its first sentence is "Eating a vegetarian diet is one of the best things you can do to stop climate change – it's also delicious and loads of fun!" It then carries on "Eating a veggie diet means 2.5 x less carbon emissions than a meat diet."

The only scientists that support this view are scientists who are not meat eaters and, unfortunately, scientists who can prove the opposite is true are hounded and left largely unread. Allan Savory, an ecologist, started what he calls Holistic Agriculture Management which advocates using bunched and moving livestock to what he claims mimics nature, as a means to heal the environment, stating "only livestock can reverse desertification. There is no other known tool available to humans with which to address desertification that is contributing not only to climate change but also to much of the poverty, emigration, violence, etc. in the seriously affected regions of the world. Only livestock can save us." He believes grasslands hold the potential to sequester enough atmospheric carbon dioxide to reverse climate change. Praised by cattle farmers, his controversial ideas have sparked opposition from other academics; ranging from debate on evidence for treatment effects to the scope of the potential impact for carbon sequestration. As you can see his detractors are academics sitting in educational institutions while he has been 'praised' by farmers who have benefitted by his system, farmers who have for decades seen the land they are on become barren and then returned to lush green pastures, with photographic evidence to back it up.

Savory received the 2003 Banksia International Award and won the 2010 Buckminster Fuller Challenge. Prince Charles called him "a remarkable man" and noted farmer Joel Salatin wrote, "History will vindicate Allan Savory as one of the greatest ecologists of all time."

In contrast, James E. McWilliams described Savory as having "adherence to scientifically questionable conclusions in the face of evidence to the contrary". George Monbiot said of him, "his statements are not supported by empirical evidence and experimental work, and that in crucial respects his techniques do more harm than good." However, this comment has itself been subject to criticism in a later article published in *The Guardian* by Hunter Lovins entitled "Why George Monbiot is wrong: grazing livestock can save the world".

I could go on all day about the pros and cons of Savory but to sum it up, do your own research and you will have to conclude that the scientists are against it while the farmers are for it. Furthermore more and more research shows, to quote,climatechange.ucdavis.edu,"Unlike forests, grasslands sequester most of their carbon underground, while forests store it mostly in woody biomass and leaves... When fire burns grasslands, however, the carbon fixed underground tends to stay in the roots and soil, making them more adaptive to climate change."

The other claim by non-meat eaters is that it is better for your health. I will start with the age old argument that humans are descendants of hunter gathers and our biological system from the jaw and our teeth to our digestive system. Scientific American May 2013 states, "There is no doubt that human evolution has been linked to meat in many fundamental ways. Our digestive tract is not one of obligatory herbivores; our enzymes evolved to digest meat whose consumption aided higher encephalization (an evolutionary increase in the complexity or relative size of the brain, involving a shift of function from non-cortical parts of the brain to the cortex (a dictionary definition) and better physical growth." So this shows that the body needs meat. Furthermore it goes on to state "Killing animals and eating meat have been significant components of human evolution that had a synergistic relationship with other key attributes that have made us human, with larger brains, smaller guts, bipedalism and language. Larger brains benefited from consuming high-quality proteins in meat-containing diets and, in turn, hunting and killing of large animals, butchering of carcasses and sharing of meat have inevitably contributed to the evolution of human intelligence in general and to the development of language and of capacities for planning, cooperation and socializing in particular. Even if the trade-off between smaller guts and larger brains has not been as strong as is claimed by the expensive-tissue hypothesis, there is no doubt that the human digestive tract has clearly evolved for omnivory, not for purely plant-based diets. And the role of scavenging, and later hunting, in the evolution of bipedalism and the mastery of endurance running cannot be underestimated and neither can the impact of planned, coordinated hunting on non-verbal communication and the evolution of language."

Non meat eaters often cite that vegetarian or vegan diets are healthier or you, well here is an extract from Healthline, a predominantly Vegan/vegetarian nutritional magazine, written on 31/10/2019. "Vegan and vegetarian diets are both very healthy ways of eating. They have been linked to multiple health benefits and a lower risk of excess weight, heart disease and even some types of cancer. However, a few nutrients are either difficult or impossible to get in adequate amounts from plant foods. Therefore, it's very important to be aware and supplement your diet with them to maintain health or physical performance. Here are 7 nutrients commonly lacking in vegetarian and vegan diets." They then go on to list the seven with reason and function for their necessity, I will only list them, you can do further research if you like. Vitamin B12, Creatine, Carnosine (this supplement is well worth researching due to its beneficial influence on health ), Vitamin D3, Docosahexaenoic acid, Haem iron and Taurine. The reason that I mention these in particular is that in order for your brain and muscle to survive and grow, non-meat eaters need to take them as supplements and guess what? They are ONLY available through meat and / or fish. So vegans and vegetarians out there are still contributing to the meat and fishing industries. I say all this because every discussion I have had with non-meat eaters ends with 'agree to disagree'. This for me is because, and I emphasize it is my humble opinion, non-meat eaters do not want to look at facts that contradict their beliefs. I have nothing against non-meat eaters, I eat plenty of fruit , vegetables, etc. and I enjoy them but I do not want to be told that my eating habits are wrong or destructive or anything else. I like meat and I will continue to eat it, but I will concede that meat farming methods should be improved upon and even some of the present methods should be illegal.

Lastly I would like to show that even with our badly managed environment, farming does not produce the most greenhouses gases but 5.5% methane gas which breaks down rapidly.

**Power Plants (1/15)(Source: Reuters)**

Greenhouse Gas: Carbon Dioxide
Share of Global GHG Emissions: 25-30%

**Residential Buildings (2/15)(Source: Reuters)**

Greenhouse Gas: Carbon Dioxide
Share of Global GHG Emissions: 11%

**Road Transport (3/15)(Source: Reuters)**

Greenhouse Gas: Carbon Dioxide. Share of Global GHG

Emissions: 10.5%

**Deforestation, Forest Degradation & Land Use Change**

**(4/15)**

**(Source: Reuters)**

Greenhouse Gases: Carbon Dioxide, Nitrous Oxide, Methane
Share of Global GHG Emissions: 10.3%

**Energy Industry Processes & Losses (5/15)**
**(Source: Reuters)**

Greenhouse Gases: Carbon Dioxide, Methane
Share of Global GHG Emissions: 8.3%

**Commercial Buildings (6/15)**
**(Source: Reuters)**

Greenhouse Gas: Carbon Dioxide
Share of Global GHG Emissions: 7%

**Cement, Ceramics and Glass Production (7/15)**
**(Source: Reuters)**

Greenhouse Gas: Carbon Dioxide
Share of Global GHG Emissions: 6%

**Livestock (8/15)**
**(Source: Reuters)**

Greenhouse Gas: Methane
Share of Global GHG Emissions: 5.5%

**Iron & Steel Manufacture (9/15)**
**(Source: Reuters)**

Greenhouse Gas: Carbon Dioxide
Share of Global GHG Emissions: 4.8%

**Agricultural Soils (10/15)**
**(Source: Reuters)**

Greenhouse Gases: Carbon Dioxide, Nitrous Oxide
Share of Global GHG Emissions: 4.4%

**Chemical & Petrochemical Industries (11/15)**
**(Source: Reuters)**

Greenhouse Gas: Carbon Dioxide
Share of Global GHG Emissions: 4.3%

**Oil & Gas Production (12/15)**
**(Source: Reuters)**

Greenhouse Gases: Carbon Dioxide, Methane
Share of Global GHG Emissions: 3.1%

**Waste and Waste Water (13/15)**
**(Source: Reuters)**

Greenhouse Gases: Methane, Carbon Dioxide
Share of Global GHG Emissions: 3%

**Coal Mining (14/15)**
**(Source: Reuters)**

**Aviation (15/15)**
**(Source: Reuters)**

Greenhouse Gases: Carbon Dioxide, Water Vapor, Nitrous Oxide, Aerosols
Share of Global GHG Emissions: 1.5%

I leave you to do your own research on the above, but to me it clearly shows that all the main sources of pollution need to be addressed and different sects of society cannot pick and choose what they think the main cause is. Furthermore you can note from the above that livestock provide 5.5% of methane gas, a less damaging gas than agricultural soils which produce 4.4% carbon dioxide and nitrous oxide, both more damaging gases.

The cruelty reason for pescatarians does not ring true. Animals, in certain countries are still inhumanly killed, but well known charities and organisations throughout the world are trying to combat this. However the fishing industry is just as cruel. From the line hobby fisherman who catches his fish through a barbed hook that goes through its mouth and is then suffocated or beaten to death, to the fishing trawlers which catch tonnes of fish which are then suffocated, which is a slow painful death compared to a quick bullet or bolt through the brain. Pulse fishing, another cruel method, sends short electric pulses into the seabed to force the fish into to open seas in order to be caught and then suffocated.

Whether plants feel pain is still an open discussion, many scientists scoff at the idea while others accept it as a fact. What is true is that experiments on plants has shown that some plants send electrical impulses throughout its system and ramps up its chemical defences against herbivory. It is also widely known amongst the scientific community that plants perceive and communicate stimuli and damage in sophisticated ways. Whether this can be claimed as pain is still open to debate.

I believe that whatever we eat can cause damage and pain to both living things and the environment but seeing as we need to eat to survive we should take as much care as we can to cause minimum distress and to not anthropomorphise anything in our food chain. So I will end off this rant with another quote from Grace Slick and Paul Kantner with the lyrics of her Song Earth Mother:

"Once the earth was a garden
It gave us all we need
Then it grew so barren
All because of greed

Once the air was for breathing
And clouds caused rain to fall
Then it filled with poisons
Strangling us all

Water was once for drinking
And giving life to the land
Then it was used for cooling
The machinery of man

It's not your fault you're ill now
It's the men who went before
Your children are at your side now
Don't worry anymore

Your children are your salvation
They see your life as their own

They recognize no nation
They dance around your throne"

Incidentally Grace Slick is now a vegetarian.

# Chapter 16

Arriving in Jo'burg I went to stay with good friends, the same ones who had gone in with me, as cash was low I needed a job quickly, but as I had arrived at a weekend I went to Pretoria to see my brother and immediately got another job managing a small photographic laboratory with one of his partners in Cape Town. I got a new second hand bike, sold to me by a mate Paul who had bought it from his brother, Jed, who had emigrated to the UK. Jed and I had shared a flat in Jo'burg for about a year but he had fallen in love with the girlfriend of a mate, Mitch, who had come out from the UK to stay with us for three months. Well that trip was cut short as Jed and Karen were caught in their affair and they returned to the UK only for Karen to come back a month or so later and stayed with us.

Anyway the bike was the Honda Bol d'Or, a 900 cc racing bike made street legal by Honda in order to participate in the 24 hour endurance Bol d'Or motor cycle race in France and had won the race 4 consecutive times from 1976 to 1979, plus on a couple of other occasions. On Sunday evening I jumped on the bike and rode to Cape Town, completing the trip in 9 hours, approximately 1,400km, a great ride, that bike could hold 200kmph and make it feel like you were going slowly! I went straight to the lab arriving in time for work. I enjoyed Cape Town a lot. It is was a diverse city, with a lot of anti-apartheid sentiment amongst the voting population and was also the best cultural centre in South Africa. There were many places where all races could get together and enjoy the multi-cultural aspects of the Cape. However these places were also political hotbeds and once again I found myself drawn into the political environment. Since leaving Jo'burg I had not really used my photographic skills as I was now only a manager of a laboratory and this lead to two extracurricular activities; setting up my own lab at home to develop and print professional photographs and secondly to visit the troubled areas with my camera. Not long after I arrived the photographic goods I had bought in the UK arrived, so I went up to Jo'burg to pick it up, and also phoned Mick to find out how things were going. He had decided to rip me off, and hence, in turn I had not kept my deal with a long-time friend who had needed the money at the time. This was one of the worst moments of my life.

Cape Town is a beautiful city and I had a wonderful time there although I had a few bad experiences regarding work. Arthur, Patrick's partner and also the owner of the lab, was a regular visitor to Cape Town and had a flat in Sea Point a few kilometres from Strand Street in the Centre of Cape Town, where I was working. I was staying there until I could find a place of my own. The Lab had been running for a few months with Arthur popping down from Pretoria to run the place and it had problems, leading to my appointment. It didn't take long to realize that the financial problems were substantial. The daily takings were put directly into his personal account while the business was in the red and the debt was increasing on a daily basis. At the end of the first month none of his three staff, including me, got paid. Arthur was coming down the following week and would sort it out.

When he arrived he explained that he had a hiccup, paid us, encouraged me to find a place to stay and he would give up the flat and contribute to my rent, as he was still coming down regularly to visit his girlfriend in Cape Town. I found a lovely house in Fish Hoek, apparently the original farmhouse in the area. It was about a 30 to 40 minute ride to work, depending which road you take. The motorway which started a few minutes from work, winding its' way round the back of Table Mountain, past the university, through the back of leafy suburbs with mountains and reserves on the other side and ended almost at Muizenberg, was the quickest route but going through Camps Bay to Llandudno, Hout Bay and then along through the winding seaside cliffs over Chapmans Peak, down to Noordhoek and on to Fish Hoek is a bikers dream ride and must be one of the most beautiful scenic routes in the world!

Not long after I moved in Arthur arrived for a visit and we knocked back a couple of bottles of wine which brought out him babbling about his money worries, unfaithfulness, my brothers' financial woes which resulted in many problems for him including depression. It was at this point that I decided I did not like Arthur, he was a great guy to be around, fun and outgoing, but his blatant disregard for his wife and family along with his arrogant disregard for his 'business partners' who he ripped off on many occasions left a bad taste in my mouth. I decided then and there that I was holding back a little of the daily takings in order to pay the staff their wages at the end of the month. This proved to be a good move as on various occasions he did not have the money to pay the staff.

It was about this time that my younger brother, Michael, came down to spend the university holidays with me. Arthur immediately offered him a job canvassing the beach for tourists who wanted beach portraits done. This was not a total washout but did not reap the benefits he expected and consequently he didn't pay my brother. I took some funds from the lab and paid a portion of what was owed to Michael. The result of this was that Arthur told my older brother, Patrick, that I was stealing from him, and what was worse, even after explaining what had happened, Patrick believed that Arthur had paid Michael directly, in full, and that I had, in fact stolen from Arthur. However as Arthur did not fire me or even mention the incident to me assured me that I was in the right, but I was disappointed that my own brother did not believe either of his two younger brothers. Michael went on to get a job as a waiter in a restaurant owned by long-time friends, brothers Wynne and Robin for the duration of the holidays.

I had started frequenting a local pub and restaurant in Kalk Bay, The Brass Bell. This was a great place for young adults, with bands playing every Saturday afternoon. I met a lot of good people there and the atmosphere was always upbeat. The music was in the downstairs bar which had a large patio extending onto the rocks with the waves crashing against the wall of the pub. One of the people I met there was Mike. He was a drunkard, never worked, lived off an inheritance as both his parents had died, but also one of the most fascinating intellectuals I had ever met. We often sat down with a few bottles of Tassies (a cheap red wine, rumoured to be a collection of wine from the bottom of various barrels and bottled) while discussing life, the universe and everything and to this day some of the best philosophical discussions I ever had. However when he got too drunk he would get violent and turn into a mumbling idiot. Through him I met a lovely lady, Cathy, we became firm friends. Her boyfriend Stuart was in the South African Navy based at Simonstown and was away at sea most of the time, hence Cathy and I spent a lot of time together, going to restaurants, music festivals, drinks at the Brass Bell and just in each other's company. This actually made Mike jealous as he really fancied her and thought we were having an affair, but her boyfriend Stuart was fine with the situation, even appreciating the situation so that Cathy had someone around her when he wasn't there. I also soon discovered that Cathy was an agoraphobic and being a motor bike rider with her as a passenger actually helped the situation, which was a surprise to me. In outdoor situations she would cling to me which, until she told me about her agoraphobia, I found annoying. Cathy had her 'safe' places, the Brass Bell, some restaurants and was trying to control her problem by trying new places for which I admired her. Sometimes these new places would have a successful outcome, sometimes not, however she was always totally relaxed at her flat, my house or the Brass Bell.

Another friend I met there was Kelly. He working for an advertising company and lived close by in Kalk Bay and had a girlfriend, Mary, also a great person. I had acquired a dog, a Rottweiler bitch called Jessica, who went out with me on regular occasions, within walking distance. A habit I had acquired was riding to the Brass Bell on a Saturday afternoon, drinking while listening to the band and then on to Kelly's for dinner and more wine and then due to my state I would walk home returning to pick up my bike, with Jessica the following day. Mary happened to live on the second floor and we would often sit on the balcony with a cup of tea overlooking the bay. On one such occasion, we were sitting there with Jessica lying by my side when two guys approached and starting fiddling with my bike. Before I knew what had happened, Jessica was up and jumped off the balcony charged at the guys and chased them down the street. She returned limping and the vet informed me that she had strained both her ankle tendons. She was limping for the rest of her life, but once again, an animal had proved her love and loyalty.

Another bloke I met in Cape Town was Ralph, and he was the technician for the processing machines. Ralph was a real womanizer, sleeping with 2 to 3 women a week. During the nights that he was without a woman he would pop around to drink coffee, listen to music and just talk. It was through Ralf that I learnt the extent of Arthur's debt and he warned me that his company was coming to take over the lab, leaving me without work, once again. This didn't last long and while stock etc. was being taken, a competitor, Heime, came in and offered me a job in a lab he and an associate was opening in Fish Hoek, obviously I accepted. This also offered me the opportunity to print larger photos at home as the lab was only offering 5x4 and 7x5 inch photographs, larger ones were sent off, but it was agreed that I could print off positives, something a lot of professional photographers used so I was happy with the arrangement, as this meant I could buy the chemicals and paper at a good price, collect business through the lab as the lab had nothing to do with printing from positives.

Accounts were settled at the end of the month and if I owed the lab money it was deducted from my salary and if they owed me money it was added to my salary. It was a good arrangement that went on for about six months and after the first couple of months when I was setting up my services, I started to make a decent profit. This is when things started to go wrong. The partner, I can't even remember his name, worked in Fish Hoek and would regularly come in to check up and do the accounts at the end of the week. One day he asked me if I would like to resign to carry on with my own business without the worry of the lab. I declined and said that I was not quite making enough money to cover my living expenses yet. A week later he asked me again as his son, only 18, had decided he wanted to go into the photographic business. Again I declined. At the end of the month I got a visit from Heime who took me out for a cup of coffee to inform me that he was really disappointed that I had stolen from him. I started to protest when he brought out the current month's income and expenditure which showed that I owed him R750, a considerable sum in those days. I pointed out that I had not received my salary for the month and that my accounts for the month had not been completed and that from the 750, the lab would have some payments owing to me. He wouldn't have it, he believed his partner, I was fired and the partner's son was running the business the next day.

My experience of employers in South Africa was negative as every single job I had there ended with a unfair dismissal and most of them with nepotism. I was really pissed off. However the up side was that my business at home started to do better. I had the South African Navy as a client and they brought in quite a lot of work, along with Ralf bringing in clients for me.

Soon things started to go wrong for me. On Easter Saturday I went along to the Brass Bell and got way too drunk. My mates refused to let me ride and I remember stumbling home and falling into bed. The next day, I got out of bed and my motor bike wasn't there, so I grabbed Jessica and went off to Kalk Bay. The bike wasn't there either. I canvassed the area and eventually one of my neighbours had seen the bike being loaded onto a white bakkie earlier on in the day. It had been stolen! Then another bit of bad news came at the end of the month, my landlady wanted the house back. I could not find a place big enough to have a studio and a photographic lab in so I had to pack it up and I moved in with a friend, Vernon, in Kalk Bay. It was only a temporary move as he was looking after a house, right on the sea, literally across the train tracks and you are on the rocks picking up mussels. His girlfriend who I had only met once had just been through a really rough time with an ex-boyfriend. The ex had been extremely violent for years, she had reported him on various occasions but as he was a police officer nothing was done. She broke up with him, removed his belongings from the house and changed the locks. He still managed to break in on various occasions and rape her. Her reports fell on deaf ears. Eventually she hired a body guard who slept in the house and was with her 24/7. Her ex broke in, shot and killed the bodyguard and eventually her ex was taken away. However due to his position in the Police force he pleaded guilty to involuntary manslaughter and received only 5 years. It was not long after this that she met Vernon and formed a relationship with him but, as she had been notified that the ex was getting out of jail, she decided to leave Cape Town and left Vernon to sell the house and settle her affairs.

I spent two months living there and generally had a good time, but as I didn't have much work I was running low on money. We had a great party there with a pig on a spit and the band Ntsikola came and played. Nitsikola were a mixed race band who played township jive, one of the great sounds to come out of Cape Town.  My ex landlady had a cottage at Betty's Bay and she would occasionally let me use it over weekends. One weekend myself and about 7 or 8 friends went out to relax and get out into nature. For the second time in my life I experienced what I can only describe as telepathic communication. Vernon had come out with us and was smoking grass quite heavily, I confined myself to a few beers and others were either smoking a bit or drinking or both. Vernon was getting a bit loud and obnoxious and I was getting fed up with him, so I took a beer to go outside and thought to myself 'what a wanker'. He followed me outside and an argument pursued, not a heavy one more like a 'what's wrong' discussion. During this I noticed Kelly and his girlfriend staring at us and we stopped, and Kelly  said ' that was really weird'. I asked him what and he said 'it looked like you two were having an intense conversation but you weren't even talking.' I freaked and headed to the hills to be alone with my thoughts.

Every now and then I sold photos to the newspapers which resulted in me going into the townships quite a lot. The last time I was in Khayelitsha a protest was expected. I arrived and rode though the township on a borrowed bike until I came to an intersection with burning tyres and every intersection I could see down the straight road had burning tyres. I stopped next to a CBS crew and a gathering crowd. Foreign press was always welcome, as they, 'got the truth out to the world' and I often would take photos alongside them. A short time later a Casper arrived and the crowds grew thicker but no enmity could be felt, it was more like the beginning of a party. A Commandant got out of the Casper and told us to move on. The CBS reporter showed his credentials and refused after which a heated discussion ensued. When the Commandant asked for my credentials and I didn't have any, just working freelance he said that unless I leave he would have me arrested. I moved on down the road and stopped again to watch the scene unfold.

Half a dozen troop carriers arrived with three more Caspers, Police piled out with sjamboks swinging and tear gas being fired into the ever growing crowd, the civilians fled the police while the pop pop of gas canisters and the screaming of people being beaten could be heard ringing out in the previously quiet township. A small group of police had surrounded the CBS crew, knocking down the TV camera and jostling the personnel, making it difficult to get any footage.

When a group of Policemen headed in my direction I headed home, I had enough photos of the beginning of the 'violent' protest and I didn't want to get involved with the police.

It was also around this time that Mike took in a couple of lodgers, two guys about to finish their conscription with the South African Navy. They were both complete and utter stoners, from rising in the morning to hitting the sack at night. One of them, MM, had his sights on the UK when he finished and was always asking a myriad of questions, where to stay, how much, what to visit, etc. and of course, the availability of hash and grass. At first his questions seemed like naïve curiosity but after a while they began to become monotonous and boring and so I would change the subject or wander off to talk to somebody else.

Heading into the townships on a regular basis and making some contacts who would inform me of what was happening and where. Along with this information came advice on good spots to take photos out of police view. I attended a few rallies and protests until one day I was caught by the police, held for a few hours and let go. This brought me once again onto the police radar and after three years in Cape Town I decided it was time to leave and once again head over to Europe. I am not really fond of Europe, for me it is too hedonistic and although this is a sweeping statement I find it generally true. The Europeans I came into contact with were mostly politically ignorant or were too concerned with the triviality of day to day events offered by the tabloid press. The Africans were far less selfish and far more concerned with the people. This was true even for the misguided supporters of Apartheid.

I bought my ticket to London via Paris and spent the next few weeks saying my farewells. One evening at Mike's place having a farewell dinner with most of my close friends there MM informed me that he was on the same flight as me and asked if he could stay with me in the UK. Reluctantly I agreed depending on the friends I was staying with but was sure that a couple of nights would be OK. Arriving in Paris in the early morning we headed straight to the Gare du Nord and headed to Calais. While embarking onto the ferry MM got stopped by Customs and Immigration, I assumed it was due to his South African Passport and continued onto the ferry. A short time later a customs official approached and asked me to follow him. We went into a small room and I was thoroughly searched and then left alone for about an hour, missing the ferry. The Customs officer returned and I was informed that I was under arrest for conspiracy to smuggle 12 kilos of marijuana into France. MM had smuggled the grass and had informed the Customs that I was his accomplice organizing the sale once in London! I was flabbergasted! I was shocked and totally unaware of his choice to import the marijuana. I pleaded, asked for evidence, asked to speak to MM, alas all to fall on deaf ears. I was put in a Police car and delivered to the prison in Lille.

# Chapter 17

Entering prison was a shock, sure I had been in prison in Botswana, far worse than European prisons but Botswana was for a belief, and this? This was for nothing. The word of someone I had met and only associated with when other friends were around. I was really pissed off. After the initial shock I calmed down and adapted to my environment. It was a 23 hour lockdown with exercise being half an hour in the morning and half an hour in the afternoon, showers twice a week, consultations with the doctor when needed, library books once a week, a visit from the British Consul and occasionally taken to the lawyer who tried to persuade me to plead guilty. I was in a cell with another English guy who had stolen an ambulance in the south of France and only got caught in Lille, on his way to the ferry. Apparently he got tired of hitch hiking. So for the first few months all I did was the permitted exercise, read and contemplate. MM had been placed in a different prison, pleaded guilty and was sentenced to 18 months. I had many offers from various prisoners to shiv him, put him in hospital, etc. This was not me and so I refused all offers, however quite a few of the more hardened criminals did not understand why I refused their offer. Fortunately the prison I was in was a short term prison, up to 5 years, and those who were awaiting their court dates, so there were not too many hardened violent criminals. Work was also available, mostly prison duties, cleaning, cooking, library, laundry, etc. along with a pallet repair workshop and farm work. I put my name on the list and waited, but the list was long.

I came to terms with my incarceration while admitting that it was probably past actions catching up with me. Other than reading, exercising and talking to the same person day in and day out there was very little to keep my mind occupied. As some people were released, cell mates changed and I was put in a cell with another Englishman, a Londoner named James he is a nice guy with intelligent conversation who had work in the pallet workshop. He put in a good word for me with the owner and I eventually started repairing pallets. Sounds easy! However it is a really physical task as old pallets come in on a lorry and dumped. Our job was to take the good wood off them and construct new ones, if you didn't complete 12 a day, ie; 2 an hour, you were off the work detail. So that is basically my time spent in prison. Two incidences of note that happened in the prison.

One was an incident that made me think about society as a whole. One morning while being lined up on the way to work one of the prisoners being released that day was screaming and shouting and holding onto the stair rails, refusing to let go. Eventually 3 of the guards managed to carry him into the holding cells awaiting release. It turns out he was a repetitive petty criminal, shop lifting, graffiti, minor vandalism and so one. His problem was that he didn't want to leave. He has nowhere to go and just ends up on the streets and so in winter he commits a crime and gets put in prison where he receives shelter and three square meals a day. So when he was being released into mid-winter he was not going to leave. As it turns out, on release prisoners are given a bus ticket home, but this guy got to the bus stop outside the prison and vandalized it, so he was back in prison that evening.

The second incident is a bit more gruesome. Arriving in the workshop one morning and settling into work James pointed out that the guards had all left. A group of the French prisoners grabbed this one guy and started to strip him. Those of us not involved questioned what was going on and were told in no uncertain terms to leave things alone; this prisoner was a paedophile who had raped a 10 year old child. They stripped off his trousers grabbed his scrotum, put a six inch nail through it into his work bench, grabbed a bottle of paraffin, used for the heaters and set his balls on fire leaving him a prison made machete, basically forcing him to castrate himself. All the ruckus eventually brought the guards back who hauled the paedophile off to the doctor and then hospital, while we were confined to our cells for the next few days as an investigation ensued.

Fourteen months later I learnt that MM had been released; he had been sentenced and served his time. I had received no notification and therefore contacted the British Consul who sent me a lawyer two days later. I was released 10 days after that, the charges against me dropped. The whole time I was in prison I was given the run-around regarding my case. My appointed lawyer had told me that I was being charged but there was no evidence against me, I was taken on two occasions to see the prosecuting attorneys who informed me that I should plead guilty and that the case has low priority and will take a long time to get to court if I don't. After that I received monthly letters informing me that the case was ongoing and two visits from the appointed lawyer basically saying the same thing. Well, I got out about two months after James who had offered me a place to stay if I needed it. I don't believe in karma but I did accept this punishment as payment for past transgressions.

# Chapter 18

It has recently been pointed out to me that many people do not understand drugs; what they do, what they are and language around them. Here I will give a brief explanation of my interpretation and please remember that all drug users have different experiences with drugs. This extends from the legal drugs like sugar and coffee to the heavy illegal drugs like heroin, morphine and alcohol.

I bet coffee and sugar caught your attention. Let's have a look at the effects of them. As we all know most natural foods have some form of sugar in them, so like the accepted designation of 'drugs', I'll only discuss the 'overdose' of sugar and later coffee. The first obvious impact is obesity, heart disease and diabetes. (I am not going to go into statistics, you can do that yourself.) Sugar is addictive due to its dopamine release and once addicted people suffer from irritability, emotional lows and hence crave more. Coffee is more often described as an obsession but the physical effects include tiredness, headaches, insomnia as well as shaking, especially of the hands, when coffee consumption is extreme. Fortunately most coffee drinkers do not have this extreme addiction reliance, although we all know someone who 'needs' their coffee, especially in the morning. Excess coffee causes physical symptoms like nausea when people attempt to quit.

Nicotine is one of the most addictive drugs and causes many health problems. One of the reasons for the high addiction rate is that the high from nicotine is really short and hence leads to the craving for another one. The National Institute on Drug Abuse states, 'only about 6 percent of smokers are able to quit in a given year. Most smokers will need to make multiple attempts before they are able to quit permanently.'

Marijuana has many names, including but not confined to Mary Jane, pot, weed and grass. It also comes in various forms like hashish (hash), a solid compression of the extract tetrahydrocannabinol, the main active ingredient, and oil. The extracts are obviously easier to smuggle and hashish has been the preferred European form for many years. However the extract of the tetrahydrocannabinol often uses toxic and poisonous liquids, like petrol in Morocco or butane and carbon dioxide in parts of Asia. If the processes are done well you can be left with good high grade hash. However more often than not the producers are in a hurry for a profit and therefore skimp on the process making it low grade and mixed with ingredients like beeswax, milk powder, ketamine, boot polish, henna etc.

The choice between hash and grass is always personal. Grass is a psychotropic drug while the process of turning it into hash reduces the psychotropic effect. Marijuana is psychologically addictive but can lead to dependency as the user craves it more and more as the brain gets used to the cannabinoids. Marijuana can lead to mental illnesses including psychosis, schizophrenia, social anxiety and depression.

Alcohol is the most popular drug worldwide and, to me, one of the worst. Alcohol has both psychological and physical addiction which leads to heavy withdrawal symptoms, sweating, shaking, nausea and one can go into shock and could die. This is why alcohol addicts are advised to enter programs which medically monitor them.

Cocaine, to me is the worst drug, not because of its physical or psychological addictiveness but because of the sheer pleasure in bestows on the user! The feeling of euphoria while being active and stimulated is the best high a person can ever have and therein lies the danger. Cocaine is a massive market with massive profits and yet suppliers get more and more greedy mixing it with corn starch, talcum powder, flour as well as other drugs like amphetamine and synthetic opioids like fentanyl.

Opium, morphine and heroin are the last drugs on my list. These all come from the same source, the poppy. It is an analgesic, (pain killer), which dulls your sensation physically and arguably mentally. The overall effect is one of drowsiness and takes you into a painless dream world where everything is great, no more problems or hassles. Addicts often turn into themselves, hide from society and generally associate with other users. The introversion feeds their addiction and soon they become physically addicted. Addicts often try to come clean through 'cold turkey', instant stopping. This method of withdrawal is brutal and usually takes up to three days or more. It is not as dangerous as alcohol withdrawal in that it is not life threatening. Withdrawal symptoms begin slowly, sweating, irritability which proceeds to delirium, inability to eat and violent retching, accompanied by intense stomach pains due to nothing to bring up and yet the retching continues.

Eventually the user will drift off into a peaceful sleep for at least 24 hours.

This is a small selection of street drugs, but are the main ones used with a lot of derivatives coming from them, eg: oxycodone from opium and crack from cocaine. I must further state that many people I have met can use the drugs recreationally without becoming addicted, much the way society uses alcohol. A pick-me-up at the end of the work day, a relaxant after tough work, a confidence booster when going on a first date and so on. My advice is just be careful whatever your choice of drug is. Furthermore if you are in a position of trust or in a career that illegal drugs can end: stay away from them!

# Chapter 19

From Lille I headed to Crouch End, near Muswell Hill, in north London. James was squatting in an old doctor's surgery with three other people, Dave, a Professor of Fine Arts who had spent years in Denmark lecturing at a University. He supposedly fell in love and went out briefly with Beatrice Welles (Orson's daughter) while doing his lecturing tour in Europe, although I have never been able to verify this, he did have numerous photos of the two of them together in private settings and his friends corroborated as they were the ones who told me about him. Dave was also the first manager of Eurythmics, however this is not reflected in their history but people who know him do verify that he was with them for a while a love sick puppy for Beatrice, Dave turned into a full time junkie and fell into despair, gave up personal hygiene, spent all his money on heroin and ended up on the dole. At one stage while I was living in the squat (it was actually quite near to where Dave Stewart squatted in earlier days),Dave tried to blackmail Annie Lennox claiming to have compromising photographs of her. This came to nothing except to frustrate Dave who believed Eurythmics had ripped him off.

Next was Jonnie, a Welshman and hash dealer, only hash. He was well connected and dealt in large weights. His partner, I have forgotten his name, was a really scary dude, well dressed and always armed, was in charge of importation, with rumours of a tonne at a time. This rumour came about when an importing ring was bust in Spain and things dried up around our area, but that didn't last long and Jonnie was soon back in business.

The last member of the squat was Ty, another love sick male continually chasing his ex-girlfriend who actually played with him, encouraging and then rejecting him, although I do not think that she meant it, she just enjoyed flirting. Ty was a petty criminal and a part time junkie. He worked for a friend of Dave's, Arthur, a drug dealer and thief. Arthur had just been released from prison after a five year stretch and was getting his crew together. He was a really nice guy and I was unaware of his profession when I met him. After a week or so of spending daily time with Arthur, Ty and James in a pub, Arthur was aware that I was looking for work and offered me a job as his driver having just lost his licence. I agreed but when we got home James warned me about Arthur's chosen career so I politely declined. Fortunately my job hunting paid off quickly and I soon got work in a professional photo processing lab. It was quite a small lab catering to commercial photographers with a staff of 4 including myself. Unfortunately this lab was underfunded and went into bankruptcy during the second month I was working there. So I decided to take a break and visit a friend in Wales.

# Chapter 20

I spent a few days in Wales as a tourist escorted around by a friend Enzo, half Italian half English. It was basically an historical tour visiting castles, ruins and battlefields. Although along the way we visited farms and country crafts. It was during this visit that I decided to make my way back home overland through Africa. I bought a Subaru All Wheel Drive estate quite cheaply in Wales and headed back to London. There I stayed a few days, packed up and Irish Peter decided that he needed a holiday and joined me as far as Spain. We set out on the night ferry to France and drove straight through to Spain and slowed down, taking five days to drive down the coast to Valencia where we set up our last camp together and spent another four days on the beaches in the area. At the campsite we met a group of Madrileños who we had a good time with in the bars at night, my first attempts at the Spanish language and generally just having a good holiday.

I dropped Peter on the road north of Valencia as he started to hitch back to the UK, while I went on to Algeciras arriving mid-afternoon and then catching the 20:00 ferry to Ceuta, on the northern tip of the African coast. Ceuta is part of Spain and was one of the best tax free ports in Europe. It didn't take long to get through the border and by the time I arrived in Tetuan twilight had settled in. I got a room in a boarding house and through my window I could see the lights of the city and hear the cacophony of trade along with the hustle and bustle of the crowded streets and the mosque loudspeakers blaring out from the minarets crisscrossed the cityscape. I descended into the narrow streets and wandered around the souk markets with their colourful merchandise blowing in the gentle breeze amongst the artefacts and relics, seemingly from a bygone era. One rather large shop was filled with Persian carpets. As I started to roam around the shop the owner approached and started to find what I wanted. I explained that the rugs were lovely but that I had just arrived and was not willing to buy yet. He persisted showed me a beautiful rug and ordered some Moroccan tea from a minion, then invited me to sit down and started to haggle. I did not want to buy but only admired the rugs but he was insistent. In the end I lied and said that I didn't have room to travel with the carpet and so I would pop in on the way back and maybe buy the rug then. This was still not accepted and he proposed that I buy it now and he will hold it for me until I return. I said sorry, thanks for the tea and left with him following me out of the shop and into the street. Welcome to Moroccan business haggling! I did however manage to reduce him from 700€ to 300€! So I left without the rug and found a little restaurant and dined on Moroccan red chicken and couscous before returning to my room.

The following day I arose early and set out for Fes and spent the day driving in the Atlas mountains, real mountains! Not the little ones of the UK. The Atlas are over 4,000 metres and are comparable in size to the European mountains although the vegetation is very different and little snow could be seen at this time of year, July, but only on distant peaks. Driving through I encountered valleys with rivers and wadis, while the higher passages had beautiful scenes of the gigantic mountains covered with oak, cedar, speckled with bushes and grasses before thinning into the rocky peaks. The temperature seemed erratic, cold when driving over the higher peaks the roads traversed, while warmer when descending. The roads had picnic spots, some with water taps and I stopped at many to record my travels with my camera. Fez was about a five hour drive and I managed it in eight and quickly wound my way through to a campsite in the southern part of the city.

Fes is an incredible city! It is well over a thousand years old and looking over the city you take in a view of the ancient and the modern. The towers and minarets are like fingers pointing to the heavens while arches straddle the roads, with parks adding a pleasant green to the surroundings. This was the first time I have ever enjoyed slow traffic, giving me the chance to absorb the beauty, the poverty and vibration of a cluttered city. I arrived at the campsite, set up the tent and started to cook dinner when an oriental young man approached me asking for some sugar for tea, I asked him to join me as I had just put on a kettle, which he did. He was a Japanese youngster, I can't for the life of me remember his name and as he was touring on a motorbike I started talking to him about bikes. His preference was for off road bikes and he had a Honda 500 Endurance. During our conversation I learnt that he had ridden from Japan and was headed to Cape Town! One hell of a ride! We talked about his ride and my travels and the places we had in common and the next day we went on a tour of the city, on his bike which made things a lot easier.

One of the old buildings that fascinated me was an old prison. It was six or seven stories tall and the cells started on about the third floor. The cells were open with no bars or walls facing the outside, just an open room with no doors and open to the elements, like dozens of caves along the building. The prisoners' food and other goods was hauled up by the prisoners using ropes. The bottom floors were obviously for the guards and other staff. The prison had been out of use for over a hundred years, but still conveyed its sorriness and cruelty.

The city was full of contrasts, the glamorous University, originally built as a mosque in 859, becoming a university in the 1960's, the Blue Gate of Fes, the gentle rolling hills upon which it is founded, the hustle and bustle of a living city. The poverty also stands out with brightly clad women carrying water on shoulder poles or milkmaids' yokes, dirty, starving street kids looking for food and money, willing to do anything for a meal while fat cats drive past in their shiny Mercedes, the perfect condition of the roads falling into disrepair and potholes the closer you get to the poorer areas. A beautiful and neglected city reflecting the range of classes from the rich and important to the starving and downtrodden. Yet the people, rich, poor or in-between were friendly, accommodating and willing to talk and help. I loved this city.

A few days later I was on the road to Meski. Meski was on the main road south to Algeria and the last real stop to get provisions for driving into the Sahara and once again I was planning on resting up a few days before the trek through the desert. Arriving at Meski was reminiscent of approaching Fish River, I could see nothing but flat rocky desert and wondered whether I had got something wrong when I saw a small small sign in Arabic and with 'MESKI' in the Latin alphabet fading below. Slowing down I turned into a dirt road disappearing into the distance. Driving for less than ten minutes, palm treetops starting appearing and soon enough an expanse of green spread out before me, with a small river running through and a very large pond in the middle. It was easy to see the camping site and after setting up the tent etc. I went exploring. Close to the southern end of the oasis was a bazaar with everything you need and a lot of what you would want as a tourist.

A Persian carpet shop once again caught my attention and I started browsing. The salesman was on the ball and within a few minutes we were sitting down having a cup of tea and talking about the history of Meski, in perfect English. It is on one of the old Caravan routes which has been around for centuries and still has caravans passing through. It was a few days north of a fort called Sijilmassa which was one of the main trading centres and had a gold mint, minting the gold from regions as far away as Sudan. Due to its power Sijilmassa had a lot of political intrigue even being independent in the 10th century. In the 16th century the city was destroyed after a Prince was assassinated by its citizens and the population spread out from the city. However it was rebuilt in the 1700's and then in 1818 once again destroyed by nomadic tribes. Meski then became a major stop on the North African route.

After the history lesson we started talking about the carpets. Many of the carpets have the story of the owner's family, some telling of adventures, some the lineage, while the majority are just designs that take the weaver's fancy. It was one these that I decided to buy. The one I wanted was bed length and thick so when sleeping on the hard ground it provided a softer mattress and this is what it was made for but had an Arabic spiral design in the centre within the typical rectangle and a flowery border forming another outer rectangle, mostly shades of red, and brown with white bordering. The shop owner wanted £500, knowing the Moroccans liked to barter, I contemplated bartering, but with a £500 opening I knew I couldn't afford it, apologised for wasting his time and got up to leave. Well he stopped me and asked what I could afford, so I told him £50, he laughed at me but I eventually got the rug for £90! I was really quite happy and it was a lot more comfortable than just the sleeping bag on the ground.

I spent the following day taking in the oasis and the palm trees with their dates hanging in massive bunches while the locals scramble up to harvest them. The thin silvery river disappearing into the desert on both sides of the shiny pond, the natural pool fronting the bazaar, locals huddle around eating points while meals are prepared on fires and makeshift barbeques. As I watched the yellow and pink sunset reflecting in the pond with its finger of light disappearing along the river path, my thoughts led to my departure and what lay ahead in Algeria. That evening I went to have dinner in one of the makeshift restaurants under the starry sky at the edge of the oasis and starting chatting to another diner, an Algerian. I told him of my plans and that I was heading off in the morning. Fortunately I had bumped into him as he informed me that the border I was heading to had been closed for a couple years as the roads had fallen into disrepair and taken over by the desert and I would have to travel to Oudja in the north-east in order to cross. So the next morning I started heading east instead of south.

The road to Oudja was a reasonably well made tarmac road through the desert and about an 8 hour drive. Besides the desert views, the occasional camel or local when I thought,' where do they come from', as I passed nothing besides a village or two hundreds of kilometres apart. I was driving along a straight road for as far as I could see, the surrounding terrain was flat and sandy, it was hot and the road was producing a shimmer blurring out the water mirage on the tarmac when, in the distance slightly to the right of the road, an animal was running straight at me, the blur and distance made it phantasmal and I caught myself slowing down and staring. Passing a local walking along the road to who knows where, the animal came into view, it was a wild dog running flat out towards the car, as it got closer and closer the resolute animal continued its charge, slowing almost to a stop the dog ran straight into the car and dropped dead. Cautiously I got out of the car and examined the dog, definitely dead. The walking local lady caught up and said "Merci, c'etait enrage", (it had rabies), while she grabbed the dog by its leg, dragged it off the road and carried on to her destination after declining the offer of a lift.

I arrived in Oudja around midnight and decided to sleep in the car and headed to the border which opened at 07:00. A queue was already tailing out of the building and down along the road. Parking the car and taking my papers, I joined the queue to arrive at the counter and hour or so later was refused entry into Algeria. It was difficult to find a reason as my papers were in order but on the way back to the car I met a New Zealand couple who were also refused. They had stated that they were turned back because their car was British, but they were allowed in if they left the car behind. This was just ludicrous and totally unbelievable and I started to enquire into reasons among others that had been refused entry. Algeria was going through turbulent times (riots broke out in October 1988) but officially British Citizens were still allowed into Algeria. After spending the day at the border post and speaking to many people, Moroccans, Algerians, British, Europeans and other international travellers along with two more attempts to cross I made my conclusions as thus: Algeria was entering a state of turmoil and although no British / Algerian conflict existed a portion of the population blamed Europeans for interfering with their internal politics resulting in an Algerian Border official taking his frustrations out on British Citizens wanting to enter Algeria. This was born out over the next few days as I waited around Oudja hoping that circumstances would change.

During this time I met a Moroccan about my age who invited me home for lunch where I met his whole family, mother, father, grandparents, brothers, sisters and others that I didn't quite manage to place. During the lunchtime conversation I learnt that these refusals of British nationals had been going on for about a month, some stated that the British Government had slighted the Algerian Government and this was an unofficial reprisal, although nobody could tell me what is was. The next day the family took me on a picnic up the mountains, which also turned out to be a petrol smuggling exercise. The men of the family, about 10 of them at least, joined a stream of men heading off across the frontier all carrying two 20 litre jerry cans on a milkmaid's yoke and returned about an hour or so later with the jerry cans full of petrol and diesel. The picnic was great with all the locals enquiring about my travels and origins, with many queries about Europe, particularly France and England. During all this I noticed that one of the sons was contentious and continually threw offensive glances my way. I kept out of his way and generally had a good time with the family and an afternoon swim in a cold river before heading back to town, loaded with petrol. Arriving back still wet from the swim I took a change of clothes from my car and asked if I could change after which we had a farewell tea as I had decided to leave, where to, I don't know. After tea I went to collect my bag with the wet clothes only to find that my tee-shirt had been used to wipe a bum and was full of shit. The son who had been visually aggressive came up to me indicating the tee-shirt and said 'that's what I think of you foreigners'. I ignored him, returned to the lounge, said my farewells and drove to the camp site. The incident started me thinking as in all my years of travel this was the first sign of aggression towards me and it was a little startling.

The following day, without a plan I set out along the mountain route heading west and with so much beauty surrounding me I decided to take a slow drive over the next few days soaking up the tranquillity of the mountains. Instead of the main road I took a more northern route, but still a reasonable tarmac road which turned out to have many good side roads and diversions and at the end of the first day I was at Monte Arruit, only 135km from Oudja and checked into a boarding house for the night. After settling in I went out for dinner where I met Bram, a Dutch guy about my age who was travelling with a Moroccan teenager who he was taking to Amsterdam with him. However before that he was spending a week on a farm belonging to the boy's family. During the course of the evening I was asked if I would like to stay a few nights to which I agreed, if it was OK with his family.

After a late breakfast I set off following Bram through the winding Atlas Mountains with the sun dancing through the gently waving trees. Ahmed, the Moroccan teenager, was travelling with me in case I got lost. He was quite chatty speaking good English with a strong desire to live and work in the UK. The hour it took us to get to the turn off to the farm he had not stopped talking once. It was still a reasonable tarmac road, narrow and a windy climb up the mountain until we came over a crescent and a beautiful fertile valley spread out below us like an infinite garden spreading as far as the eye could see. The continual U-turns descending into the valley was tortuously slow until finally we reached a dirt road where we turned off onto the farm and the crops spread off to our left for what seemed like miles – marijuana!! If you have never seen a marijuana plant – they are beautiful, 2 to 2 1/2 metres tall, five, seven or nine fingered serrated leaves spreading up the plant like a Christmas tree with beautiful flowering heads, just the right time to visit a farm! I was reminded of my youth in Zimbabwe when my brother in law, Mike, would take me out to the mealie fields and we would stand on the roof of the bakkie and look out over the fields for the marijuana plants, which the labourers were growing, sticking out over the tops of the maize.

The farm house was a typical French Moroccan colonial house, double story, plus upside-down V-shaped attic room windows, sharp sloping tiled roof, long verandas surrounding three sides, outside staircases leading to the upstairs veranda, or rather balcony, again on three sides. However recent extensions had been built joining one side of the veranda to a massive workroom, equal in size and height to the house, all the structures looked a bit run down, paint dirty, stained and peeling, woodwork a bit shaky in some places. However the interior was in great shape with large rooms, the entrance hall led into a large lounge on the left with folding glass doors opening onto the veranda, while on the right was the dining room leading into a massive kitchen with its own dining room table. Ahmed's family was numerous, what seemed like dozens of siblings, cousins, uncles and aunts all helping run the family business. Bram and I were not the only western visitors, Bram was already acquainted with them and so I was introduced to an American couple, in their mid-twenties, James and Madge, from Kentucky. Upon learning of my colonial African descent, James, particularly, started a political conversation which quickly turned into a condemnation of any white person in Africa. The ignorance was staggering and I just accepted an offered beer and went for a walk around the farm with Ahmed. While walking around the fields James and Madge came running past, naked and disappeared into the fields, the workers just laughing. Not long after returning to the veranda James and Madge returned, their bodies covered with marijuana oil and bits of the buds which had rubbed off on them and scratching them along the arms and bodies and disappeared around the back of the house, apparently to collect as much of the resin as they could and then lick the rest off each other! Another variation on chocolate with sex!

Anyway I spent two relaxing nights on the farm and felt very welcome the whole time, I was shown the processing areas, the drying racks, harvesting the best parts of the plant, the dissolving dishes with a variety of stages, the sticky hash left behind, the compressing into kilo blocks and the marking and wrapping for transporting. I was actually amazed at the ease with which I was accepted into family and shown the production of their crops.

Both Bram and I left on the same morning with Ahmed going along with Bram to Holland. We got onto the main road and headed towards Tetuan, while my thoughts were to head on further west. It was a long drive, expecting about 6-7 hours. However a few hours later a massive queue was holding up traffic, crawling along at, if we were lucky, 10 km per hour. Very few cars were coming from the other direction and with the windy roads in the Atlas I expected a major accident. About an hour later some policeman came into view, selecting some cars which could proceed on the other side of the road while the majority were held in the queue. As the policeman approached my vehicle we had a conversation that went something like this: ”Good morning officer”

“ You American?”

“ No, British”, as I was travelling on a British passport.

“ You wait here”

“What is going on?”

“ Looking for drugs.”

At this stage paranoia started to set in, having just come from a plantation, but I hadn’t partaken or had any drugs. About this stage he waved a car on from behind me, so I enquired, “ Is that someone important?”

“No, he has many kilos of hash.”

“ Oh dear, is he going to jail?”

At which the policeman burst out laughing and continued, “No, no, no he pays our bonus. You see the Americans don’t understand that Hashish has been in our culture for centuries, but they insist we stop or no trade. So we put on a show, stop many cars produce little hashish put a few Americans in jail, they take them home to USA after a month or so, and the Americans are happy and we get trade and money for helping.”

I could not help laughing inside and as a smile overcame my face, the policeman laughed again and waved me on. The jolly Moroccan policeman has remained a laughing image in my mind ever since, although the incident was another wakeup call as to the corruption of politics as I could not believe that the USA was not aware of what was happening, and yet publicly they condemned the trade but paid drug producing countries to uphold the farce. The same was true in Turkey who gave foreigners very heavy sentences, including the death sentence while the drug trade used Turkey as a main route uninterrupted.

A little further down the road I came across Bram with his Mercedes on its roof with he and Ahmed, unharmed, standing beside it. I stopped and they were OK and so I offered them a lift to Ceuta. During the ride Bram asked me to take Ahmed to the Canaries where he would meet me in about a month after sorting out his affairs in Holland. I thought 'why not?' and after crossing to Algeciras, said farewell to Bram and headed to Cadiz.

## Chapter 21

The ferry to Gran Canaria was about a day and a half with a brief interlude at Tenerife, to unload and load up again. Arriving in Las Palmas I drove straight to Maspalomas where I rented a holiday apartment for a week and then took a walk around the area. I can honestly say that surprise is an understatement. The shopping centres were extremely busy, hawkers abound. Walking through the streets and peering into hotel grounds showed people crammed around swimming pools, eating and drinking to their hearts' content. However the beach was the object of utter bewilderment! People compacted together, worse than the London tubes at peak hour, as far as the eye could see with the people merging into the seascape on the distant horizon. How could people want to pay for a holiday like this? I descended onto the beach and carefully positioned my feet at designated points between towels, legs, arms and any other obstacles encountered. After 10 minutes of this I gave up and returned to the promenade.

The next few days were spent discovering the island with Ahmed, which has a lot to offer once you get away from the tourist traps. That is not to say there weren't tourists in the more remote areas but not many were seen. Anyway, Gran Canaria has quite a few things to offer, unique rock formations, volcanic craters, mountain trails, etc. Ahmed had found some Moroccans he had become acquainted with and left to live and work with them, hawking goods around the tourist hotspots. This was also where I discovered the Spanish custom of Siesta. What a great idea! It is not that I enjoyed the afternoon snooze, not yet anyway, but the fact that the shops closed and restaurants were open with relatively few people around, mostly locals, as the tourists had all returned to their hotels to enjoy the all-inclusive packages they had paid for. This left me plenty of time to leisurely explore the malls, shops, etc. The hawkers and street entertainers hang around the malls, waiting for Siesta to end and were really forthcoming on where to go outside of the tourist areas.

My apartment was close to the beach and almost all night, every night, I could see vehicle lights and hear heavy machinery on the beach. One morning I decided to get to the bottom of this and I approached a worker leaving the beach and with a spattering of Spanish replies in halting English I gleaned the information I was after. The beach was laid over volcanic rock that had wound its way to the sea millennia ago, so in order to serve the tourist trade sand was imported from the Sahara and spread nightly on the beach! What a palaver! The tourists can't even find natural beaches and take their vacations on manmade beaches! My dislike for tourists took a giant leap. About this time I was due to either renew my apartment or move out. A solution offered itself when I was casually walking along a beach away from the tourist traps, not far from Maspalomas when I came across a massive cave. There and then I decided that this was my next temporary abode. It was a reasonably long walk from where I could park the car and it took me the better part of a day to set up my campsite in the cave and out of sight but I was extremely pleased with the result. The cave was deep so the tent was out of sight and the fire to cook could only be seen if you were at sea. Furthermore even during the day the beach was quiet and a small climb led up to the cave from the beach.

This move left me with more money to spend and so I decided to explore the night life. One of the first places I started frequenting was an English pub that had reasonably cheap meals and I started to take my dinner there. At about nine, after I had eaten, an Englishman, Rob, started a music session playing his guitar and singing popular English songs. Soon he and I built up a friendship and we started spending some days together with his wife, Paula. He showed me around some of the lesser known places, including some of the cave houses on the island. We also partook in some of the tourist activities, diving, jet skiing, etc. Paula also worked as a magician's assistant and chorus girl in one of the biggest shows on the island and she got us front row seats to a show. It was the one and only cabaret type show that I have ever been to. The auditorium held about 500 people and the act I enjoyed the most was one of David Copperfield's tricks, The Disappearing Aeroplane. To this day I consider the best bit of 'magic' I have ever seen. The show also had the standard type of entertainment, singing, comedians and, of course, the French style burlesque with plenty of topless girls prancing across the stage.

A few days later while sitting in the front of my abode I saw a gangly figure traversing the beach, struggling with his cameras, reflectors, tripods, suitcases of props, etc. Offering to help him I met Matt, an aspiring photographer who had come to the Canaries in order to complete a swimsuit photo shoot which would either give him a permanent job or leave him scraping by as an unknown freelancer. As it was quite early in the morning he explained that he wanted to get set up so when the beach fills up he could approach some of the beautiful young ladies to pose for him in his array of swimming gear. Thinking firstly it was not a good idea to approach strangers and secondly that this particular beach was pretty deserted most of the time I invited him up for a cup of tea. During our conversation I told him I may be able to help with proper models, i.e., Paula's workmates. That evening at the pub I enquired of Rob about the possibilities and the next day he arrived at my cave with four beautiful young women with Matt arriving about half an hour later. We spent the day, directed by Rob, to some of the best (and deserted) beauty spots on the island and hundreds of photographs were taken. After the shoot we retired to a bar for a relaxing drink, where I informed all concerned that it was time for me to return to the UK. Rob immediately asked what I was doing with the car as he didn't have transport. So Rob bought the car, I bought my ticket and spent the last few days out of the cave and with Rob and Paula.

# Chapter 22

I arrived back in London just before Christmas and moved back into a squat with James and fortunately got a job virtually immediately with another Pro Lab in Bicknell Street, right next door to Gary Glitter. This lab was a really good set up, really busy and had its in-house photographers who were also the owners. The lab was run by Brian who had been there for over twenty years. I got on well with the owners who, unfortunately, were away quite often leaving Brian in charge and he and I had, how shall I call it, a personality conflict? This got to me and I looked for another job which I got in Joe's Basement in Wardour Street in Central London. Joe's was one of the original Professional photographic houses in London. It opened in the sixties and immediately became the go to place for photographers like David Bailey, Terence Donovan, Brian Duffy, Eric Swayne, John Cowan, etc. It was a great place to work, all the staff great people and an entourage of famous people passed through. The lab itself was awe inspiring, four floors of laboratories and studios. I was in the E6 process receiving department and started off printing reasonably small photographs, up to about 24inches squared. Tim, one of the other darkroom workers, was printing massive billboard size photos on a vertical enlarger onto a suction roll paper easel mounted on the wall. I loved Joe's basement and learnt more about photography than at any other stage of my life. I was on the night shift, 19:00 to 04:00 which included a mandatory lunch hour when I would wander around the West End bathing in the glory and seediness of London's night life.

Almost opposite Joe's Basement was Brewer Street which had a Turkish Restaurant from where you could sit and watch the comings and goings from Raymond's Revue Bar and this was generally where I took my lunch between 01:00 and 02:00, although I only took half an hour. Sitting here one evening when it was full, a lovely young lady asked if she could sit at the same table. Not being used to being approached by beautiful women, I obviously agreed and she was quite chatty and soon we struck up a conversation. These night time lunches turned into regular meetings. Her name was Jane and she was a stripper at Raymond's. At first I was quite taken aback and didn't know how to respond, but she quickly put me at ease as it was only a job and no 'funny business' went on. However the stories she regaled me with were entertaining, some funny and some frightening. Tales of old and young men masturbating, drag queens approaching men who were shocked while others pleased when discovering the queen was male, the proposals reaching dozens every night, the assumption that because you took your clothes off for a living that you were a prostitute. The stories went on but the sad and frightening stories revolved around stalking and attempted rapes, but Jane assured me the girls were well looked after and if they had had a creepy encounter on any night one of the bouncers would escort them home. The seediness of Soho had a closed protective side that Jane had taught me, however I refused the offers of entry into the club but I enjoyed our numerous conversations. When I finally left Joe's I went to say goodbye to Jane who said "you are a funny old one, wise and distant and if I hadn't got to know you I would have pegged you for a policeman", after which she kissed me farewell on the cheek .

I was happy at work and my time off was enlightening. James was a mechanic and doing his own thing including driving around London looking for cars ticketed on public roads for parking over three months, when they were either towed away by the council as abandoned, disposed of or sold. What I was unaware of was that anyone could claim these cars and obtain the paperwork from the council and then obtain a new set of keys and the car is legally yours. One day James picked up a virtually new BMW 325i Coupe! It took him about a month to get all the paperwork done and sold it for a fortune. About six months later a knock on the door and James was confronted by the original owner who had been in the States for a year and wanted his car back. James obviously refused and was taken to court. The original owner lost the case as the car had been abandoned and so James was within his rights. Chris had also met a lovely Irish girl Rachel, called Rack due to her obvious asserts, who was a preschool teacher. Unfortunately James had started recreational heroin use once again.

I met quite a few people with whom I became friends. Peter, an Irishman from Belfast but living in London, invited me up for a week when he went back to visit friends and family. I spent the week being shown around as a typical tourist and learning about the politics. As many things were taboo and could end you up in trouble I had to learn to keep my mouth shut and asks questions later in private conversations at home. Peter was a former UDA member. The UDA had a military wing called UFF which had been declared a terrorist organisation way back in the early 70's, targeting mostly Irish Catholics. The Irish are a lovely people, fun loving, outgoing and talkative. The accent was a bit hard at first but I got used to it quite quickly.

Kevin was another person I spent time with. He was married and had a young daughter. Both he and his wife worked with the daughter at preschool and we would meet in a pub over weekends. One evening I was invited to dinner and his wife cooked a lovely meal which he just shovelled down to which I was quite surprised as he was well brought up and well mannered. He obviously saw my surprise and explained that he didn't like eating as he had lost his sense of taste and smell in a car accident which landed him in a coma for three months, the result of which led to him not liking the texture of food in his mouth and hence got the meals over with as quickly as possible.

James and I frequented an Irish pub owned by Rack's parents where we would be locked in after closing and carry on drinking. Remember these were the days when pubs closed at 22:30 and 23:00 on weekends, so this was a nice perk. The pub had weekly quizzes, darts and pool tournaments and was just a nice place to spend time when I could.

Arthur and Ty were the people who entertained me the most. On one occasion Arthur had his crew break into various houses and stole Credit Cards. In the UK stolen Credit Cards are blocked as soon as they are reported missing but it took three days or longer (this is about 40 years ago, before the age of modern computers) for the block to reach mainland Europe. So Arthur had Ty and someone else immediately go over to Holland on a spending spree and bring the goods back to the UK, small things, cameras, Hi Fi systems, clothes, etc. which could then be sold at local markets and hence make a fortune. On one occasion Arthur found out that Ty had ripped him off, threw him in the boot of his car and drove around with him in it for three days, no food or drink and he went through cold turkey so, when Arthur opened up the boot, Ty was lying in his own vomit, sick and weak from withdrawal of heroin, while Arthur made him clean up the boot before taking him home. Ty had learnt his lesson from Arthur but the first thing he did was steal my cameras in order to get more Heroin. I got home after work and was really pissed off. When James got up at around 08:00 I told him and we went to confront Ty, who of course denied it. Fortunately it was a Saturday so I didn't need to go to work and I wanted to go to the Police. My camera equipment was hidden in the walls and I thought nobody knew where they were so James, Jonnie, Ty and I sat down to discuss the situation. I was not involved with the drugs at all but Jonnie was a dealer of kilos, Ty was working Arthur, a full time heavy drug dealer and thief. Basically I couldn't go to the police yet. So we headed up to a pub in Crouch End which was known as a place to offload stolen goods and fair enough my cameras had been sold the previous evening by Ty. Arthur and Jonnie brought in the heavyweights while I went shopping. When I returned to the pub, my cameras were back and Ty was in debt to Jonnie for £1,500, what he had got for my equipment and basically indentured to Arthur until he had paid back Jonnie. Everyone was happy except Ty.

Another little quirk about this pub was that it was a place where you can sit and relax while someone will do your shopping for you at the Tesco's up the road. You give them the list, they go shopping and bring you back your trolley full of food, etc. for about half price. They just fill up the trolley and walk out the entrance without paying! After they did it for me on the first occasion, I didn't do it again as I was expecting the receipt and a small charge! However I enjoyed the pub and would go there for Saturday lunch and enjoy the atmosphere. It was full of petty criminals and dope smokers. As you have probably noticed I enjoy watching society and people and this brief time in Crouch End I saw people at their worst and their best. Crouch End also had a lot of good things, Eurhythmics had their studios close to the main street and helped up and coming musicians record without charge or with low fees. Muswell Hill was just up the road which was a rich area and a great place to buy clothes at charity shops, Alexander Palace was within walking distance with its many exhibitions, particularly cars and bikes, which as you know I love. All in all I loved this stay in London but once again it was time to move on and I got offered a job as a photographic assistant in Colombia.

South America is a place that had caught my imagination ever since I was a child staying with my grandparents in Pretoria. My granddad had a collection of Time Life travel books and I would often sneak into his study and browse through the one on South America and I fell in love with the place. The photographic gig was only about four weeks and I wanted to stay longer and a friend had given me a tip about teaching English and so after scouring newspapers I found an advert, applied, went to an interview and got the job, starting about a week after the shoot finished.

# Chapter 23

Before moving on to South America I would like to explore my psychological and social attitudes as I was now a 33 year old man and my family was always telling me, some of them lecturing me, on the fact that I should settle down, etc. My younger brother Michael had visited while I was staying in London and although happy to get together, my circumstances had not encouraged him to stay over even one night with me, his brother, who he had not seen for at least 4 years. So my family relationships felt strained and in my mind dated back to my desertion leaving me the black sheep of the family. Communication over the last few years had been virtually non-existent and my touchstone was friends from my school days who were 'solid family folk', with whom I was in constant contact.

My experiences formed who I am and although drawn to the seedy side of life I existed on the fringes not getting involved but observing. This has led me to various controversial beliefs while leading me back to Christianity, which I had never entirely relinquished. However the subjects occupying my mind revolved around sex, politics, greed and the ignorance of mankind. I know that this ramble will be controversial and will upset some people, but I feel it is a truth that needs to be explored and thought about before we, as a society, can move forward to the resolution of this deeply troubling aspect of this society. I would also like to point out that I am not a sexist and I believe that women are the stronger sex although men, generally are physically stronger and have a more brutish nature. Let's get on with it.

I have been acquainted with a number of women who have suffered from sexual abuse and I abhor the crime, believe in castration and life sentences for the offenders. I do not believe that sexual predators can be rehabilitated. However a small minority of women make the situation worse by throwing doubt on the offences committed by all of these predators with false allegations. Figures are not really available as estimates range from 2% to 10% for false accusations (you need to do your own research) but the main problem with these accusations it is not the accusation itself, even though it can be devastating for the accused, but it leaves men empowered which is the last thing this world needs! While I believe that all people should be able to do what they want as long as it does not have an unwanted effect on any other person, this attitude is not real because of the society we live in. People need to take responsibility for their own actions and this also extends to women, the way they dress and behave can lead to men believing that some of these women are inviting them for sex. However wrong this is, it happens. A Daily Mail reporter, Rebecca Camber, wrote the article 'Rape? It's the fault of the victims, say 50% of women', which contains the line, 'More than one in ten said that dancing provocatively, flirting or wearing revealing clothing made them partly responsible.'

While I believe that women should be able to dance and dress as they wish I do believe that what Rebecca Camber wrote is true. Adverts involving scantily dressed or nude women far outweigh fully dressed women, gossip magazines push a type of beauty for youngsters to aspire to, while trying to get photos of celebrity boobs and invading their privacy at the same time. These attitudes are what empower men and make them believe that sex with whomever they please is a right; fortunately these men are in the minority in following up on their twisted desires. One only needs to look at sex scandals and who are involved to realize that the perverts are not just the men in coats flashing in the park but extends to the rich and powerful as well. Unfortunately this leaves women to protect themselves which can infringe upon their freedoms.

Do women ask for sexual violence? The short answer is no. However this overlooks men and their darker nature. Everyone has a dark side, most people can control it, and some can't. This is our fundamental mistake and for women to ignore this is a grave mistake. Women can wear what they want, dress how they want, dance how they want, go naked if they so desire, within the bounds of the law, and no other human has the right to interfere with them. That is a God given right ingrained into the law, but it ignores the nature of men. Going back to the Stone Age, I am pretty sure the males did not club the females over the head and drag them off to a cave to mate with them, but anthropologists seem to agree that mating was taken by the strongest and hence created an aura of violence. This is echoed in nature all around us from birds to lions. I don't say it is in all nature but none the less it is there. In art, sex and the naked body, mostly the female form, has been around since forever, from Michelangelo to Picasso, Dante to Dali and with the advent of the digital age to every idiot with a smart phone. Our society has become sex crazy. Playboy, Page 3, adverts, films and stills, etc. all display the female body in all its glory.

So we have to admit that the naked or topless female body is thrown at us wherever we go and this includes various public places like beaches swimming pools, night clubs, bars and so on. The film and TV industry further expound this attitude with explicit sex scenes which flood our screens and is available for kids to view from a young age. As stated previously adverts involving scantily dressed or nude women far outweigh fully dressed women. Men are lecherous by nature and enjoy these displays. Here begins the problem.

I do not believe that women enjoy being watched in this manner, a surreptitious glance of admiration – maybe some women, but not more than this, as lechery is not admiration but desire for sex without commitment. Society has hidden the female form for centuries behind layers of clothes and for good reason, men cannot control themselves, bringing about the need for brothels and the naked pictures of beautiful women. Advertising and girlie magazines strengthen the view that women are commodities. You cannot tell me that women posing naked and often provocatively in magazines are not aware that their photos are marketed to boys and men for self-gratification! It is the first sexual experience young boys have and as society moves on these images are becoming more and more graphic and more and more pornography is created and watched; without the market it wouldn't exist. So we are aware that a sexual environment surrounds all aspects of our life and we are aware that men enjoy the visual form of the female body for their own fantasies, where does this leave the women of this world in relation to the few men who cannot control their dark side? The answer, to me, is in their ignorance. Just because laws forbid certain acts and language, it doesn't mean that the thoughts disappear. To a man watching women he perceives the naked woman on the beach as flaunting her desire for sex, a woman gyrating to a song on the dance floor, flaunting her desire for sex, a woman with a low cut dress leaning on a bar top, flaunting her desire for sex, a woman with her nipples pressed against her wet shirt, flaunting her desire for sex, see-through tops, bra-less, clinging trousers or dresses and the list goes on and on. Most men, thank god, can control themselves, ignore it and understand it has nothing to do with sex, only free will, but to the few who can't this means 'come and get me'. How often have you heard a rapist say, 'she asked for it', how often have you heard 'no really means yes', how often have you heard, 'she likes it a bit rough', how often have you heard, 'she is the village bike', she is a goer, she is a slut and in the man's mind it is all true. Male dominated society encourages this by cover ups, the rich buying their way out, police don't care or don't know what to do. Sex is brought into everything and even movies now seem to have an 'essential' sex scene, why? Get on with the movie! I was watching an old film the other day, one of John Wayne's films and he had his romantic interest, and scenes without nudity and sex conveyed the message perfectly, so why do we have to have so much sex and innuendos of it? The women who annoy me the most are those who have nude photos taken, send them to mates, store them on the computer, go topless on the beach, swimming pool or wherever and then get upset when the photos reach the media! It happens and it seems that these women don't want to learn from it.

So where does this leave women? They are at liberty to dress and behave as they like within accepted norms of society while not just being aware of the beastly nature of men, but taking steps to protect themselves. This is, of course an infringement of personal rights, however you cannot legislate against the desires of men, only the actions. Men will rape women and most rapists must feel it is justified or 'she wanted it' or 'she needed it'. Rape has been around forever, only the perception is changing. It is not too long ago that rape and pillage was considered a norm. All the men were killed and the women raped and then taken as slaves, either sex or domestic. The law has changed, society has moved on and yet men still have the basic instinct that they can have any woman they desire unless she belongs to another man, but not always. Even this barrier is breaking down in modern society, as public nudity spreads certain men see this as an opportunity to, basically rape women as these women are acting like whores. The Arabs still cover their women, not because the woman will be unfaithful, but because she will attract desire from men who cannot control their desires and if those women get raped it is their fault for 'encouraging' men.

The following excerpts are from an article written by Khalid Diab of the Guardian newspaper. "Like the traditional orientalist image of the harem, Arab views of the contemporary western woman are also highly sexualised. In fact, many Arab men, particularly those with little contact with the west, have this fantasy of western women that comes straight out of Playboy magazine or the grainy images of pirate pornos". "In this view, western women are oversexed, promiscuous and have revolving doors in their knickers. A typical Egyptian male is a firm believer that any western woman is an easy catch and would not mind at all having sex with complete strangers".

A journalist with a leading Portuguese newspaper, who wishes to remain anonymous told me. "They (male Arabic society) think that all foreign women are prostitutes and they try to treat them like that." "According to this outlook, women's sexual appetites are so insatiable that, if they are left to their own devices, they turn into uncontrollable nymphomaniacs and temptresses luring men to crash into the rocks of lust."

Statistics show, (I have looked at various sources and taken the highest and lowest here), that the Arabic countries have the lowest rape rates, although these may be skewed by the fact that marital rape in not a crime, but never the less vary from 0.6 to 7 per 100,000. While the figures for Western society is between 15.7 and 32.2, with the USA and Sweden leading the way! We must also take into account that rape in Western society is usually committed by someone known to the victim, i.e.; ex-lover, friend or family. This is not my subject of discussion as I am looking at the violent and social rapist. Up until recently and still in effect in some western countries, Police investigations take the line of, how was she dressed, was she drunk, she was asking for it, men get the urges to rape – they can't help it, the victim is ruining the life of the rapist – he had so many opportunities, the victim should not have been there – behaved like that, and so the list goes on. (These are all quotes from cases that either went to court or were prosecuted). I am not trying to blame women I am trying to point out that due to the brutish nature of men, women have to look after themselves, society won't, after all you wouldn't rush to stroke a lion in the African savannah.

My conclusion is therefore that dress and behaviour of women have an influential effect on rape, it shouldn't, but does. This is not just a heinous sexual crime but also a crime by forcing women to behave in a male preconceived manner if they don't want to be molested – an invasion of privacy and women's right to freedom. I do not believe that groups like the '#MeToo' movement continue to help women in need although it was incredibly effective to begin with. Normal good men are becoming too scared to ask women out and avoid interaction with them in case it is misconstrued, the gap between male and female in the workplace could widen as employers subconsciously avoid hiring women if men are concerned about inadvertently offending someone. However, significant women are voicing their concerns. A survey by VOX resulted in the following concerns by women: 63% false accusations, 60% lost professional opportunities and 56% of perpetrators receiving the same punishment for different types of offence.

Heather MacDonald of the Manhattan Institute gave a speech at the Hillsdale College where in she said: "Our nation is about to be transformed, thanks to the #MeToo movement. I am not speaking about a cessation of sexual predation in the workplace. If that were the only consequence of

#MeToo, the movement would clearly be a force for good. Unfortunately, its effects are going to be more sweeping and destructive. #MeToo is going to unleash a new torrent of gender and race quotas throughout the economy and culture, on the theory that all disparities in employment and institutional representation are due to harassment and bias. The resulting distortions of decision-making will be largely invisible; we will usually not know of the superior candidates for a job who were passed over in the drive for gender parity. But the net consequence will be a loss of American competitiveness and scientific achievement." She then went on to state "But however pervasive the diversity imperative was before, the #MeToo movement is going to make the previous three decades look like a golden age of meritocracy. No mainstream institution will hire, promote, or compensate without an exquisite calculation of gender and race ratios. Males in general, and white males in particular, will have to clear a very high bar in order to justify further deferring that halcyon moment of gender equity."

The #MeToo movement is causing a shockwave throughout all aspects of society from Hollywood to business, race to sexism, religion to government and in the end all aspects of society will lose. The #MeToo movement has split feminist movements across the world, not only on the status of men and women but creating an image of a liberated woman who can no longer look out for herself. Men no longer know how to behave with women, how to approach someone they fancy, how to invite someone out as a friend, how to start a relationship as any move by a man could be taken as offensive. I am not talking about physical advances but trying to get to know someone.

Felicity Chaplin wrote in the Financial Review: "This may seem an old chestnut, one that feminism has held as its central tenet for decades, where even consent can be understood as an effect, rather than an exercise, of power. It may seem like nothing new; but it does beg the question: why now? Why a return to these arguments, to these views of sexuality that some critics of the #MeToo movement have labelled Victorian? Is the movement an extension of feminism, part of an ongoing project that had, only two decades ago, been declared by many to be finished, at least in the West? Or is it, to the contrary, a betrayal of the ideals of the feminist movement, of the image of the liberated woman who can not only control her sexuality but fend for herself whenever this control is threatened, replacing this image with that of the cringing wallflower terrified of the advances of men? ".

Catherine Deneuve wrote in Le Mond about the #MeToo movement "puritanical ... wave of purification driven by a growing hatred of men and of sexuality".
Michelle Perrot, a professor of history at Paris Diderot University describes "the #MeToo movement is a new moral order that introduces a new censorship against the free movement of desire."
The French 100 described the #MeToo movement and its French equivalent #balancetonporc, or 'dob in your pig', as "is driving a New Puritanism based on the hatred of men rather than directed at patriarchal culture as such."

Philosopher Slavoj Zizik, stated and quoted in from the Financial Review: "while these protests are bringing out the dark underside of our official claims of equality and mutual respect, they run the risk of turning into just another case where political legitimisation is based on the subject's victimhood status. It is precisely this notion of victimhood as a form of empowerment" and "it remains too obsessively focused on the realm of sexual exploitation within a very narrowly defined milieu, with little or no relevance for, or impact on, the lives of women in the real world".

Susan Faludi who wrote 'Backlash: The Undeclared War against American Women' in which she agrees with Zizik and further states in the New York Times that "[The] challenge today is ... how to bring the outrage over male malfeasance to bear on the more far-reaching campaign for women's equality. Too often, the world's attention seems to have room for only the first."

Consequences of the #MeToo campaigns are ruining many lives of good people as collateral damage.

"In January 2018, also in Paris, #MeToo advocates forced the cancellation of a screening and public discussion of Brigitte Sy's 2015 film, *L'Astragale*. Sy, who was scheduled to speak at the screening, is one of the signatories of the open letter to *Le Monde*."

Brigitte Sy responded: "I did not think one day I would be deprived of the right to speak, or banned from debate or showing my film, censored only because of a signature."

"Across the Atlantic, Casey Affleck bowed to pressure from #MeToo and declined to present the Best Actress award at the 2018 Academy Awards. Affleck had been accused of sexual misconduct on the set of his 2010 mockumentary *I'm*

*Still Here*. Many in the industry rallied to defend him. Kenneth Lonergan, who Affleck worked with on the Oscar-winning 'Manchester by the Sea', called the actor's treatment at the hands of the #MeToo movement abominable."

The #MeToo movement also threatens to destroy the history of cinematic art by threatening male filmmakers who have influenced productions with their unique perspective; these include Woody Allen, Roman Polanski, Alfred Hitchcock, Bernardo Bertolucci, Quentin Tarantino, Terry Gilliam and Michael Haneke. Furthermore Hanke has no accusations against his works but #MeToo targeted him because he spoke out against their movement, "filmmaking in the post-#MeToo world will face a new form of censorship based primarily around funding. Producers and funding institutions would be wary of backing a film that is likely to draw criticism for its use or depiction of sex, or because it is directed by or stars a 'suspect' director or actor", this also threatens the freedom of speech and is the result of injustice and irony as is the protest against Brigitte Sy. I would call the #MeToo movement a revolutionary one and like some revolutionary movements it started with, not just a good cause, but a great one and has spilled over into a man hating revenge trip.

Please remember that this is a personal opinion, right or wrong, so you are welcome to agree or disagree, I am not going to defend my position although I am open to discussion.

## Chapter 24

The plane to Colombia stopped off at Caracas which is on the Caribbean coast and after take-off for Bogota I noticed the plane heading north, circling and then the Andes came into full view grand and majestic, in a way more majestic than the Himalayas, as we had just left the sweltering humid heat of 30°C and within a few kilometres we were flying over snow-capped peaks! Bogota airport was a horde and cackle of loud Spanish with Colombians rushing indiscriminately in all directions. We made our way through the hubbub of the airport, hustled into a van and rushed off in snail paced traffic to a hotel in the centre of Bogota.

The streets were teaming with loud life and the fascination of a new culture put me into a relaxed observation mode. The little motor bikes and scooters zooming through the intricacies of seemingly stopped traffic, pavement cafes overflowing with the lunch time diners, the intricate mix of clothing colours, the row of small business shops interspersed with massive malls, a cultural mix of old and new architecture hinting of the colonial past.

We finally got to the hotel and straight to our rooms to rest after the long flight. We had a nice early dinner of some Colombian dish with meat and yucca with rice which was great and then we were informed that we would be going to the location for the shoot at about 08.00 in the morning and we were free until then. I took a stroll around the streets watching the night life with the food vendors cooking what you would expect along with the unknown, the bars full of happy people, street urchins looking for handouts, hawkers offering the 'best deals ever' in halting English, hippies with handmade merchandise laid on carpets or cloth blocking the pavements all the time accompanied by the hustle of the rushing passers-by. I returned to the hotel and immediately went to sleep.

Rising for breakfast, excitement started to creep in as this was my first big shoot on location. After breakfast we once again boarded a bus which slowly made its way out of the city and into the winding mountains. Six hours of napping later we were dumped at another hotel while the bus chugged off to its next job. We settled into the hotel and then took a tour of the shoot sites, which basically surrounded a lake and we ended up in a thickly forested area with a little beach stretching into the lake. We were told to get our gear and meet back at the site at 16.30 with our allotted equipment. Arriving on time I set up the lights, umbrellas tripods, cameras etc. with the help of two others. The photographer arrived at 17.30 and made us rearrange it all as it was not to his liking. We finished just in time for the light to fade, packed up headed back to the hotel and repeated the set up the following morning. We sat around all day while the photographer placed his models and then moved them around the beach and forest like chess pieces. This went on for a week while I got thoroughly bored with the situation as I learnt that I was not his assistant but his gopher, go for this, go for that. My job was to keep the cameras loaded with film and have the various lenses ready for quick changes. The most monotonous job in photography and on top of that I didn't learn anything other than the fact that the photographer considered himself god, hence no mention of Gu.. (whoops) name.

The shoot ended, I was happy and took a bus to Bucaramanga where I spent the next few years. The 12 hour overnight bus ride to Bucaramanga was both beautiful and scary. The bus drivers are obviously very skilled as they drive along unkempt potholed roads with cliff edges right outside your window as the bus meanders like a flooding river through the winding Andes. Arriving mid-morning I was met by the principle of the college I was to teach at, escorted to a home where I was to live during my contracted period. I was shown my room, a decent sized one with a double bed, desk and en suite bathroom, and then told to dump my things on the bed as I, along with another English teacher, Alaric, were being taken for a braai at a place called Mesa de Los Santos. This a rural area about 2 hours drive from Bucaramanga, up the mountains. It was a beautiful spot but I was too tired from the bus ride to appreciate it. While we were waiting for meat to cook the principle booked a horse ride for me which I really didn't feel like and expressed my opinion. She had already paid for it so reluctantly I was led to an old nag and handed over to the proprietor who helped me mount and then led me off as if I was a five year old child on my first ride! I was so embarrassed and tried to get the reins from him so I could at least ride on my own but the only response I got from the leader was 'English no ride'. He had no further English and I had no Spanish so I continued atop the old nag led by an old man who was not enjoying himself either. It was a short walk as I quickly got across the fact that I would like to return.

Alaric was laughing his head off as the same thing had happened to him when he arrived. Alaric, an Englishman of Italian descent, was a young university student studying law taking a gap year and we became good workmates but never really close. Like me, he had never taught before he went out to Colombia and gave me some insight to the college which was basically the times and students ages and levels.

Although the classes were held in the evenings between 17:00 and 22:00, I was asked to visit the Director on Monday morning. Isabel, the recruiter in the UK had asked me to deliver a VHS video player and to hand over US $1,000 which she had entrusted to me. I went to the school and as I was counting the money to hand over another teacher entered the office, a young girl, Patricia, 18 or so with perfect English. After the brief interruption the Director/Principle starting asking about myself, basic questions like what do you do, have you taught before, where are you from and then stared in disbelief when I said Africa and then the same question I have had ever since leaving Africa, "Why aren't you black?" Well, getting back to the discussion, we moved onto the school, the students and the methodology. She believed in natural acquisition or the mother tongue method and hence no text books or writing materials were given out to the students at the lower levels. The teacher was given a little stuffed toy while all the students sat in a circle while the stuffed toy was thrown to them and then the student would do the assigned task; e.g. lower levels would be something like a morning greeting conversation while higher levels would be involved in longer and more intensive conversations. At first I was wary of this method but it did seem to work, taking students from Beginners to Intermediate (for those of you not in the know, Intermediate would give students a workable day to day grip of the language) in less than three months. At the higher levels, still no text books were given out but writing was included.

As I arrived home I got a phone call from Isabel as to why I had only handed over the VHS and not the money. Fortunately Patricia had walked in and witnessed the handover and I was cleared as a 'miscommunication' had occurred. This incident taught me two things, corruption was rife and the school would not last long. Isabel launched an investigation which concluded that the Director, who had been friends with Isabel since school days, had been stealing since the beginning of their partnership. This conclusion took about 4 -5 months and things went on as normal during that period. Also at home, another teacher, Andrew, had arrived back from a jaunt around Colombia. Andrew was a great guy and we became good friends.

Three months later I had a week off as I needed to travel to Bogota in order to renew my visa. The renewal was quick and easy, in and out within an hour. I decided to return to Bucaramanga via Barrancabermeja, a petroleum producing town situated on one of the largest rivers in Colombia, Rio Magdalena, the largest being the Amazon. The Magdalena is also the main artery to the Caribbean and the basin contains the production centre of Colombia. I arrived in Honda and was quite disappointed by the river, it seemed that it was hardly navigable but there were plenty of long canoe type bus boats that could take up to 12 people up and down the river, some had canopies, others didn't. I booked a ticket for the following day and left for El Dorado, the next stop around mid-morning. The day was hot and sticky with high humidity but the boat ride was refreshing and the river opened up slightly not long after we left Honda.

The river was also busy with traffic in both directions carrying people and goods. The trip to La Dorada did not take too long, arriving during siesta most things were closed but the 'almuerzo' restaurants were serving meals. These restaurants were great and had become a staple for me. They served a set menu of three courses; soup, main dish, desert and a drink, all for the incredible price of between 600 and 1000 Colombian pesos, in those days between 50 pence and about £1! This was also around the time my main meal changed from evening time, which I was brought up with, to midday which I now much prefer. After lunch I took a walk around the village while looking for a place to stay for the night. No one spoke English, my Spanish was still virtually non-existent and I was continually stared at. Communication was through gestures and I finally got a room in a small boarding house for 500 Colombian pesos, including a small dinner and breakfast.

I left early the next morning for Puerto Boyacá arriving late morning. The river was getting wider and wider with a lot more traffic, cattle boats were plenty but also an assortment of cargo carriers, ranging from fruit and veg to other livestock and grains going downstream, to electrical goods and other domestic products going upstream. We stuck quite close to the western river bank where I saw police and army bunkers fortified with both heavy and light gun posts and artillery. The river traffic was patrolled by police gunships, occasionally stopping a cargo carrier for inspection. Upon gesticulating to the gunboats and bunkers I got a two word response: 'terrorist' and 'narcos'. I was aware of the civil unrest problems but not the extent as I was really in a bubble in Bucaramanga, the district capital of Santander.

Arriving at Puerto Boyacá I settled down in a bar overlooking the river and had a few beers of the local brew, Áquila, a beer I liked. The river was busy with trade on the 'docks' really quite active. When a boat arrived the locals gathered around to see what was being brought in and it was everything from toys and electric domestics to cars and bakkies. The boats quickly unloaded and then carried on their upriver route and the crowds quickly dispersed. I wandered around and found an Almuerzo restaurant also overlooking the river. It was quite large with a glass front and sides leading in both directions from the entrance, the tables were bare and a few people had gathered for lunch. I chose a corner table near the window and ordered my lunch with another Áquila. I became aware of people staring at me again as this was quite common but a young boy of, maybe 9 or 10, would not take his eyes off me, so much so that I could see his mother getting agitated and embarrassed. I started to feel a bit disconcerted and tried to rush my lunch. Half way through the mother got up and approached and in reasonable English, the (best I had heard since leaving Bogotá), apologized and carried on that her son had never seen a gringo as no foreigners had been here for about 10 years. I accepted her apologies and as she left I began to ponder why, it must have something to do with the bunkers and patrol boats on the river. I put all this aside as I wandered back to the boat stop as I was taking the afternoon boat to Puerto Barrío. I had discovered that the boat busses only did small hops and so multiple boats were needed to travel downstream. The river was getting wider with a lot more traffic, especially the livestock boats. The patrol boats were also more frequent and this brought home the fact that Colombia was in the middle of a terrorist war.

Arriving at Puerto Barrío I found another little boarding house for the night before taking to the streets exploring. The towns along the route from Honda all had similarities in architecture and structure. A central park with people lazing on the benches, mothers watching their kids while others were strolling to the various small shops and chatting in the doorways, often with kids sitting on the steps blocking the entrance. The square had statues in the middle, often of local heroes, some of Simon Bolívar, the man who brought independence to a few South American countries. Surrounding the square was a church, with mainly women entering for a while and leaving, government buildings with slow traffic while men leaned against the white arches smoking and chatting and the tavernas with outside tables and customers staring bleary eyed while discussing something of importance. One curiosity I noticed at almost all the eating and drinking establishments along the river was that they all had bags of water strategically hanging from the roof.

The next morning I set off for Barrancabemeja in the stifling heat and watched as the river once again grew in size. Barrancabemeja was a bustling port with boats loading and unloading and I looked around at the frenzied activity while I disembarked and made my way to the bus station. The port lived up to its reputation as a place you do not want to linger in. I was approached dozens of times with merchants wanting to sell drugs along with girls who were fluttering their eyelids and flashing their breasts as I hurried along. I made it to the bus station without incidence, purchased a ticket to Bucaramanga, which was leaving in an hour and I settled down to another beer and watched the organized chaos unfolding before me in the suffocating 40ºC heat and humidity. The bus ride back to Bucaramanga was in a cosy air conditioned bus driven by a maniacal driver winding his way up the mountains as fast as he could!

Bucaramanga is situated on a plateau in the eastern Andes with an altitude of 959 metres, a temperature between 18 and 28, is sunny and humid and the locals will tell you it has only 2 seasons, rainy and not rainy, which seem to alternate every 3 months, although I consider this a misnomer as the 'rainy season' still had plenty of sun and periods of no rain. The rain was more like short and strong falls. Bucaramanga is also in an active seismic area and so has quite a few tremors, but not a lot of really damaging earthquakes, generally up to 5.1 whose magnitude scale is defined 'often felt but only causes minor damage'. Bucaramanga is also called the 'La Ciudad de Los Parques' and 'La Cuidad Bonita de Colombia' - City of Parks and Colombia's Beautiful City respectively. It has about half a million people and the lowest unemployment rate in Colombia, the Magdalena Valley is about three hours down the Cordilla to the heat where you can enjoy water sports on the river while going up the Cordilla for three hours puts you in snow and freezing country, although to my knowledge no winter sports are available, due to the fact that I am a sun and warmth lover.

Back teaching my students asked me about the trip and when I informed them about the Honda to Barrancabameja trip I was informed by one and all that I was crazy and lucky to be back without incident. Ignorance is bliss, I had a great trip. Two things were of importance to me when I got back, one was to become more politically aware of what was happening in Colombia and to make a larger effort to learn Spanish. My environment within Bucaramanga was not conducive to learning Spanish as I lived with English people, taught English 5 hours a day and then, tired after work, socialized with other teachers and students who all wanted us to speak English. So I made friends with a hippy selling his crafts on the roadside in a shopping mall. When I first approached Freddy he assumed that I wanted marijuana and / or cocaine. He didn't speak English, I didn't speak Spanish, but through gestures and pointing to a watch I gathered that he wanted me to come back in an hour. Returning an hour later Freddie packed up and led me off on a 10 minute walk to a little Taverna called Pacho Natcho and introduced me to Natcho, short for Ignatius. Nacho spoke perfect English after having spent a number of years in the states and after chatting over a beer for awhile he asked me how much I wanted. 'How much what?'
'Cocaine'.

'Sorry, but there has been a misunderstanding, I just wanted to talk to Freddie in order to learn and practice Spanish.'
After this was cleared up we carried on drinking, Freddie and I eventually became quite good friends, as did Natcho and I. Freddie was a new age hippie and sold handmade artisan goods every day on the sidewalk at the Cabecera in Bucaramanga. He made jewellery but also sold clothes made by others and so I became a regular sitting with Freddie for an hour or so every day, while learning Spanish. This is a good way to learn a language, using real life situations and soon enough I was chatting to other hippies selling their wares and had the confidence to chat with almost anyone. One problem with this way of language learning was that as the people I spoke to learnt to understand my convoluted Spanish they stopped correcting me as communication was sufficient. This led to years of problems with verbs, tenses and word order which took me ages to iron out, bad habits die hard! However once you become aware of these problems and counter them from when you first starting learning a language, it is the best way.

Natcho was a different kettle of fish, he ran his bar and an empanada business now on his own as his partner had left and gone back to the states. Natcho was talkative but said nothing. I gathered from the little he said about his time in the States that he was affiliated to a cartel, this was also backed up by rumours and some of the things he said inadvertently. In Colombia there are mini Police Stations spread around the cities manned by only two or three policemen. One of these happened to be about 100 metres from Pacho Natcho and one evening I asked if the close vicinity of the police wasn't a problem for his 'secondary' business to which he replied 'they are taken care of'.

This period of time was the height of Pablo Escobar's power and war against the government with politicians being assassinated as well as reporters that wrote articles about him together with the bounty he put out on police it was no surprise that the local police were paid to look away. Pablo Escobar also helped communities to a tremendous degree, building schools, hospitals, football fields and even the first metro system in Medellin. This 'charity' work made him beloved by the people he helped and feared by those who opposed him. During these years Escobar is estimated to have had over 4,000 people killed including 657 policemen, an estimated 1,000 journalists and 4 presidential candidates. The drug war was in addition to the guerrilla war raging in Colombia by FARC and ENL, both of which were extremely active with armed attacks and bombings throughout Colombia including Bucaramanga while I was there. Escobar's sicarios bombed the Van Guardia Liberal newspaper officers as well as a police station while the guerrilla groups shot up places regularly and kidnapping was prominent. However the people of Bucaramanga, and Colombia as a whole did not let the fear rule their lives and life carried on as normal.

A little over a month after my trip down the Magdalena we entered the Christmas holidays and the college closed and so I decided to take a trip through Colombia, ending up on the Amazon.

The first leg on the trip was to San Agustin. It took three bus rides totalling over 24 hours but well worth it. San Agustin is an archaeological site holding one of the largest indigenous necropolises in the world, dating back to 3,300 BC. The area full of stone artwork, ceramic, wood as well as high quality gold pieces (now in the Gold museum in Bogota, which I was to visit later due to the influence of San Agustin). There were also sacred caves with stairs leading down to tombs. Surrounding San Agustin are various sites hosting anthropomorphic sculptures of faces, polychrome sculptures of magical and religious zoomorphic masks, mythical animals, ancient tool making sites, sarcophagi and so the list goes on. It also transpired that the River Magdalena had its source in the surrounding mountains.

I happened to be in San Agustin for Christmas and on Christmas Eve, returning to the Hostel I had decided to have a quick drink and dinner from a street vendor. This was not to be the case. Colombians celebrate on Christmas Eve and not Christmas day. The streets rapidly filled up with revellers and the whole town became one big party, music, eating and drinking going on until after sun up. I am not a party person but this was a fantastic night and I flopped into my bed exhausted and drunk well after the day had broken over the majestic mountains. After spending Christmas day asleep and recovering I caught the bus to Popayán on Boxing Day, spent the night and the next day travelling on to La Pedrera, situated on the Caquetá River which flows into the Amazon River. I had been told that there weren't any passenger boats but with luck I would be able to travel with a merchant taking his wares down river. The bus ride was almost unbearable; the tar road ran out, turning into a mud path with the bus sliding from side to side almost crashing into the humid, sweaty and encroaching jungle at every curve.

La Pedrera was the final destination as the road ran out and further travel was on the water. As I got out of the bus I spotted three men dressed in typical local garments armed with AK's talking to the bus driver, who was headed towards a Taverna. The three men left him and approached me, ' Gringo?'

'No' I replied.

' Hablas Español?'

' Poco.'

'Speak English?'

'Yes'. All the time my heart was racing like a two stroke.

'Where you from?'

'Zimbabwe'.

'Where is that?'

'Africa.'

'Passport'

I handed it over. 'It is British'

'Yes, but I was born in an ex–colony', he handed the passport back.

'We are closed to tourists, the bus leaves at 8 tomorrow morning, be on it,' Looking at my camera bag he continued, 'no photos'.

The three of them turned around and walked away. I slowly headed to the Taverna and downed a beer and got another. Although I was weary and continually watching over my shoulder the evening in the Taverna was jolly. Although I was cautious of my intake, the locals plied me with drink and told stories about the area. I apparently was the only Gringo seen in the last 5 years, the last was an American who came on a yacht, was suspected of being DEA and disappeared in the multitude of the tributaries leading to the Amazon, his yacht was found deserted.

Unbeknown to me La Pedrera was a narco trafficking staging point. The cocaine came down river from Peru, made its way through the tributaries to La Pedrera where it was transferred by donkey through the jungle and up the mountains to the Magdalena River where it went to distribution points ending in the States. I was waiting for the bus to leave at about 7am and the bus driver arrived at about 7:45 leaving promptly at 8AM. Once the bus was out of town I felt relieved as I settled down to the harrowing journey back to Popayán.

The next leg was to Manaus in Brazil, of which I knew nothing about except that in the colonial heyday it was an important trading centre, I just wanted to see the confluence of the Rio Negro with the Amazon. Landing in Manaus was the first surprise, it was massive! I thought it was a provincial relic of a bygone era, but boy was I wrong! Before even landing my plans had changed and I decided to stay a few days. Situated bang in the middle of the Amazon jungle, local reservations start a few miles out of town. The old colonial architecture is splendid although decaying in much of the town, but the old opera house stands majestically displaying its former glory, conjuring images of the rough and refined days of its colonial past. The port is also enormous, being the main trading centre up and down the Amazon and has ocean-going cargo ships delivering goods. The main road south to Porto Velho (situated on the south side of the Amazon, while Manaus is on the north bank of the Rio Negro) necessitates a ferry crossing and the only land connection with the rest of Brazil was now impassable as large parts of it had been reclaimed by the jungle, leaving air and river the only ways out for its approximately 2,000,000 population. However the highlight for me was the reason I went there: The meeting of two great rivers, The Rio Negro and the Amazon River, are main tourist attractions especially where the two rivers run side by side creating one river with a dividing line of black from the Rio Negro and muddy silver (at the time of year I saw it) of the upper Amazon. It may sound simple but you have to see it in order to appreciate the distinctive demarcation flowing off into the distance in this 10 kilometre wide river, in the rainy season. The next day I flew off to Tabatinga and walked across the border into Leticia, back in Colombia.

Leticia is my kind of town, small, busy, with friendly people. Most of the buildings are wooden with a few solid colonial buildings and even fewer modern brick buildings. I found a Hostel overlooking part of the port, but not really. It was more a place on the river bank looking more like a bay of the Amazon River where small boats and canoes of the indigenous Amazonians would bring their goods to trade. Looking south from the Hostel porch one could see across the river to Peru, which appeared in the far distance. The hostel had no electricity, running off gas, candlelight and lanterns, downstairs was a porch with a taverna where you could watch the hustle bustle of the informal port. The port for larger vehicles was around the corner, out of sight.

The following day I was awoken by the sound of a bugle at sunrise and decided on a walkabout. The town was small and could easily be walked around in 30 minutes. I discovered that a zoo existed about 10 minutes' walk outside of town and so off I went to have a look at the local fauna, even though caged, which I hated. The zoo was disgusting, the animals caged in wire pens hardly big enough for the animals to turn around in, I didn't stay long. Once outside the gate hawkers bombarded me with animals for sale, anything from boa constrictors, jaguars, parrots, alligators, monkeys, toucans, sloths, etc. What caught my eye was a miniature monkey, with a body the size of my finger and a tail twice as long, I knew I couldn't buy it but I was fascinated by it. The seller started at $100 and came down to $10. We argued about transporting it back to the UK, but quite rightly he countered that anything that small could easily be hidden even in your pocket! The next subject was how to keep a monkey still on a plane, apparently it came with a tranquilizer that would knock it out for 24 hours, these guys had an answer for everything, and his mate next to him was trying to sell me a baby Anaconda! The only way I could get rid of these guys was to promise to buy one when I come back from my Amazon trip.

Walking back to Leticia by a different route, an army barracks appeared in a large clearing with the sun setting over the jungle canopy. A small group of soldiers marched out and once again a bugle reverberated through the town over the river and disappeared into the jungle as the Colombian flag was lowered for the day, a welcome custom signalling the end of the day. That night while having dinner and a beer on the porch of the hostel a Brazilian guy appearing to be in his late thirties sat down, introduced himself Diogo and we started chatting. He was a tour guide taking tourists into the jungle, for 3, 7 or 10 day walks and as a three day tour was leaving he was trying to find a couple more people to complete the numbers. I agreed and then I enquired about the local area and Leticia. Leticia was founded by a Peruvian Captain and Governor of the adjoining Peruvian department, Loreto, and named San Antonio. Colombia and Peru fought over the territory eventually giving it to Colombia in 1922 for their recognition of Peru's claim to land south of the Putumayo River, also being claimed by Ecuador. The name changed to Leticia, as legend would have it, when a high ranking soldier stationed in the area fell in love with an Amerindian (the local name for the indigenous people) named Leticia.

After the history lesson we started talking about the life of the town and bought a copy of the local paper. On the front page was a photo of an anaconda that had been killed by locals and slit open to reveal a young boy who had been taken. Contrary to popular opinion this is not a common happening as some media outlets would lead you to believe, as for the majority of locals this was the first incident known to them. Still horrific. The photo was enough to make your skin crawl.

The bugle, once again woke the town up at sunrise. After a 6am breakfast I was at the dock awaiting my tour by 7am. There were 8 of us as we set out by boat across the river into the Brazilian part of the Amazon jungle. The first spectacular sight was a flock of parrots on the lower limbs, five metres above our heads squawking and flying from branch to branch. A sense of awe overtook me as for the first time in my life I saw wild parrots by the hundreds, some with long tails, some short, the myriad of colours displayed with open wings as they flapped and glided through the dense jungle. The jungle was thick but the route was obviously well used and marches were generally 2 – 3 hours with half hour breaks. The animals are not easy to see other than the continuous presence of monkeys and parrots, but we still saw quite a few, particularly sloths, too slow to run and hide! However the guides were fantastic at spotting the game and directing our gaze.

The first night was spent in a Kokamas village in an open sided dormitory, while I don't know what dinner was, it was tasty and as we were all tired the night overcame us early. As did rising the next morning. Breakfast was a porridge-like substance with goat's milk and we set out for the second day's walk. This brought sightings of Tapirs, Toucans, a variety of other birds and a massive fright! The leaves are continually falling and although the path is easy to follow the humidity is high and the leaves are slippery, leading to somebody slipping every now and then. During one of our breaks, as usual we were looking for a place to sit, rest and drink some water, preferably a log on raised ground. The guides were not as fussy as the tourists and just sat on their haunches anywhere. Suddenly one of the guides jumped up and moved us on. We stopped a few metres away while the guide returned to where he had been to clear away the slippery leaves from next to where he had been perched. All at once various reactions of surprise ranging from a screech, howl, shriek to exclamations and whispers when a digesting anaconda was unveiled. It hardly moved and although the guide assured us that in this state it was not dangerous, we all took a few steps back, while the guide carried on uncovering the anaconda. Apparently it was a female about 10 metres long with an outlining bulge at least a metre long, having probably eaten in the last 36 hours. All this did not comfort me and I was happy to move on but spent the rest of the day weightily scanning the jungle in every direction.

The second night was spent in another village and followed the pattern of the previous day. The last day's walk brought the most spectacular sight of all, a Jaguar! Unfortunately I did not see it at great length as Diogo had seen it first and pointed it out to us but all we could see was its head peering out between some flora and then it disappeared back into the jungle. Mid-afternoon we reached the river where the boat was waiting to take us back, but first we went downstream to where the pilot had seen some game. Cutting the engine and pointing, the pilot indicated to where some capybaras (large, cute rodents about a metre long) were grazing by the river's edge while birds rested on their heads and backs. Getting back to Leticia worn out, I ate and drank the evening away, retiring early and spent the next day resting before joining a riverboat for a cruise up the Amazon into Peru.

The riverboat had 15 passengers and 4 crew, offering a luxury cruise up to San Jose de Saramuro on the Marañon River, a tributary of the Amazon. On boarding the riverboat the passengers were introduced to each other and the crew who spoke good English, the trip was to be 10 days. The rest of the tourists were from the United States and a mix of people from various South American countries. An old man celebrating his 80th birthday, a middle aged evangelical pastor with a cadre of young women in their late teens or early 20's were among the passengers. We left mid-morning and crossed the river to go through Customs and Immigration into Peru and then headed slowly upstream. The day was hot and humid and various animals could be seen along the banks. We were summoned to lunch by a gong and assigned seats according to our rooms. I was placed with Bruno and Mary. Bruno was the old man I mentioned earlier and Mary was thirty something and the only woman travelling on her own. After lunch the boat was anchored and tied to the banks while we were taken in two speedboats to a Ticuna village. The village was spread out with a football field in front of a small square in the centre where the villagers would congregate. The headman came out to meet us and showed us around the village which was made entirely of wood and all the buildings were on stilts in case of floods. The villagers were in traditional dress. The women were wearing knee length white dresses with indigenous patterns painted brown, headbands of similar design – some with feathers in. The men wore similar designed skirts from the waist down and large feathered headbands while the kids just wore loincloths. Some of the people wore western dress, but only one or two. The families lived in the houses, generally one large room which had the living, eating, cooking and sleeping areas neatly separated with some houses having areas partitioned with material, not all had walls and those that did were only waist high.

Under the houses, hanging from the floor of the house and on the stilts, were tools, gourds and other household implements. The locals were keen to sell their crafts and crowded around at the square after the tour, but were not pushy like the hawkers in towns, they just waited patiently until you showed interest and then an interpreter would help the negotiations. We returned to the speed boats and leisurely cruised along the banks looking out for game until we reached the riverboat hot and sticky, so I headed off for a cold shower. The riverboat started off upstream and the passengers were soon enjoying a drink on deck as the jungle slowly chugged by.

Bruno turned out to be a fascinating and entertaining man and throughout the trip we spent time together. He was orphaned as a baby and was brought up with his grandparents who were Republican politicians and his grandfather was the Ambassador to France, twice in the late 1920's. Bruno spent part of his youth in Paris in the 20's and made his way after school to the hangouts of 'The Lost Generation' and 'the Crazy Years', which included writers like Scot Fitzgerald, Hemingway and Gertrude Stein and many artists including Picasso, Arp, Ernst and Duchamp as well as musicians and composers like Igor Stravinsky and

George Gershwin. Bruno was a teenager hanging out at the cafes Le Jockey and Le Döme in the Montparnasse area of Paris where apparently he became a regular gofer for these young artistes and sat around while they discussed the woes of politics and the world. Bruno became a freethinker and for many years rejected all forms of religion.

On his return to the States he entered politics but preferred the background and never ran for any form of office, even being offered an advisory position to the first George Bush Presidency, which he rejected as he loathed the man calling him a pompous charlatan. His stories regaled the passengers every evening as we drank sundowners while waiting for dinner. However he never mentioned why he disliked Bush so much and would not be drawn on the subject but his face let you know his dislike.

The second day we stopped again, taken on the speedboats and on a jungle walk where once again I encountered the breath-taking sight of a flock of parrots. Other than that we only encountered a few sloths and insects trying their best to eat us. The flora of the jungle is incredible as are the continuous sounds surrounding us.

The third day we took the speed boats up a tributary for about an hour and a half and stopped on the banks in front of a small village where we were to have lunch supplied by the local family. Alighting the boats onto a shabby jetty the smell of coriander was overpowering as it grew all around us as we were led to the stilted house. A toothless old lady greeted us indicating for us to sit on the floor around a huge table, as we did so she drifted into the kitchen area returning with a handful of small empty gourds then made another trip to the kitchen returning with a huge gourd filled with liquid. One of the speedboat drivers told us to take a gourd if we wanted to taste the local alcohol, which I decided to do. She poured out a generous quantity to those of us who wanted to try it. It was disgusting! Thick and slimy, it reminded me of how oysters slid down the back of your throat like snot. It was all I could do to spit it out. However I drank some of it and asked how it is made. Some vegetable, I don't know what it was, is thoroughly chewed by the ladies of the community and then spat into a container where it is left to infuse for a few weeks, then strained and placed in the gourd from which we were served. I was drinking brewed spittle!! After that I didn't enquire what lunch was, but it tasted good and soon afterwards we returned to the riverboat. Upon reaching the boat various pink dolphins were frolicking around and I had never even heard of them until I got to Manaus and then considered them an urban legend. Observing them for about 10 minutes I noticed that the river was absolutely calm. So I stripped off and dove into the river from the bow, about the same height as a high school diving board. What a mistake! The water looked calm but the flow was strong and by the time I surfaced the river boat was about 50 metres up stream so I frantically swam towards the bank, the pink dolphins no longer a priority as it took another 50 metres of downstream movement to eventually reach the bank, boarding the riverboat to stares and sighs of incredulity. I dried myself off and settled down to a nice cold beer.

This evening the evangelical pastor was encouraged by his entourage to part with the reason for his trip. Not really impressed with him, mostly due to the young women who were mesmerized by him, I settled down to expect the bible punching, hypercritical rhetoric of a seasoned hustler. Bruno and I sat at a table next to the railings drinking beer while the preacher took centre stage. His speech was calm and collected not at all like my image of an evangelical preacher. He would smuggle bibles into Russia and hold secret masses in homes throughout the country, being able to enter the USSR as a businessman selling tool making equipment to the Russian government provided a cover for his true intentions. He got caught while holding a mass in Moscow and sent to Siberia without trial, he simply disappeared, along with some of his parishioners. The camp he was sent to was a labour camp filled mostly with petty thieves, religious people and minor dissidents. Manual labour was from pre-dawn to sunset with sparse food and drink with a scarcity of warm clothes.

The camp was not enclosed as anyone foolish enough to attempt escape would die in the vast, unpopulated, freezing wasteland while the guards didn't really care and considered the camp some form of punishment as well. Yet he was rescued. The nearest train station was over 100 kilometres away and the track to the camp was unyielding and driving was a herculean task with the end of winter approaching. Two of his devoted followers braved the trip and snatched him from his daily labour tasks when outside the camp. They gave him a change of clothes, a new ID and got on the train with him. They headed east to a small town on the east coast of Russia where his friends left him on a boat to Japan. On arrival in Japan he went straight to the American Embassy where he was interrogated by the CIA who accused him of being turned by the Russians. During his stay at the camp he had lost a finger to frostbite after an accident during one of his day's labour. The CIA took this as evidence of torture and did not believe that he was a preacher. He spent six months in CIA custody before he was released. I must say my opinion of him changed.

Chugging up the river the following a day loud clunk reverberated throughout the riverboat and we started drifting. The reaction of the crew was prompt and the two speedboats were used to pull the riverboat to the shore where it was tied up. We then set out on a sightseeing trip up one of the tributaries. Returning for lunch we were informed that the propeller had dropped off and the drive shaft had caused some damage. Mechanics were being dispatched but we are likely to be stuck there for a few days. We were assured that day trips to into various parts of the river and jungle would continue. I don't think anyone minded, I certainly didn't. The trips carried on and we returned to the boat exhausted for a few days when we were informed that it was not possible to repair it while on the river and that the Peruvian Air Force was sending a plane to collect us at an airfield about 4 hours away the following day.

We left early and crammed into the speedboats with our luggage and arrived well over five hours later. A small two propped plane awaited us. One of the riverboat crew started talking to the pilot and then informed us that the plane was too small to take us all. It only had 6 seats apart from the cockpit. We were 15. After another discussion the crew member asked us whether some of us would mind sitting on the floor, we didn't. We were loaded onto the plane with the luggage at the back among the remaining 9 unseated passengers. The cockpit had no door and we could see straight through the windscreen. We taxied to the beginning of the runway and then started the take-off procedures. The plane gained speed but no height. The pilot started to shout to us in Spanish, which none of us understood. He shouted a few more times when Mary, who fortunately understood a bit told us the pilot wanted us to quickly rush to the front as the plane started to leave the ground. The group rose as one and ran to the front of the plane only to feel the nose of the plane dip as the tail rose and a few seconds later we were edging above the tree tops. The plane gained height and a green carpet of jungle spread out before us as the Amazon River meandered through it. It is a sight you have to see in order to appreciate and I spent the full two hour trip staring out the window at the unbelievable expanse below. Landing at the Air Force Base went off without a hitch but a group of military personnel with crates of beer were gathered where the taxiing stopped. My immediate thought was what a great welcome but as we were led off in a different direction to a hangar I asked the person leading us what that was all about. Fortunately he spoke English and replied, 'It is a celebration of the pilot's first solo flight!' I'm just glad that we were informed after the flight!

At the hangar we were met by a representative of the travel agency who informed us that we were being taken to a hotel while things were sorted out. We were taken in various motorized rubber dinghies for about an hour up one of the tributaries, which was smaller muddier and darker than any we had visited to date. We eventually stopped and disembarked on a jetty leading to a large elegant wooden structure, which was our hotel. It was beautiful! The furniture was of Spanish colonial design, massive and really comfortable; the bed in my room was a double four-poster. I met Bruno for a drink on the veranda and took in the scenery. The river in front of us was about 100 metres across with the trees stretching as high as you could see with bits of blue interspersed silhouetting the treetops. The jungle surrounded us and the noise coming from it was continually changing, squawking of parrots, singing of birds, dripping of water gathered in leaves, flapping of wings, jumping of fish, chattering monkeys, buzzing of insects, while the chorus of stridulating grasshoppers and crickets filled in the background. A waiter approached and asked if we would like dinner where we were, both Bruno and I agreed to this and as a consequence we met the fattest parrot I had ever seen as he climbed up the chair leg and onto our table to steal our food! I enquired as to his history and was told that he had lived directly across the river and used to fly over to get titbits from the guests, however over time he got too fat to fly and now just perches on the veranda and solicits food from the guests. The Hotel staff asked guests not to indulge it, but some people still do.

As it got dark oil lamps were systematically placed along the wooden handrails and produced a cosy atmosphere with the dancing shadows animating the walls behind us. After a few drinks I retired for the night only to be woken in the morning by the natural song of the jungle and proceeded to have breakfast where the agency rep had organized a river trip upstream, left us in the capable hands of the tour guide and informed us he would return in the evening. The trip was slightly different to the other villages we had visited. This one, although constructed the same, on stilts etc. was actually in flood so the dinghies were tied up to the legs of the buildings and we entered up ladders. This household took us on a canoe trip around the area visiting shops, neighbours and the community centre where a lot of people were gathered doing daily chores, cleaning vegetables, making dough etc. The tour lasted about an hour and then we returned to the hotel and relaxed. Just before dinner the agent returned, gave us a full refund for the trip and let us knows we were welcome to stay another two nights or we could return to town with him in the morning. The next morning I said my farewells and departed for Iquitos.

Iquitos, to my surprise is a reasonably large city, approximately 400,000, with colonial Spanish architecture dating back to the 1700's, including a beautiful cathedral. It had a fair amount of traffic, but as is typical in a lot of Spanish speaking countries, scooters are everywhere. The port looked a mess, with boats, large and small cluttering the banks overflowing from the harbour, boathouses made from wood and palm leaves dotted the river village and the market was just off the harbour with a variety of food stalls emanating an aroma that makes you feel hungry. I had a meal of pinchos cooked over a coal fire with potatoes and peppers skewered along with the meat. The hostel was basic so dumping my stuff I explored the city a bit, ending up with a beer and chatting to some locals in bad Spanglish. This was the first time I had encountered hyperinflation and the cost of a beer was 1,500,000 Intis (less than USD 0.50) and the bed for the night was 4,000,000!! The locals asked where I had come from and where I was going; in the instant I decided to travel overland to the Peruvian coast, only to be informed that there was no road out of Iquitos. I was dumbstruck! Here was a thriving city in the middle of the Amazon jungle, cars, motor bikes, scooters and even small busses along with the puk-puks, bicycles and animal drawn vehicles and yet no road in or out. So I jumped on an overnight cargo boat to Yurimagaus, where the road started.

At the Yurimaguas bus depot, a cubicle on the square, I enquired as to when would be the next bus towards the coast to be informed it was only coming in about 10 days but the helpful agent gave instructions as to where I could get a ride with some commercial vehicles, so off I went and after a few hours I secured a lift in an old Chevy pick-up, probably already a classic, leaving at 6am the following day. Arriving on time I jumped in the back with half a dozen or so fellow travellers and we set out. About 15 minutes out of Yurimaguas the tar road came to an end and the dirt/mud road began. The trip was expected to take between 24 and 36 hours, depending on conditions and with the road winding and the pickup sliding around all over the place we felt like marbles in a tin can rattling around and getting banged from side to side. A few of the passengers chuckled at my obvious discomfort at what felt like a nonstop fairground ride, 24 hours of this was really not what I expected. However there turned out to be quite long stretches of good flat roads where one could enjoy the Amazon jungle scenery with the trees on either side of the road forming a long tunnel until the next corner with the sun shimmering through the leaves and occasionally catching glimpses of the blue sky through the tree tops. Even with the engine sounds the jungle could be heard humming with its teaming life. Night came and the only stop was to fill up with diesel from the jerry cans in the back with us, sleep was haphazard with us nodding off and abruptly waking as a corner bounced us between our dozing neighbours.

Morning broke and I wish I had been more prepared as my travel companions ate their planned meals, while my ignorance and stupidity left me starving! At least 24 hours had passed so it can't be too much further. The morning revealed that we were climbing the Andes and the spectacular views which presented themselves were well worth the discomfort of the ride. Morning mist hanging over the tree tops, the screeching of the jungle birds and insects echoing through the trees, all spreading on a silver green carpet as far as the eyes could see. The indifference of my travel companions reminded me of how I had taken my home in Africa for granted until I left, some things remain the same wherever you go. Rounding a corner we braked to a halt as lorries queued up in front of us until they disappeared around a corner. A street market of food vendors had sprung up and everyone except me knew what was going on. Walking up the road a bit I discovered that there had been a landslide with no way through! Estimates as to when it would clear varied from a few hours to a day, depending when equipment arrived to help clear it. People from the cavalcade had already started clearing. The road just ended in this massive sea of mud interspersed with glimpses of greenery and colossal branches, it was impassable, but at least I had a nice hot meal!

The rest of the day I spent watching the workers clearing the landslide and I was impressed with their knowhow and ability considering the lack of tools. As it got dark I returned to the pickup where my travel mates had picked up a couple of crates of beer, I contributed to the cost and sat down and got tipsy with them in this most glorious of settings. By midday the following day the way was clear enough for the lorries to get passed, often with the assistance of another vehicle. One thing I noticed was that the majority of the lorries loaded with goods, were Volvos, this in a country whose primary importation of vehicles is from the United

States. Our pickup was through by 15:00 and less than an hour later we had crested the Andes and had a wonderful view through the foothills and down into the plains below stretching as far as the eye could see. The Jungle was still there but seemed to have been tamed and slowly gave way as we entered Jaén, the end of the trip, in the evening. The driver dropped us all at the bus station, a real bus station and not a cubicle! I decided to enquire when the next bus to Chiclayo was. It was about to leave, so a quick decision saw me on the bus. The road was tar and comfortable, at least as comfortable as a bus driving down the mountains can be. I dozed all the way and on arrival received directions to a decent hotel. I booked in, dirty and ragged, showered for about an hour and went to bed and slept soundly.

I spent a day in Chiklayo walking the streets, enjoying the sea view, a beer or two and my meals. I realized that my trip had gone on longer than intended and so the following day I took the bus, or rather two busses to Quito, the capital of Ecuador and the second highest capital in the world, the highest being La Paz in Bolivia. The preservation of the historical centre, cannot be equalled anywhere. The old town is like stepping back in time, the palace overlooks the Plaza Grande and a cathedral all of which are in pristine condition. The Plaza is crowded along the sides with a market which starts early, around 6am, I had a hotel room right above it which woke me up! Along with the market was a selection of food vendors where I consumed my daily victuals served by the locals dressed in their colourful traditional dress. Due to the elevation Quito was cold, even though the north of the city had the Equator running through it. From the plaza you can look onto the snow-capped peaks of the Andes mountains. Spent two nights and one day relaxing in Quito before catching the bus back to Colombia, except at the border the bus did not go through customs and immigration. We disembarked, walked through the border and then embarked on another bus on the Colombian side! Forty eight hours later back in Bucaramanga I learnt that the partner in London had pulled out of the partnership and the school closed. Luckily, Gladys, the owner of the house was content to let us carry on living there. She did not live there herself but had her physiotherapy rooms in the front part of the house. Gladys also worked full time in the local hospital and did her private work in the early morning, evenings and weekends, so all in all was happy to have us, Aleric, Andrew and myself living there.

I immediately got a job at another language institute called CELAI, run by an American, Mr Fritz, who had been living in Bucaramanga for over 30 years. Nobody knew his first name and even the Board of Directors called him Fritz, while everyone else used their first names. The methodology at CELAI was similar but better constructed as books and grammar lessons were an integrated part of the course but conversation was the prime focus. It was here that I started to enjoy teaching and although I spoke English correctly and had done English Grammar for 'O' Level, it was here at CELAI that I really started to look at the English Language and it's usage. I was given the Intermediate to Advanced conversation groups and Fritz insisted that more conversation was had when people were drinking alcohol, so every Friday lesson I took the adult group to a taverna across the road from the school to drink and talk with my students! This went on for three months when I had to leave the country in order to renew my visa. I booked my flight back to the UK and was to take the bus to Bogota the night before my flight but my plans were scuppered by an attack carried out by FARC who blew up a police station and another attack further along the road to Bogota. The busses were cancelled and nobody knew when they would be restarted, certainly not before morning, too late for me to catch my flight. Eventually finding a taxi with four other people we decided to take the risk. The driver left around 1am and Bogota was about a 12 hour drive, I may just make the airport in time. After eight hours of a cramped and worrisome journey, we were stopped once at a roadblock put up by local militia, we arrived in Tunja, informed us that he wasn't going any further. Disappointed we all got out, headed to the bus station, booked a ticket, had breakfast and caught the bus two hours later. I knew I was not going to make to the airport on time, but after arriving in Bogota I had to find out what would happen to my ticket so proceeded to the airport anyway, albeit it three hours after takeoff. I made my way to the Avianca desk and presented my ticket, only to be led away to a group of people also from my flight. Due to a technical problem the flight was delayed 24 hours and we were all whisked off to a nice 5 Star hotel and treated like royalty, picked up the following day to catch our flight. God was on my side!

# Chapter 25

Arriving back in England was a let-down as I hadn't wanted to return at all as I was enjoying Colombia. I wanted a quick turn around and I applied for a three year work permit at the Embassy, but was granted one with renewal one year at a time. I had booked into a Backpackers in Nottinghill and soon after got a job with them cleaning rooms for 4 hours a day, 5 days a week in return for board and lodging. This fitted in well with my plans as I was hoping to return to a nightshift at a photo lab. However that was not to be and I found it increasingly difficult to get work. One day at the tube station I bumped into Jonnie, from the squat in Crouch End. He had settled down with a woman and was still working with his importing buddies. We had a drink, he gave me his phone number and we parted ways, however it was nice to catch up with him. Work was proving a non-starter, but I needed to replenish my pocket for Colombia as the teacher's income was hardly liveable, so I headed down to my old stomping ground in Haywards Heath.

As luck would have it, in the first pub I went into was Neil an old mate and a nice, crazy guy. He had been a cook aboard the Queen Elizabeth 2 when it was requisitioned for the Falklands no-war (war was never declared and Argentina still claims the Falklands are an Argentine province, but they are administered and act as a British Overseas Territory). Go figure. Neil had also settled down with a girl in a farm cottage and led the life of country folk. He had a spare room and invited me to stay, I thought my luck was changing. I started to look for work, which was as difficult in Sussex as it had been in London. Nick had become good friends with Neil and was a frequent visitor. One day they asked me if I knew anyone who could supply them with a kilo of hash. I told them I was out of that game but gave them Johnnie's number. The following day Jonnie contacted me and asked if they were trustworthy as they had asked for the goods on tick, I said that I trusted Neil 100%. However Nick decided to rip Jonnie off and a week later he was at the house demanding his money or the hash back, he gave us 24 hours. I tried to explain to Nick that Jonnie and his partners were not people to mess around with as they can be pretty heavy, he chose to ignore me. When Jonnie returned the next day, I persuaded him to leave the problem with me, which he did by taking my photo equipment as collateral, because if he went back to his partners empty handed Neil, Nick and myself would end up in hospital, probably with permanent damage. Over the next week Neil and I tried to persuade Nick, but he wouldn't come around and refused to listen. In the meantime two of his other mates had become keenly interested in Colombia and the availability of cocaine. These guys even asked Nick whether I was trustworthy and stupidly he said yes. So a plot was hatched. Nick and his two mates discussed the costs of buying a kilo of cocaine, two mules, flights and other costs which came to a grand total of £5,000.00. These three people gave the money to me, I retrieved my photographic equipment from Jonnie which cost £2,000.00, including costs and interest, the original debt being £1,000.00 and I set off back to Colombia and my teaching job with a little cash in hand. A total of two months in England and I was happy to leave again.

Arriving back in Bucaramanga I stayed at a hotel for a few days and then found a room in a family house. Andrew was still there but Aleric had left. Andrew was working at CELAI already but I decided that I wanted to have a short break before starting the job. I met a girl. Betty, a chemist, and we seemed to get on and we even dated for a while until I realized that she was a gold digger when I informed that I wasn't rich and didn't have money, she didn't believe me, until one day while out at a restaurant I told her I had no money left (which was untrue) and she dumped me like a ton of bricks. I was actually quite pleased that she had dumped me as various people had told me various nasty things she had done to men who had dumped her. All the while I had been thinking about cocaine and decided that I would like to try some, it was supposed to be a wonderful drug. So I went out and bought a gram. It WAS a wonderful drug, nothing like the crap I had tried years before in the UK. This gave a euphoric sense of well-being with an unequalled energy and sex was fantastic! This happy feeling, unfortunately led to me wanting to stay high and within a week I was snorting about 3 grams a day. Around the time of the breakup with Betty I realized that I didn't want to do the coke anymore. So I bought 10 grams of coke and with Freddy we buggered off to the Caribbean coast, to a place called Arrecifes in the Tayrona National Park.

First a bus to Santa Marta, a night there where Freddy picked up a lovely looking girl, brought her back to the hotel for the night, where I politely refused seconds, and then caught another bus to Arrecifes ending with an hour's walk along a donkey path to a restaurant, with hammocks slung up on the veranda, which was where we slept. The sea looked so inviting, with the weather hot and after the walk we were hot, tired and sticky so I stripped off to my underpants and rushed into the sea. What a disappointment! The sea was like getting into a warm bath! We spent a week there, finished the coke in two days, and I have never touched it again, I have even become afraid of it.

The restaurant was stocked by donkey trains, bringing alcohol and food. Fish and seafood was always fresh as the owners would buy fish daily from the local fisherman. The days were spent discovering the coves and beaches in the area and a full day's walk to a recently discovered, 1972, lost city, 650 years older than Machu Pichu. We walked along the coast for about half an hour before starting the ascent through the jungle mountain. Not far up we encountered ancient steps leading all the way up to the re-found city. Although it was a great outing, a hard hike and generally a beautiful trek, fortunately the city was still not on the tourist route due to the guerrilla conflict, so we had to explore for ourselves as no guides were available and the feeling of finding the jungle covered walls and steps leading to different landings was phenomenal. The area still had scars in the earth from the treasure looters who inadvertently brought the site to the attention of the authorities, hence bringing one of the most significant archaeological finds in South America to light. It appeared quite massive and as the day drew on we contemplated staying the night or leaving early to avoid stumbling through the rainforest at night. We decided to go back as we were not really prepared for what we encountered and nobody in the area seemed to know its origins. Later, back in Bucaramanga, the museum had a small section on it. Apparently some of the local tribes visited it regularly but did not want it discovered, it had been a political and manufacturing centre with a population of between 2,000 and 8,000 inhabitants starting from its construction in 800AD until the last permanent inhabitants left in the late 14th century and the local Tairona people finally fled the area in about 1514 when the Spanish Conquistadors pledged war on the local tribes and with the 'help of God' forced obedience and slavery on local tribes until they became Christian. The Tairona resisted Spanish conquistadors for about 100 years, this is a retelling by the Kogi tribe, still around today and fought alongside the Tairona against the conquistadors.

After Arrecifes we headed to Sierra Nevada de Santa Marta. I knew nothing about it except that this massive mountain, 5,775 metres, grew out of the earth from what appeared to be flat earth from where we were at Tairona. A tip we were given at Arrecifes was to take as many seashells as we could with no explanation given other than the locals would appreciate them. Although travelling through the Andes, the peak still seemed to rise up from nowhere and could be seen on virtually the whole trip except where the rainforest hid it along the snaking road to Valledupar (pronounced - badger do par) also the home of vallenato, an accordion music. As we got closer the peak, Pico Cristóbal Colon, it seemed to grow higher and higher into the heavens being incredibly impressive, not really due to its actual height, but its meteoric rise from sea level in such a short distance, about 50km as the crow flies. However the bus ride did not reflect the distance as we had to almost circle around the mountain to get to Valledupar, 255 km and about 6 hours on the bus. Entering the city I was really surprised! I was expecting a small provincial town and yet here was a city of about 200,000 with a lot of construction all around. Later, talking to the locals, we learned that a growth campaign which had doubled the population in a decade was still attracting migrants to join its booming economy. The economy was based on cotton, beef and dairy farming, along with the services needed to cater to the influx of people; health, construction, banking, telecommunications, etc. The people were optimistic.

We also discovered that tourism had not really taken off yet and the best way to get up the mountain was with a helicopter tour and as this was not wanted we were told of a village San Sebastian de Rabago, populated with Arhuaco Indians, and we could find a guide there. The rough dirt track took the bus four hours to wind its way through the mountains and dropped us on a path about an hour's walk to the village. Fortunately some of the locals met the bus to pick up supplies and loaded up donkeys and offered to escort us back to the village. At the village we were given a warm welcome and informed that it would take about 7 days and cost $200.00 each, this would include food, donkey transport, tents, equipment and the guide. We agreed and then gave them the gift of the shells, which much to our surprise earned us a 50% reduction! Enquiring as to the use of the shells we were informed that, the Arhuacos have traditionally chewed cocaine for centuries and is an acidic stimulant which also helps oxygen get absorbed into the blood, which is great for walking at altitude, when they go up the mountains for herding, etc. The cocaine leaves are chewed into a saliva ball and stored between the teeth and the cheek when climbing, however as cocaine is acidic and the seashells, being an alkaloid, are crushed into a powder and mixed into the cocaine ball to prevent acidic damage to the mouth, which is visible on many of the people who climb and stay at high altitudes for periods of time. The temperatures at the Sierra Nevada are extreme, at the base of the mountains the temperatures are between 21°C and 39°C while at the peak it is between -4° and -5°.

We spent the next day preparing for the climb with the guide organizing clothes for the colder temperatures as we climbed. I was worried about the climb as the mountain was massive and I am not a climber but the guide had assured us that it was an easy climb and we could turn back at any time. So off we set. We got off the lower slopes and out of the rainforest, with its 30 metre canopy, rather quickly, having lunch at a clearing on the verge of a change in the forest, the canopy was lower with more sunlight was getting through while drier and a scanty collection of palm trees dotted here and there. After lunch we continued trekking up, up, up, accompanied by the variety of birdsong, hushing as we got close and starting again as we passed. I also got a glimpse of a condor soaring in the rising warm air while scavenging for its next meal, squirrels stopping and staring before scurrying off while the tapirs glanced at us unconcernedly.

The night rest was a welcome break and although the guide was right, it was an easy climb, it was still a tiring climb. Rising to an early breakfast I felt as though I had played 10 hours of nonstop rugby, the porters and guide chuckled at my stiffness and assured me I would be fine after an hour or so. The second day was much the same as the first but the views got better and better. As we settled down for the second night we had just entered the páramo, like a green grassy savannah. However I was too tired to explore and retired after dinner, as did Freddy. The meals were great with a lot of meat, often three times a day, and rice (also three times a day) mixed with a variety of vegetables, some picked along the way. The next morning I wasn't feeling too bad as we set off across the paramo which was grasses and shrubs interspersed with marshes and acid bogs which we took pains to avoid, but I got my first clear sighting of the mighty Andean condor! Even though he soared above us his size and grace was awesome and I stared at him for what must have been a full 10 minutes as he disappeared into the distance. The guide and porters once again chuckled at my fascination at, what was to them, an everyday sight. The páramo also offered amazingly clear views stretching off into the distance below to the mist filled trees of the rainforest and up the mountain to the rocks and snow quickly approaching. It was also a lot colder and long leather coats were offered to us. These presented the problem of being too hot on and too cold off as we climbed and entered the rocky slopes and plush páramo leading up to the last push for the top. That night we camped next to a beautiful mini lake with a view of the distant peak, our destination.

Freddy and I were feeling excited and sat up chatting to the guide for a while before going to bed amid nervous expectation for the following day. Rising early I joined the clattering of the camp as some cooked breakfast while others broke camp. The day was muggy and the peak almost obscured and as the guide approached I could sense the bad news, the weather was changing and we could not go any further, we had to retreat down the mountain. The news flooded me as disappointment took over. With breakfast over and the descent began my spirits were lifted as I saw the valley below huddling clouds between the mountains, I had had a good run and although I never reached the top I had had a wonderful climb. The descent was a day quicker and after a day resting we took a bus to Valledupar and back to Bucaramanga.

# Chapter 26

Life started to return to a steady routine. I was working evenings with CELAI from 16:00 to 22:00, I had found a house to rent with another teacher, Lucho, but the days were monotonous. I then decided to open a photographic business. We were only using the upstairs which had a lounge, kitchen, 3 bedrooms and bathroom. Downstairs had a garage, another large lounge, two more decent size rooms, a toilet and a courtyard and this is where I set up my photographic business. One room was a darkroom for processing transparencies and black and white film and an enlarger for the film up to 40cm X 60cm. The other room was for paper processing, while the lounge was used as a studio and the garage became my shop front. It was a slow start and so I started teaching photographic classes to private students and the business started to pay for itself.

The business was slow and I took another teaching job 4 hours a week at a private school for extremely rich kids. When I first arrived at the school I was quite shocked. It was enclosed by a 3 metre wall, had gun turrets at the corners, armed guards patrolling with a vigorous security check of both staff and students at the two sets of gates entering the compound. This was due to the business of kidnapping by the guerrilla groups, which was popular at the time. Inside was like a typical school aside from a few guards posted around and a comfortable and well stocked 'staff room' for the bodyguards aside from the school staff room. My teaching hours finished up at lunch time so I had great lunches at the school cafeteria on the two days I taught, before going home. The kids were a nightmare! I was teaching two 2 hour classes to the kids in the second to last and last year at school. They were not interested in learning English and discipline was really lax. I had some kids who would gather around the front rows who wanted to learn, but the majority talked throughout the class, walked around, a couple were continually making out and one kid pushed three desks together and lay down listening to his walkman. At the end of the first lesson I paid a visit to the Headmistress who was not sympathetic at all. She agreed that nothing could be done because a complaint made against any child would result in the parents forcing dismissal of said teacher. I could not believe it! Well I carried on trying and hating it but the pay I was receiving from the school for 4 hours more than I was getting for 32 hours at CELAI.

My next problem came at the end of term exams when over half the class failed. I was called into the Headmistresses office and ask to account for the scores. I showed her the papers with kids who had only written their names, some of them had a few answers scrawled here and there, while the ones who paid attention and did their work got good marks. I was informed that this did not matter, English is an elective and the majority will probably never use it again, I must pass them all with at least 60%.

Needless to say I did not return for the next term. One positive aspect of my time at the school was that the vanity of these rich kids led to a boom in my photographic business doing portraits. On one occasion 5 girls came at the same time, aside from the chaos of 5 young girls wanting portraits together and separately, each one of them had 2 bodyguards making 15 people plus me and my assistant in the studio, what chaos! I managed to get the bodyguards down to one each inside while the others waited outside. After this I never allowed more than two at a time for portraits. This also led to some business through the parents, who were all business owners, doing some commercial and industrial photography. CELAI started giving me private corporate students in the mornings from various industries like telecommunications, petroleum, medical, chemical etc.

It was at about this time that I realized that I was inadequately prepared to be a teacher, other than just conversation, and decided that it could be a good second career, so I visited various universities, UIS, UNAB and SENA. Both UIS and SENA offered me a job, I taught English to some of their students and they taught me to teach. I didn't have to pay for the course and I got paid for my teaching. I landed with my butt in the butter. My time was filling up, which was great but everything was a few hours here and a few hours there, but soon enough I gave up teaching at CELAI in the evenings and just kept the one to ones.

This proved to expand my horizons within, both physically and socially as most of the teaching was on site. One USA petroleum company had a Director from the states who had been in Colombia for 23 years and refused to learn Spanish, instead he put all the staff on English courses. One day on the field site Gerardo, a student and I were distracted by shouting out the window, men were lining up and pulling on something leading to one of the oil wells. We went outside to offer our help when I saw what it was. One of the wells was shut down for maintenance and an anaconda had decided to go down the well and was spotted by a worker who shouted for help while grabbing it. Soon at least a dozen people were holding this solid piece of muscle and dragging it out of the well. This, to me, looked over 10 metres long and as its head appeared out of the well it tried to defend itself by turning on the person closest to it. However the workers were quick and they managed to catch it below the head before any harm could be done. It was taken to the river, upstream of civilization and released. Good English lesson that I thoroughly enjoyed!

Through the English teaching I got a great photographic assignment from the Colombian petroleum company Ecopetrol. The pipeline near Barracabemeja had been blown up by the FARC guerrillas and aerial pictures of the pipeline were needed. So I loaded up and got into a helicopter. The photos needed had to be parallel to the ground and not at an angle and were also needed for 3D retention. So I was strapped into a harness with my ankles strapped to the floor of the helicopter while I was lowered out until my body was parallel to the ground, with me screaming instructions to the guys holding me and then passing them onto the pilot as we proceeded along the pipe line. All in all I took over 50 photographs hanging out the helicopter. The camera was a medium format camera which required the back changed six times, all while hanging out the door.

A while later I was approached by another English language school to give conversation lessons to the advanced students, however it would require a three month course in learning their methodology. This was a system designed to teach English to German spies by the Nazis in WW2. At first I was enthusiastic but soon I began to doubt the method. It consisted of repetition and nothing but repetition. The beginning levels would start with a few simple sentences, 'My name is', 'good morning' etc. No context or translation would be given so for an hour a day these few sentences would be led by the teacher then repeated by the class, first chorally and then individually, then written and then repeated. This would carry on for days on end until the students had the same accent, intonation, stress and speed of the teacher. This would start off slowly with exaggerated speech patterns and gradually become normal speech. The teacher's accent and speech pattern would eventually be emulated by the students. Only by the intermediate classes would translations and explanations come into the teaching.

So you had students speaking perfect English without knowing what they were saying. In order to stop teachers jumping ahead or missing parts of the lesson, each class had a camera with audio recording which the Director would review before the following lesson. He also would decide when the students could move on to the next part of the course. The teachers were given stress leave of a week every three months and had a psychologist to talk to if needed. This system produced some of the best speakers within 6 months but also had the highest turnover of teachers, I only managed three months which was basically at the end of the methodology course but my doubts were unfounded, it worked! The down side was the turnover of teachers and the high dropout rate among students, but those that stay the course speak English like a native.

# Chapter 27

I moved on to another school in the evenings, again teaching classes from Intermediate to Advanced. The Advanced class was conversation only, by request, but I threw in correctional grammar. By this time I had completed both the University course and the Meyers Institute course so my handling of the class was getting better and I was developing my own teaching style, nothing out of the ordinary, but all teachers have their own style.

The Advanced class was on a 3 month course and after my last lesson I did it. I asked Mariana out. Mariana was part of a group of Dentists who wanted to improve their English and we fell in love. She comes from a decent Catholic family, her dad an engineer, her mum a housewife, her brother and one of her sisters are also engineers, one sister a highly specialized doctor and the youngest sister an architect. Her dad was great and we got on from the word go, however her mum didn't like me, thought I was a gold digger and was very protective of her family. However after a short courtship, about 4 months, we decided to get married. Her mum was up in arms, she didn't believe that I was Catholic, but in Colombia you have to produce your baptism,First Holy Communion and Confirmation Certificates as well as go on a Marriage Counselling course once a week for 10 weeks, so that obstacle was overcome, but only just. I obviously didn't have these papers with me and asked my mum to send them. She couldn't find my Baptism Certificate and so my younger brother, Michael, managed to contact an Irish Catholic priest in Mongu who responded in the broadest Irish accent, to the request for the baptism certificate " Jesus, Joseph and Mary! Michael do you think I'm a bloody miracle worker?" But he found it, certified it and mailed it all for free!

Anyway time was getting short and not all the papers had arrived and with Mariana's mum's strenuous opposition to our marriage we talked about eloping. However everything was alright in the end. Andrew came over from the UK to be my best man, arriving on my doorstep a few days before the wedding at about 4am with a crate of beer (Colombia has 24 hour liquor sales) which we finished by about 6am and went out for another crate which we polished off before sleeping for a good part of the day. About this time I was picked up by the Immigration authorities as my visa had expired. However one of Mariana's friends was dating a police lawyer who we had consulted and he had informed us that with the wedding so soon after the expiration it wouldn't be a problem. Mariana called him and he explained the situation, but they were having none of it. In their opinion I was marrying Mariana in order to live permanently in Colombia, this was not so as at this stage of our relationship we had not thought much about the future, we just wanted to be together. Fortunately Mariana's friend's lawyer boyfriend had a contact in the Immigration department and the problem was sorted 24 hours later.

After that Andrew wanted to start organizing my bachelor party which we discovered was not a Colombian tradition as the night before was when the groom serenaded his bride and the wedding gifts were brought to the house! This was a shock to me, the idea of singing in front of people was frightening to me, I hardly even spoke at gatherings! Well Andrew organized the bachelor party for two nights before the wedding, which turned out to be a fun drinking evening and I was happy that it was two nights beforehand. A band had been brought in for the serenade and I had to liaise with them about my choice of music and particularly what song I was going to serenade Mariana with. This was Eric Clapton's 'Wonderful Tonight'. About 150 people were attending the Serenade party and the time came, I knew I was going to embarrass myself as I approached the band to start the serenade after I gave the short traditional speech, the singer of the band informed that he would do the singing and not me. Boy was I relieved! The tradition held that a serenade was part of the ceremony but the groom could opt to have the band do the singing. Nobody had told me that, they all just assumed that I knew the tradition, so I went to join my bride while the band sang an Eric Clapton song;

It's late in the evening, she's wondering what clothes to wear
She puts on her make-up and brushes her long blonde hair
And then she asks me, "Do I look all right?"
And I say, "Yes, you look wonderful tonight"

We go to a party and everyone turns to see
This beautiful lady that's walking around with me
And then she asks me "Do you feel all right?"
And I say, "Yes, I feel wonderful tonight"

I feel wonderful because I see
The love light in your eyes
And the wonder of it all
Is that you just don't realize how much I love you

It's time to go home now and I've got an aching head
So I give her the car keys and she helps me to bed
And then I tell her, as I turn out the light
I say, "My darling, you were wonderful tonight
Oh my darling, you were wonderful tonight"

The next day one of Mariana's sisters, Cristina, was sent with her boyfriend to babysit me as my nearly mother-in-law, thought I was going to abscond. I later discovered that all morning, including in the car on the way to the church, Mariana was being told 'don't worry if he is not there, you still have your family'. Well, the wedding went off without a hitch beside a small language mistake on my behalf. The Spanish word for ring, as in, with this ring I thee wed, is 'anillo' while a screw is 'tornillo', guess which one I inadvertently used. I also discovered that my wife had collected all the clothes of mine she didn't like and had used them in the torches leading up to the church entrance.

The musician for the wedding ceremony had not arrived due to their vehicle breaking and so the hymns etc. were sung by the assistant server to the priest, a baritone, who I thought sang beautifully unaccompanied by any instrument. Mariana was upset by the lack of musicians but later appreciated the baritone who stepped in at the last minute. On the way to the party, driven by Mariana's' brother, we had a bottle of champagne while waiting for the guests to arrive before us. The reception was wonderful but I discovered another Colombian tradition: champagne for the toasts and then good whiskey is the only drink other than soft drinks for the kids. As I am not a whiskey drinker I quickly sought out one of the waiters and had him stash a few bottles of champagne away for me. The reception was great, good food with plenty of dancing, ballroom earlier on with more modern styles coming in later, including various styles of line dancing.

We went off to our room not long after 1am as our flight to our honeymoon destination, the Caribbean island of San Andres, left at 6 am. The island was beautiful, sunny and the hotel was an all-inclusive four star, actually being met at reception with a cocktail while the bellboys took our luggage to the room where we were led a short time later. It was a great honeymoon in a tropical paradise.

# Chapter 28

Settling down into married life was not at all difficult aside from the whimsicalities of my mother in law. I know we all have mother-in-law jokes and stories, but in the end we appreciate our in-laws. We spent Sunday roasts or braais with the family, as is normal sometimes with more family members than others. On one occasion not long after the wedding, Amanda, my mother in law, asked us to move in with them. I was against it as I still had my photographic business operating from home. However over time I relented, made arrangements to use another photographers studio, and started sending the processing to a pro lab in Bogota and we moved in. After about a month, Amanda informed me that I was to give up my jobs, notice the plural, as teaching and photography were not real professions. Acquiescing to the conversation I asked what was I to do. Apparently I was to work as a foreman on my father-in-law's engineering sites, I could hardly contain myself as I politely refused the position. That Friday Amanda left to see the grandchildren in Bogota and in the evening Orosman, my father-in-law sat down with drinks to inform us, that we had been kicked out of the house and must find somewhere before Amanda comes back on Monday. I was flabbergasted! We found a bedsit the next day and moved in. We were there only a short time as we found a flat quite quickly. Sunday meals resumed as if nothing had happened.

Mariana was born on the 27th December and had never had a birthday party so our first Christmas together I decided to give her a party with a pig on a spit, but I wanted it to be a surprise. As the pig would take a large part of the day to cook I asked my in- laws to keep her away from home while I prepared everything, which they gladly did. The guests had arrived by 20:00 and so I phoned Mariana to come home, which she did, looking tired and dirty. My in-laws had kept her busy by emptying the pool and having it scrubbed clean! She quickly got showered and changed and thoroughly enjoyed her first birthday party with separate gifts for birthday and Christmas! Life carried on, work and family life as usual except that we were trying for a child without success, so appointments were made for fertility tests.

Mariana went first and then made an appointment for me. I went to my appointment entering a rather full waiting room, went up to the receptionist and gave my name. She replied in strong loud voice 'You are here for the sperm count'. I felt all eyes turn onto me. 'Yes', I whispered. Handing me a playboy magazine and a plastic clinical cup with a lid, she once again boomed: 'Go through that door over there to masturbate and put all your sperm in here.' Turning around I felt all eyes on me as I slunk through the waiting room and into the masturbating room, and then slunk out a again handed it over and exited as quickly as I could.

We took our first holiday together by going to Rio Hacha and then on to Punta la Bela in La Guajira, a desert region of Colombia. We spent one night in Rio Hacha before moving on to Punta la Bela.  On the way we passed salt flats with flamingos, other than that the journey was difficult along bumpy and corrugated, unkempt roads with the sea always close to the north and scrubland all around us It was a tiring, slow and difficult journey but we finally arrived in Punta la Bela in the early evening and discovered that we couldn't find a hotel. It was a small village with a main dirt road less than five minutes' walk from one end to the other. Going down towards the south the settlement could be seen spreading out into the scrubland. The main road had a few restaurants, bars and other small shops all made out of wooden posts and a few beams supporting the palm leaf roofs and the basic structure. I loved it! Not finding anywhere to stay we went into a restaurant to have a meal and asked the proprietor if he knew of a place we could stay, to which he answered we could sling hammocks between the poles in his restaurant, so after a delicious meal we set about establishing our quarters. Our host was gracious and as the evening was setting in we took a walk around the town and returned to be entertained by the locals as we got plied with alcohol and snacks. When we decided to retire our host kicked out his patrons, asked us what we wanted for breakfast and lunch and then left us. Waking with the sunrise our host had been up for I don't know how long but he was preparing breakfast of eggs and sausage. As our usual morning ablutions were calling I enquired as to where the toilet was upon which he led me outside and pointed to a shack a few hundred metres up the beach. Mariana trotted while I went into the sea, quite far out to have my morning piss and then closer to shore I washed, returned to a table to await Mariana and breakfast. Mariana mentioned that although it was a shabby shack the facilities were decent and clean.

After breakfast we asked about any nice deserted beaches and were informed about a beach about an hour's walk away. Our host then quickly prepared a picnic basket and sent us on our way. The walk led us past the only brick building in the village, the local church, in which we had a gander before continuing through the desert heat which was slow going and even though we had walked for an hour or so, it was probably only 2 kilometres from the village centre. The beach was totally secluded formed by a horse shoe sand dune, which at this time of day also provided shade. We spent the day there enjoying the solitude and after the picnic we decided to head back when I noticed something awful. I had lost my wedding ring! I didn't know how to tell Mariana but I had to and we spent about another hour looking before heading back. Arriving back at the restaurant the owner asked us when we would like dinner, the crayfish we had asked for the previous day. He had been out early to catch the crayfish which was currently being cooked in a sand oven buried in the beach outside his domain. When dinner arrived the crayfish were enormous, one could have easily fed us both but not wanting to appear rude to our host we soldiered on and finally finished our meal feeling stuffed like a turkey and retired to the section where we had slung our hammocks to have a quiet drink before retiring. The week went on in this relaxing fashion, our meals being prepared for the time we desired with our main meal, usually seafood, caught in the morning and prepared for us while we explored the area. Too soon the week was up and we really didn't feel like returning to civilization, so we ask for our bill and were really shocked… a whole US $20!!! This was for the sleeping arrangements, three square meals a day, snacks and drinks. I could not believe it and asked him to repeat the cost, we gave him $100 and began our trip back to Bucaramanga.

Mariana was a church going religious catholic but I still did not like the church as an institution even though my dad had given me the family bible which had accompanied me on my travels for years (since after my return to independent Zimbabwe) which I read almost every night before going to sleep. I went to mass to please her but upon arrival at the local church I was quite shocked. The church was not just full, but overflowing with people of all ages, families with kids to great grandparents! Outside the entrance the people were 20 rows deep, with speakers outside the church for the congregation to follow the mass. I never made it inside but did not want to return to stand in the heat for an hour every Sunday while being respectful to a pair of speakers droning on in a foreign language. We compromised and went to an earlier mass, when there weren't so many people, but it was the same, I still did not get inside but at least it was cool! The first time I actually got inside a church was when we were doing our marriage course along with another couple, months before, and the rigidity of the catholic faith was clearly visible. All Mariana´s friends were Catholic and were churchgoers and as I got to know them and talked to them I realized that they were quite aware of the shortcomings of the Catholic institution but they treated the ceremonies and their devotions as separate from the politics. They could forgive the transgressions of the clergy understanding that they were human with all the problems and frailties that humans have. This was the beginning of my acceptance of

The Church. I had always placed the clergy on a pedestal, as I had done with any form of authority as a child and, I suppose, I still believe that the clergy should lead by example, but I have to accept that the church is led by people on this earth and people are not infallible. I do believe the Catholic institution led by the Vatican needs to acknowledge the problems within and change to accommodate the leaders of the church as human and accept them as such. For example priests were only forbidden to marry in 1139 and so with the ongoing sexual problems within its ranks, why not let priests marry again as in other Christian denominations. Anyway Mariana brought me back to the church and I slowly started attending mass more and more.

Not long after replacing my wedding ring we decided to leave Colombia. It is a great place and I love the country but work for me is haphazard and very low pay. My mother-in-law took this hard and tried to bribe us to stay by buying us a beautiful flat. We actually moved in and spent the last six months living there before leaving. We took two last short holidays, both long weekends, before leaving. One was back to the Caribbean coast where Mariana's sister, Amanda, had a time share at a resort where all the family gathered to enjoy the servitude in the luxury of the sun, sand and sea. The second and last was to El Cocuy.

This is the highest mountain range in Colombia reaching 5,300 metres, (notice range, not peak) 30 kilometres long, 22 snow-capped peaks and has the largest snow mass in South America. It is situated between the provinces of

Boyacá and Aruaca. Coming from Bucaramanga we headed towards Bogotá turning east to climb the mountains just after San Gil and headed to the town of El Cocuy, a small town of about 5,000 indigenous inhabitants and its grand architecture a mix of colonial and republican. The town is known as The Snowy City, Haven of Peace, but as we were running late due to terrible roads we decided to stop on the way back and pushed on to the cabañas which were the highest we could travel by car. We continued climbing, the air was getting really thin and the car kept spluttering and stalling. It was getting dark when the car stalled and would not start, I was at a loss as not only was the engine stalled but it was already freezing, night temperatures dropping to about -10°c. I had no idea how far we had to go as when we booked we were told to carry on to the end of the road. After about 15 minutes I once again tried the engine and it started, and so we continued another 500 metres and around a corner there were the cabañas just in front of us, about 50 metres away. The car stalled once again, but we were there. The caretaker had seen us and brought the key to the cabaña and to inform us that a fire had already been started and the rooms were warm. However we were so cold that we said would just unload and go to bed early. So much easier said than done! Unlike at Santa Marta De Sierra Nevada we had ascended quickly and buy the time we had dragged our rucksacks and walked the fifty metres to the cabaña we were exhausted! The air was so thin; we waited half an hour before we made another trip to bring the rest of our belongings from the car and to have a cup of coffee to warm us up in the meantime.

I hadn't thought about physics and chemistry for years other than dark room chemicals and I was about to learn a lesson. I grabbed the camping stove out of the backpack and hooked it up to the gas while Mariana got the cups, coffee etc ready. Striking a match was difficult but eventually I had a lit match in my hand, turned on the gas and even on the lowest setting the gas came out so strong that it just blew the match out. Second try I put the match on the outer rim of the jetting gas and it lit but with ferociousness I have never seen, but at least it was alight. I put on the water to boil and waited, and waited and waited. It literally took half an hour to boil. Anyway with the boiling water we made our coffee and took a nice sip of hot coffee, but wait, it's not hot but only just warm. Bloody altitude! After coffee I got the remaining things from the car, fed the fire and curled up and went to sleep. The next morning the cold woke us up quite early, we breakfasted and went to find the caretaker.

Obviously we had to spend the day acclimatizing but the caretaker informed us that with horses we could make the trip to the summit the following day. We spent the day slowly exploring the area, there was a lake nearby where we walked over rocky outcrops interspersed with shrub land and grass. Looking east up the mountain almost immediately the vegetation stopped and turned to stone and rock rising like a scarp and disappearing into the distant sky. The good news of the day was that, although not 100%, we felt at ease and ready for the climb on the morrow.

The horses and guide were ready by 09.00 as were we with our flasks of tea and packed lunch and we set off immediately. At first the horses seemed reluctant and kept wanting to turn around and go home but they soon settled down. The path was rocky, stony and steep enough to slip off the saddle if you weren't holding on tight enough, while at one point the path was verging on an abyss that looked to be 1,000's of metres straight down, but the guide assured us that it was less than a 1,000 and the horses had done this trail hundreds of times. We were on this verge for about half an hour and I soon got used to it and let the horse do its thing while I held on and admired the scenery.

The day was turning hot and about 2 hours after setting off we came across a little lake in the hollowed rocks as we turned away from the chasm, we climbed down to rest and have a cup of tea. The guide had brought his own victuals, watered the horses and soon enough it was time to proceed. The going was tough and I thought that we should have acclimatized for another day, but it was mostly my muscles clinging on that encouraged the thought as my breathing was heavy but fine; we were also ascending quite quickly. Later we reached the snow line and skirted around it as the guide did not want the horses on the snow and advised us that it was deep and could be treacherous if you didn't know the paths. It was not long after that we reached the western edge of the cordillera and the horizon was filled with a view of Los Llanos, the plains and heart of the Colombian ranching and farming district, stretching out from thousands of metres below us and expanding from the edge of the mountain range as far as we could see. The view was impressive and we spent about an hour exploring the beauty before us and praising the architect of this alluring planet as we started to return to the cabañas.

The way back was easier as we were now going downhill although at times we had our feet straight out in front of us as the horses singled out the track along the steep and dangerous trail back down. When we reached the path along the abyss I elected to dismount as I was not comfortable with the horses picking up speed in anticipation of home, feed and warmth. The guide and Mariana stayed mounted until a particularly steep section of the path had Mariana slide down the horse's neck while clinging on for dear life and ended up looking straight into the horse's mouth while he calmly waited for Mariana to complete her acrimonious dismount. We then both continued leading the horses down until I felt it was safe to remount. However the horses knew they were nearly home and trotted speedily along until we arrived back as the sun was setting over the valley below.

We said our goodbyes and headed to South Africa with a 5 day stopover in Rio De Janeiro where we did the typical tourist things, Christ the Redeemer statue, cable car to Sugar Loaf Mountain, markets in Ipanema, Copacabana, Costa de Silva bridge, etc. On to Johannesburg.

# Chapter 29

When the door of the plane opened and that unique smell of Africa hit me I knew I was home. No matter how often or how long you are away from Africa, it is home.

We were met by Paul and Sue at the airport and we stayed with them for a short while until we rented a granny flat in Randburg and then into a Country Cottage past Fourways. I also got a job quite quickly at The Language Lab in town. It used to be part of Wits University but was sold off to one of the Professors and his business partner. Mariana got pregnant. Although marriage changes your life, the advent of children does so more dramatically. I was chaperoning my students around a tour of the SABC Radio and TV studios when an announcement came over the intercom system, 'Will John Jefferys please make haste to Flora Clinic as your wife is giving birth'. The whole of SABC erupted into a roar of congratulations! I phoned the school who informed me that was correct, somebody was on the way to take over from me and that one of the partners had picked up my wife and taken her to the hospital. I got there as fast as I could only to find it was a false alarm, however Mariana was being kept in for the night as the birth was 6 weeks early. I stayed until about 02:00 and then went to Paul and Sue's house where we were house sitting and looking after the dogs. I had just got into bed when the phone rang and I was recalled to the hospital. I got there just as Mariana was being wheeled into surgery with nurses and doctors all around and our obstetrician on the cart doing something to my wife. I caught a glance of this as Mariana entered the surgical area and I was allowed no further. However a nurse informed me that the baby had a prolapsed cord and with a preterm breach she had to have an emergency caesarean delivery. As is usual with hospital and extremely worrying to family no more information could be given.

An agonizing period of time went by before my daughter Silvia Daniela was born at about 03:00 Saturday 20th July 1996 as a wave of love overcame me accompanied by prayer and worry. She was whisked off in an incubator and I was informed that Mariana was fine and being stitched I could see her in about 15 minutes. In the mean time I went to visit my daughter, who was no larger than my hand. I had a brief chat with Mariana before the sedatives took over and she fell asleep. I drove back to the house to get clothes and things that are needed for hospital stays and the dark cloudy sky started to lighten up as snow fell, a rare event in Johannesburg. Daniela was in hospital and grew rapidly and was able to leave after about 4 weeks and then family life started. My mother-in-law came out to spend some time with her grandchild, I carried on with my teaching routine and Mariana studied for Dental exams in order to practice in South Africa. The first exam was a written exam after which she had to work for the government, supervised by a government dentist, while attending lectures an afternoon a week for three years. The time in Africa was great, Mariana worked at a government hospital and spent time in various other health centres around the area, working with children and underprivileged people. One of the perks was that the Hospital was close to one of my aunts, Angie, with whom Mariana became quite close and learnt more about my dad's family than I ever did! I also learnt one of the family's worst kept secrets. My dad was the oldest male of 13 children; when he was about 6 or 7 the family went on a picnic when my grandparents went for a walk leaving my dad in charge of the other kids. Unfortunately a baby was bitten by a snake and died. My father was blamed and packed off to boarding school, hardly even coming home for holidays but rather spending them with friends from school. When he matriculated he went home where his father wanted him to work together in the Hotel business. My father didn't want this and so travelled up to Northern Rhodesia, Zambia today, met my mum and the rest is history. He was cut off from the family and for many years had no communication with his parents and some siblings.

Two of my Uncles, Tony and Johnny made sure of this. The day my father left money went missing from the safe, and although my father never had the combination he was blamed by these two brothers who apparently witnessed the theft. Angie told us it was a frame up as they didn't want my dad changing his mind about coming back to the Hotel. Years went by and I must have been about 10 or 11, so my dad had not seen his parents for at least 15 years after leaving school and as we know not much during his school years, when he was asked through one of his sisters to visit his parents, which we did on the way to Cape Town on holiday. We really don't know what happened at the reunion but we stayed for a few days and everything seemed to be alright although I never saw my grandparents again. Angie informed us that my granddad had changed his will to include my dad who he welcomed back into the family and on his deathbed Anthony and Johnny presented a piece of paper to my granddad as a paper that needed signing for the business. It turned out to be a new will cutting my dad out of it. Angie told my dad that three of his sisters, herself and I think Joan and Pat would testify to the fraud in court. My dad was not interested, he was not happy with the way he was treated by his brothers but did not want to drag mud onto the family name, he was content to know that he and his parents were reconciled. Years later my dad decided to visit his brothers in order to reconcile and so with my younger brother, Michael, they travelled across parts of South Africa to Port Elizabeth. On the appointed day my dad and Michael arrived 5 minutes early, just in time to see Tony and Johnnie getting into the car to leave. Tony shouted across the road, 'Sorry we have to go to an appointment.' When my dad enquired about the appoint he had made with them, they just got into the car and drove off.

My mum died while we were living in Johannesburg and my dad came to stay with us for a year and surprisingly took great interest in Daniela, as he had never been a 'child person', he believed that a child should be seen and not heard, a contradiction really as kids and babies are among the noisiest beings on the planet! It was nice being back in Africa and I took my wife to see all the haunts of my youth, CBC, although it had moved, Waterkloof Primary, Pretoria Boys High, Hartebeesport Dam, etc. We also visited many of the rural destinations like the Pilansberg National Park, Kruger Park, Hazyview, Cape Town, driving through the Karoo and up along the garden route, St Lucia etc as well as many visits to my brother in Umdloti. We also took a trip to Zimbabwe to spend time with my sisters which resulted in

Mariana and I dumping Daniela on my sister and set off for a trip around the country, first to Wankie National Park, which was great and the Victoria falls, which I was really disappointed with. Considering that we had lived in Livingstone and had wandered around the area freely, often having lunch at the Victoria Falls Hotel, the area was like a bloody circus! The falls was fenced off with a US $50 charge, bungee jumpy from the bridge, helicopter tours buzzing overhead and the cheapest meal at the Victoria Falls Hotel, two salads and two beers for US$100! I was disgusted and flabbergasted. However the bush was still great. From there we headed to Mlibizi and took the ferry to Kariba where we spent a few days camping before heading back to the farm and our daughter.

Back in Johannesburg things carried on as normal with Daniela starting nursery school and karate at three years old; I had a failed attempt at a business partnership but achieved another teaching certificate, The International House TEFL Certificate, while later I had an operation on my spine and Mariana carried on as usual.

After we moved back to South Africa I found The Church easier going and more welcoming, even after my eldest daughter, then about two, picked her nose and offered the contents of her finger to the priest we were talking to! The Church in South Africa was a lot more family oriented and made you feel welcome and part of a community. The church building had a glass partition at the rear with speakers, as a place where families with babies, young and / or undisciplined children could partake in the mass without disturbing others. During this period my faith grew stronger and Sunday mass was welcome instead of just a self-imposed chore. Religious discussions with church members and friends from other Christian denominations became more frequent. As by now I had read the bible through twice, nightly reading was around things that I learnt from other people or things that I contested and thought were twisted to suit individuals. Anyway in South Africa my Catholic faith grew stronger.

However the violence was increasing and where ever you went in Jo'burg it looked and felt like a prison. Houses had razor wire atop their 2 metre walls, guard dogs ran up and down the fences trying to get at you as you walked along the road, car hijackings were an everyday event, car insurance premiums were more expensive than the expensive and desirable cars, even people who did not like guns were buying them for protection. Gated communities were more and more plentiful and becoming mini towns with their clubs and shops supplying basic needs. Rape had become the norm, accepted and in one year I knew three women who had been raped, one of them being a sixty-five year old who I worked with. Gunshots were getting more frequent, first at weekends and then almost every night. I did not want to bring up a daughter in this atmosphere, so, through my brother who had an emigration business, I started the emigration procedure to Australia. My sisters were both emigrating to New Zealand and my younger brother to Australia, my older brother had done the papers to New Zealand, but never left SA. The average wait was three months but my wife being a native Spanish speaker had to do the IELTS test which she passed with flying colours. As a Dentist she also had to do a medical exam which was only held every few months and so we had to wait.

During this waiting period an incident happened at the nursery school. The school was on a parallel road to one of the main roads, William Nichol, with an embankment separating them. The school had its 2 metre wall with its razor wire on top, a double zig zag gate with an armed guard controlling the ins and outs. One day an attempted car hijacking happened just down the road on William Nicol but unfortunately for the car jackers, police were right there and the hijackers fled on foot towards the nursery school with police chasing. The car hijackers pulled out a gun and threatened the guard who did not have time to draw his weapon letting them into the school. By the time the police arrived the criminals were scaling a wall at the end of the playground filled with young kids and the police opened fire on the escaping pair. Fortunately no one was hurt but we packed up and left South Africa within a month and went to the UK.

However leaving SA, or rather entering the UK, proved to be a bit of a problem. I phoned the British Consulate to enquire as to the procedure for Mariana, due to her Colombian citizenship and I was informed that no problem would be encountered as both Daniela and I were British subjects, but we needed to bring the marriage certificate about a week before leaving. So we prepared. We sold everything we needed or wanted to sell, including our cars, (the last car to be handed over at the airport on our departure), packed up our belongings which were sent to the UK to an address to be notified and even gave our beautiful cat to my older brother. So a week before leaving we went to the Consulate to organize Mariana's visa with all the required papers plus any that we thought would be pertinent. Her visa was refused. I was flabbergasted - why? We had been married nearly eight years with one child and one on the way, what was the problem? We received the stock answer, 'we do not have to divulge our reasons'. We went home seriously pissed off and thought about our options, which being a Friday gave us the whole weekend. Andrew's father was a political correspondent for the Guardian, so I phoned Andrew hoping to get some advice from him. He advised me to return to the Consulate on Monday morning with all our cash and assets, inform them that after the end of the month we would have nowhere to stay and we would be forced to move into an Hotel and when our resources ran out the Consulate would be liable for my and Daniela's expenses as destitute British subjects stranded in a foreign country. The advice worked and we had the visa on Monday afternoon.

# Chapter 30

I never thought I would be a racist until I lived in the UK. Sure blacks in Africa were uneducated and segregated along with a myriad of evil laws, but the blacks themselves were not disliked or treated badly by the majority of whites who had grown up with institutionalized racism. Anyone who lived there knows that the majority of whites treated blacks well, on a one to one basis, even if the belief was that they were inferior and hence had the institutionalized racism bred into them. I am not making excuses but racism is worse in the 'first world' countries, Europe and North America, than in Africa. Here are a few quotes by black statesmen, political leaders and University Professors.

Booker T Washington, 1901:
"There is a class of coloured people who make a business of keeping the troubles, the wrongs, and the hardships of the Negro race before the public. … Having learned that they are able to make a living out of their troubles, they have grown into the settled habit of advertising their wrongs — partly because they want sympathy and partly because it pays."

"Some of these people do not want the Negro to lose his grievances, because they do not want to lose their jobs. … There is a certain class of race-problem solvers who do not want the patient to get well, because as long as the disease holds out they have not only an easy means of making a living, but also an easy medium through which to make themselves prominent before the public."

If you look at the date that this was written, over 100 years ago and still relevant.

Martin Luther King:
"Shallow understanding from people of good will is more frustrating than absolute misunderstanding from people of ill will. Lukewarm acceptance is much more bewildering than outright rejection."
This quote is relevant for the 'new liberals' who pretend to know what the blacks are going through and 'speak' for them. The only place these white liberals are wanted is out of black affairs.

"My country 'tis of thee, sweet land of liberty, of thee I sing. Land where my fathers died, land of the Pilgrim's pride, From every mountainside, let freedom ring!"
This quote is from his 'I Have a Dream Speech' in 1963. I include this quote as recent comments regarding Martin Luther King promote the premise that he was not a patriot, this clearly shows that he was and loved the USA.

Glenn C Loury:
"Turmoil in the United States over police violence is the result of a distorted representation of the problem, says Brown University economist Glenn C. Loury. According to Loury, an African-American, the "empty thesis of racism" distracts us from the real problems of black Americans.

People speak of 1619, when the first blacks landed in America, and they speak of slavery, which was abolished more than 150 years ago. They talk of "centuries of oppression." But, they don't talk about how the social condition of blacks in America well may have been healthier in 1950 than it is today—racism exists, of course, but it does not sufficiently explain what is going on here, when I see the high rate of criminality and violence that is endemic in black communities, I see a failure in development, in people reaching their full human potential. Still, it's a common mistake to think that we are still in the middle of the twentieth century and that the decisive obstacle to the successful inclusion of blacks in society is racial prejudice. Many people insist that we debate racism, face the injustices of history, and so on. It's also about which values are respected in the social environment and which are not. And violence—that's culture too, the willingness to kill, which is astronomical in certain African-American communities, you are afraid to say that in certain cities police officers fear young black men because those men are too often armed and known to be willing to use their weapons. These are facts—but you are afraid to acknowledge them.

Every year, more whites than blacks are shot by the police in the U.S. But it is true that the number of blacks killed by police, relative to population, is higher. However, the problem of police violence affects all ethnic groups. Moreover the likelihood that an individual will come into conflict with the police depends on the frequency with which that individual behaves in a manner that attracts police attention. Criminal behaviour is not equally distributed across all population groups. African-Americans are overrepresented in prison because they commit more acts that can be punished with prison. Blacks make up an average of around 40 percent of inmates in prisons and jails, but they make up no more than 15 percent of the population. If you look at the statistics, there is no evidence to support the hypothesis that this overrepresentation can be explained by racist prejudices of the police or the courts. Rather, the numbers show that this is due to an overrepresentation of blacks who violate the law. It's legitimate to ask why black men commit more crimes than whites. But it is a fact that they commit massively more homicides; almost 50 percent of homicides, while representing maybe 6 percent or 7 percent of the U.S. population. Or consider robbery: many more whites are victimized by blacks than vice versa, speaking in absolute numbers, not per capita.

The main threat to the quality of life of people living in black areas is the criminal behaviour of their fellow citizens, most of whom happen to be black. Black people in American cities are victims of rape, robbery, and murder to a very significant degree and the perpetrators are almost always black. The protection of life and property is the most important task of the state, and many African-Americans cannot feel safe in their homes. The police are part of the solution to this problem. Black people need the police more than other people do."

Candace Owens: A very controversial figure, but does produce some things worth listening to:
"Black Lives Matter has virtually nothing to do with black people and nothing about preserving black lives," she said. "If they cared about black lives, they would focus on black communities and the number one focus would be black-on-black violence, which is a real issue in America."
She also said the BLM movement trying to "indoctrinate" black and brown children to believe they are victims, regardless of their personal circumstance. "Victim mentality is a cancer," Ms Owens said. "They want people to have the curse of victim mentality. "I really do believe it is killing black American dreams."
"Black Americans are doing worse off economically today than we were doing in the 1950s under Jim Crow". (For those who are unaware of the Jim Crow Laws, they were brought in by the Democrats in the early 20th century to enforce segregation, disenfranchise and remove political and economic gains by the black communities.)

I am in agreement with all the above attitudes and I am also aware that there is a growing sector of the black population who also believe that the black community must take, at least, part of the responsibility for their predicament.

I believe that in general the Police are doing a good job as we all know that in order to find criminals law abiding citizens need to co-operate with law enforcement. This leads to the behaviour of the Police and the people stopped. Why do more of the innocent blacks respond aggressively or run away from the Police when stopped? This is one of the questions that need to be addressed. Among other communities violence towards police is minimal and is generally by guilty people. Therefore the black population must feel that they are being victimized. The statistics do not back that up. However the black community does have a valid concern about racism. In my opinion all people are racist to one degree or another. In some it is so small that it is not recognized by themselves or other people, but it still exists. Legislation cannot stop racism but can help stop acts of it. Too many people cry 'racism' when it is not and many people take advantage of the law when an act that is not racist but a normal process of selection. The police force does attract racists to its ranks but racists and minorities also antagonize the police and having said that I do not believe it is a majority on any side, but a small minority and this is the issue that needs to be attended to.

However the idea of making governments pay reparations for past wrongs seems to me crazy. Where does it end? Can the descendants of Vikings sue the Scandinavian government for reparations? Why don't the black Americans sue the African nations, after all they were the ones catching the people to be sold to the British and Arabs? The European slavers, at the time, were buying a universally accepted commodity which many countries were involved in, both the capture and sale of slaves. Why blame only the European slavers? The slave trade to the Arab countries existed long before the Europeans joined in and the Europeans abolished the trade in 1868 after about 400 years while the Trans Sahara slave lasted over 1,300 years and was only abolished in the 20th century, while slavery in Malawi was only abolished in 2007, a trade that was sanctioned and helped by Arab states. Modern slavery is estimated at over 40 million people, this includes domestic slavery, labour slavery and sexual slavery. The term 'human trafficking` has replaced the term 'slavery'.

Historians John Thornton and Linda Heywood of Boston University have estimated that of the Africans captured and then sold as slaves to the New World in the Atlantic slave trade, around 90% were enslaved by fellow Africans who sold them to European traders.

We are all well aware that minorities have the loudest voice and this is certainly true of blacks in the USA and Europe. Although there is reason for concern, people who jump on the bandwagon often incite situations and this only widens the gap of racism and gives racists a valid argument. 'Look how they behave, destroying property, looting, violence' etc. This escalates the situation which requires more police, racist police included, and more and more agitators as the crowds grow larger. As stated earlier you cannot legislate against racism, it is inherent in every human being (yes I hear those sighs and damnation from those claiming to be non-racist).

Some writers, politicians and academics seem to think that blacks cannot be racist even though they can be prejudiced. Their explanation of this is that racism is inherent in a socio economic system and that the blacks have never had this type of power to actually be racist. Whereas a prejudice is just a dislike of an aspect of a person. So if a white man dislikes a black man for the colour of his skin, he is a racist but if a black dislikes a white man for the same reason, he is not? They also claim that 'reverse racism' as in the case of South Africa, Zimbabwe etc. is not racism. To me racism is racism no matter what the reason.

A dictionary definition of Racism:
'hatred or intolerance of another
The case against whites for racism lies in history, slavery and colonialism. I can understand this blame and is probably a large contributor. However this is centuries ago and modern racism has an ugly head on it too. Why are other races that are subject to racism, including the colonial racism of the past do not behave in the same way? Indians, Pakistanis, Africans and other countries in or near the Indian sub-continent, including the Chinese, all suffered the consequences of violent colonial rule and yet do not manifest the anti-racist fight in the same way blacks do. Blacks who were slaves in colonies that were not British do not behave in the same manner, and certainly, at least, the Spanish Inquisition was far worse in their treatment of minorities and yet compared to the black descendants of the British empire they do not display the same aggression and intolerance.

No one can deny that racism all over the world is evil and it is fought in many different ways and levels, but it is primarily in the USA that the hatred of the government and whites, by blacks, regularly turns to violence and looting. It does happen in other countries as well, South Africa, UK, France, Germany etc, but not as often and not as big.

Racist rioting in the USA seems to be part of the culture. Since 1829 there have been 347 race riots between black or white races. The whites rioted during the period of slavery and up to and including the Civil Rights movements of the late 1950`s to the early 1970's. The black riots started in earnest in 1958 and carry on up today; that is 210 sets of riots since 1958. This figure excludes riots by other ethnic minorities, eg: Puerto Ricans, Irish and Chinese, etc. which count less than 50 since 1829. The total race riots throughout the world from 1829 to the present day is 143 excluding the USA. This is not just black or white riots but among all races including the colonial race riots of the 19th and 20th centuries. So once again I conclude that American blacks have an attraction to race riots as do the whites who have re-joined race riots in greater numbers and intensity in the 21st century.

The American Blacks believe that the white governments 'owe them' and this attitude has spread to blacks all over the world and now including the youth of all races in America and Europe. History is just that, history. If you want progress, compartmentalize it and move on but never forget your history. This is the beginning of controlling racism, not legislation. I do not think that racism can be overcome until the world has become one race and then xenophobia will become the new racism.

I really dislike Black Lives Matter due to the distortion and corruption it encompasses and encourages. Blacks don't like whites who 'think' they understand and 'speak' for them, but they encourage it, it swells their ranks in protests, etc.

Look at any video of BLM protests and often a majority are white and when they are not, they have a huge presence. What does that really say? To me, the black following of BLM is not as popular as they would like you to think. Check out the predominantly black chat site girlsaskguys.com. Look at one of the BLM founders Patrisse Cullors, a self confessed Marxist, buying a $1.4m house, on a teacher's salary, in a predominantly white area while owning other homes (Atlanta, Georgia, Inglewood, South Los Angeles) as well as shopping for Real Estate in the Bahamas for properties between $5m and $20m. Aside from her monetary indiscretions she has also been called a fraud by Breonna Taylor. Sir Maejor Page, a BLM activist, used $200,000 for personal use, Christopher Hamner, BLM activist, arrested for racist attack against Asians, BLM business includes cruelty to animals by locking up wild horses for up to 5 years in short term holding pens and selling those wild horses to a known 'kill buyer', who slaughtered the horses. Currently, while writing this, another 45,000 wild horses in holding are to be killed so that BLM can refill their pens in order to make more money. Anyone who supports a group like this is selfish and has no sympathy for any other life on the planet human, animal or environmental.

However it is essential that blacks need and have organisations to promote their well-being and injustices. As the BLM movement attempts to destroy history it is also destroying the good that has been done in the past, through people like Julius Rosenwald, Henry Huttleston Rogers, Andrew Carnegie, John Rockefeller and George Eastman, white philanthropists working through great black statesmen funding black education particularly in the South, including the Tuskegee Institute and over 5,000 schools for black youths. The NAACP, in my opinion, has lost its teeth and the black communities need new leadership, people who can take the works, of Du Bois, King, Malcom X, etc to a new level.

Research for USA stats from:
https://www.bls.gov/careeroutlook/2018/article/blacks-in-the-labor-force.htm
Who participates in the gig economy? (gigeconomydata.org)
24+ Crucial Gig Economy Statistics and Facts | Fortunly.com
Prevalence of Drug Use in the US by Race/Ethnicity | Drug Policy Facts
Race, Drugs, and Law Enforcement in the United States | Human Rights Watch (hrw.org)
Suzanne Roy, Executive Director, American Wild Horse Preservation Campaign

A reasonably new advent in the racist conflict is taking the knee. Is it right or wrong?
Many people assume it is a gesture of BLM which is a controversial organisation and hence leads to misconceptions as to what the gesture actually means. While BLM hijacked the gesture not long after Colin Kaepernick started doing this in 2016, and changed it's meaning from when Martin Luther King took the knee in 1965 which he did to pray, not protest or inform. BLM uses the gesture to create conflict with racism. People take the knee for different reasons, as is their right, but they should accept that the gesture is often misunderstood.
Should sports people take the knee? This is a more complicated question. Everybody has a right to their belief, spiritual, social and political but I also think that beliefs

should not interfere in sports, especially when controversial. Politics has no place in sport. Imagine where this road could lead us: a gay sportsman holding the rainbow flag during the anthem, a Muslim giving deference to Allah before a game, Christians hauling a crucifixion symbol onto the field, an image of the feminist circle displayed for the world to see! Where does it end? Politics out of sport is my opinion. The controversy around the EURO 2020 is evidence enough that when belief is brought into sport it can cause division throughout the community and may even cause opponents of the gesture to retaliate.

## Chapter 31

Arriving in the UK I went to stay with Andrew lived in Brixton. As we had tonnes of luggage with us we took a cab to his flat where we were met by his girlfriend as he had to go to work. We were to meet him at a pub at about 18:00. It was early June so the summer weather was agreeable. The three of us plus Daniela, almost 5, decided to sit in the garden and I went in to get a round of drinks and by the time I returned to the garden table Andrew had arrived and was talking to someone. I approached to greet my friend when the man he was talking to turned out to be the Pub Manager who gave us 5 minutes to finish our drinks, as kids were not welcome in his pub. Welcome to England. I had spent time in England as a bachelor but now I was to learn the family culture of England, with the family set to increase by one. (I am one of those old fashioned people who wanted the sex of my children a surprise.) Well we moved on to a restaurant which did accept kids and caught up over a quiet meal. Andrew's flat was small but accommodating and within days I had a job in Brighton at an International Language school which taught English from absolute beginner to advanced and University preparation. It could be a good job.

Once again Andrew turned out to be invaluable as his mum lived in Rottingdean outside Brighton and had a guest cottage on her property, which she let out to us until we found a place of our own. The cottage was a beautiful 16th century converted stables with the low entrance and thick walls so favoured at the time. I quickly settled into the work routine which was morning only while Mariana looked around for a property for us. I contacted an old friend, Mitch, now also married and lived in Lancing, the other side of Brighton. He brought his little girl, Kirsty, to Daniela's 5th birthday and we had a little party for her. We discussed the extortionately high prices for rent in and around Brighton. Rent alone for a humble single bedroomed flat was more than my monthly salary. Mitch told us that the other side of Brighton was cheaper and so Mariana concentrated her search in Worthing, where we spent the next nine years.

Unfortunately we were not so lucky with accommodation there, easy enough to find but difficult landlords. The first flat we moved into was a small place while we waited for our furniture to arrive from SA and just to get settled. The carpet was disgusting and had not been noticed when looking at it, as it was clean but as soon as you took your shoes off and walked around barefoot, primal ooze squeezed between your toes! The agents contacted the owner who refused to change it. A war of words broke out between us to no avail, until one day I found the agent and informed them that I had contacted the Department of Health who were coming to visit and with a 5 year old child and a baby due in 5 months I was sure the they would have to change the carpets, at the very least. The agent visited later the same day and the carpets were changed the next. Work went on as normal until the end of summer when Daniela started school and all the summer students had gone home and the college's student numbers dropped. The Director, a great guy, Rhodri, managed to find teaching work for me until December and then due to a British Council inspection the following year had myself and a couple of other teachers, who would have been laid off, organise the materials, library, computers, etc. over Christmas until February when we returned to teaching, this time with full time employment.

Meanwhile one Thursday evening near the end of November my wife went into labour and we rushed to the hospital, this time it was full term so we weren't worried. However it turned out to be a false labour and things settled down but the midwife said it could still come at any minute so Daniela and I settled to await the new addition to the family. We fell asleep and were awakened by the nurses shift change when we were told that nothing had happened and we, Daniela and I should go home, school and work or whatever and we could pick up Mariana around 13:00 or so. So off we went about our daily routine when at about 11:30 Rhodri came into the class to take over and told me to get to the hospital the baby was coming.

I arrived to find a distressed wife asking for an Epidural, which she had mentioned on admission, but it was too late so the pushing and screaming and squeezed hands began. While this procedure was underway waves of guilt overcame me as during the whole pregnancy, I wanted a larger family but with the love I had for Daniela, I sometimes felt that I had no love to give another child. As my child was handed to me a wave of love overcame me as all my doubts had been dispelled and the love of my wife was as powerful as ever as I realized that God gave never ending and unconditional love as we beamed over our new daughter, Maria Cristina, born at 12:30 on the 30th November 2001.

Cristina was a good baby just like her sister who was so happy to have a baby sister that she even wanted to sleep in the cot with her. Otherwise life went on as normal and two of my nephews, brothers, Gary and Daryl came to visit. Daryl stayed only a few days as he wanted to return home to New Zealand. Gary ended up staying for about six months and helped us move into our new house. This was situated on the outskirts of Worthing and was a great detached house at the bottom of the downs. The owners told us that we could have it as long as we wished as they were moving to Spain and would use the rent to pay rent in Spain. We settled down to a security of our tenancy and were happy to have a permanent home. Gary helped us move and due to the location we would need another car for Mariana to get around. Gary was a great help around the house, cooking, cleaning and looking after his new cousin. England was becoming a disappointment to me very quickly. The health system was not great, doctors wanted you in and out of the consultation in under five minutes after keeping you waiting up to an hour, didn't really discuss anything and always seemed to prescribe medication even if you didn't want it. The education system, once held up as the best in the world had fallen to be nothing worthwhile. It had been decided that competition was bad and that all kids were equal in everything. Biggest load of crap ever!

You try getting a job with 10 other applications that is no competition. You try to get a gold medal at the Olympics when all your school life you have been told that competition is wrong. Even in class kids cannot fail a year even if they have no idea of what they should have learnt, they are just grouped in a 'different' category but still pass the year. What a load of bullshit! Every parent-teacher meeting the same thing was said, they are doing well. This nonsense really made me fume when Daniela was first year at high school. At the first teacher-parent's meeting one of the teachers asked Daniela what she wanted to be and Daniela replied, 'a Veterinarian'. The teacher went on to explain that at her current level of maths that would be impossible. I didn't really follow as all through her primary school years we had been told that she was above average for maths. The teacher then explained the group system. Children were placed in groups according to their perceived ability and Daniela was in the lowest group, but above average for that group. I could not believe what I was hearing, if a child was not doing well in a subject how can you just ignore their potential? Daniela was in the 5th group, the lowest group when we found out about this abomination of education. We immediately put her in extra classes and within two terms she had progressed two levels. I am sure that if she had been given tuition to help improve her maths at an early age she would not have had the problem which she had throughout her school life.

Another instance of the system letting her down was on bullying. A friend of hers fancied a boy who would only go out with her if she persuaded Daniela to have sex with another boy. Daniela refused while daily pressure was exerted on her and she was ostracized by her 'friends' and classmates. Soon we noticed something wrong with Daniela and spoke to her but it took a while for her to confide in us, because as we all know teenagers don't like interference from their parents when it comes to their private lives. Anyway I took this information to the school demanding that she be moved to another class and after various meetings going from the class tutor to Social worker and on to the headmistress. The result was that they couldn't move her to another class because each class studies a different part of the curriculum each term which would result in her missing a third of the curriculum and repeating the third she was studying. So she had to stay in the class with her bullies who were only talked to and denied everything while Daniela ended up seeing a psychologist. Very good educational system!

I became a victim of the educational system when the British Council did their inspection, it was discovered that I was not qualified to teach. Never mind all the studying I did in Colombia, I got another teaching certificate from International House, an international British College. Due to the fact that I did the course in South Africa which is 10 hours shorter than the course in the UK, I was not allowed to teach in England, never mind the fact that International House did not send enough professors to South Africa to teach us or to inform us individually or the school as a whole that we would not be qualified to use the certificate anywhere else, only in South Africa. With letters of recommendation from the Principle, Director, DOS and ADOS, I was allowed to continue to teach as long as I took the Cambridge University Diploma Course, so back to studying I went. After this I also completed a Masters through correspondence at Richmond University.

Mariana was also a victim of the English Educational system. Before leaving South Africa we contacted The British Dental Association to enquire about her right to work in the UK. We explained her basic degree was in Colombia and in order to work in South Africa she had to pass the 5th year of the

Dentist course at a South African University which she did at the University of The Witwatersrand, in Jo'burg. She had also pursued a Masters at Stellenbosh University in the Cape. They said fine South African Degrees are accepted but on arrival two weeks later she was told that South African Degrees are no longer valid, even with their letter of approval and she would have to sit the exams in the UK.

After three months in the house we got notice that we would have to leave after six months as the owners had decided to sell the house in order to buy one in Spain. So for the third time in 9 months we moved house into Worthing centre. A nice 4 bedroomed house with terrible decoration, yellow, red and green walls, not striped but complete walls in the same room! Anyway it was a nice house, a manageable garden within walking distance of the town centre and facilities. The family routine continued, me working 7-5, Daniela going to school and Mariana looking after Cristina and studying for her dental exams. Wednesday and Friday evenings were spent with Daniela and Mariana doing freestyle karate while Cristina and I were in the sport centre pub. Saturdays and / or Sundays were shopping, cleaning the house and once again, karate. Our holidays were within the UK, visiting the typical family resorts like Hoseasons at Lizard Point in Cornwall or visiting the English Riviera, dropping in on family etc. Holidays were difficult as summer was the busiest time of year for me so holidays were generally just before or just after summer with my main holiday at Christmas when we shut down.

Work progressed as I made my way up the ladder, being promoted to ADOS after two years, DOS after another year and a half and then Director six months later, maintaining that position until I left six years later. The work was good, the staff great but it wasn't without its problems. The main problem arose after the Regional Director left due to a job offer at Cambridge University and, although we did not really get on/ we had similar concepts about the job and what needs to be done, so we had a good working relationship. The problem arose as his position was not filled and hence no academic direction existed, only business. The owner was a clever business man but had no idea on the academic side and it was only through the Principles and Directors of the various schools (19 in total) that we managed to get anything done. The school trebled in size under my leadership, having to expand into two more buildings and employing up to seventeen staff during summer with the winter figures peaking at over ten times the numbers from when I first arrived. I also steered the school through two more British Council Inspections, which we passed with flying colours, but it wasn't easy sailing.

The teachers were on Zero Hour contracts – basically we will give you work if we have it and you are paid by contact hour. Any teacher knows that a five hour contact requires at least 3 hours preparation as well as marking students work, talking to the students about their progress etc. So a teacher would work an eight or nine hour day get paid for five and could be left without a job at any time without notice. Furthermore the owner was convinced that no teacher should be employed with us for more than three years! I managed to hold on to my staff for the whole time I was there with endless castigation and investigation into the staff coming down from above. However the school managed to thrive with students and teachers mixing at numerous social events throughout the year. Christmas we had the staff party which welcomed family as well, so the staff became one big family.

Slowly England started to get under my skin. The weather is terrible and the politics with its extreme liberal leanings were spoiling life for everyone. The charity Bathtub boat race from Beeding to Shoreham was cancelled due to health and safety reasons, never mind the fact that in its history of over 70 years only one death had occurred 35 years previously and no other incidents had resulted in serious injury; a ranger was fired from his job because he stated that kids should be allowed to climb trees; a retired man in his 70`s was convicted and sued with assault after he shot one of two armed burglars who had entered his country house during the night; adult students had their hot drinks rights taken as they would have to descend three steps from the kitchen to the lounge with the hot drink in their hands and so the list of petty laws goes on and on. Criminals now have more rights than victims, and that encompasses all crime from petty crime to murder and rape. How can we have ever contemplated creating such a warped society. Discipline no longer exists at home, at school or in public; police have had their powers diminished to such a degree that it is difficult to arrest criminals and when they do they come under a sea of abuse. Oh yes, the woke generation.

I believe that the education today has led to the 'woke' and 'unwoke'. People today choose a side, either woke or unwoke, regarding a socio/politico stance like racism, anti-Semitism, immigration, etc. and they only know the words to support their view without acknowledging or even knowing the historical facts behind the view they are supporting. Take for example slavery; people want to tear down a statue of Winston Churchill as he was pro slavery and racist. Well, yes he was, so were millions of others including the Prime Minister who preceeded him, Neville Chamberlain, as well as Clement Attlee who was the Prime Minister at the time of the Windrush arrivals, he also preferred workers who were prisoners of war to black people. Before the ship Empire Windrush left port Attlee tried to divert it to Tanzania. 'To this day the UK government does not mention the Government dismay at black workers entering Britain, stating that the influx of migrants would create a colour problem.' (Gabby Thorpe Socialist Worker). It was only due to the need for reconstruction after the Second World War and Business pressure that the Government acquiesced. Harold Macmillan in 1962 was the Prime Minister who was responsible for the Commonwealth Act restricting black migrant workers. Harold Wilson's Tory Election Campaign was partly based on the exploitation of anti-immigrant sentiment, particularly in the midlands around Birmingham and the north. Its Conservative MP, Peter Griffiths, had been elected in the previous year's general election on the slogan "If you want a nigger for a neighbour, vote Labour." Griffiths refused to disown it: "I would not condemn any man who said that," he told the Times during his election campaign. "I regard it as a manifestation of popular feeling."

My point here is that you cannot single out one leader as an evil racist when most of those before and after Winston Churchill were also racist. The woke and unwoke generation are trying to dictate a history that falsifies facts. Winston Churchill was part of a racist generation, emphasis on generation, like scores of previous generations and many generations after him. Even in recent and present UK governments the Windrush victims are still being swept under the carpet. (Only 13 out of 91 claims for compensation have been received as at the time of writing.)

George Orwell observed: 'The very concept of objective truth is fading out of the world. Lies will pass into history.'

The reasonable new concepts of 'woke' and 'unwoke', in my opinion, is due to the ignorance of the extreme liberals who really do not understand what they are doing, but it sounds right. Every aspect of life is now a confrontation and the sides taken are woke or unwoke, that's it. Examples of woke include seeing racism when it is another form of discrimination and white privilege. Words lose their meaning and became a social position, 'he is right wing', 'she is a bigot' etc. are statements defining a position and no dialogue, discussion or understanding is needed, just 'I belong to this group'. Social problems cannot have one perspective, for example the woke want to tear down the statue of Cecil Rhodes and the unwoke want it left alone are these the only two views? To view the past to define the present? History cannot be rewritten, various opinions about the past can be debated but it is simply not a black or white choice. Statues tell a story. How often have you been somewhere and seen a statue or plaque and asked someone what it refers to? Each time you did that you learnt something about the past and local history good or bad.

Governments are now forcing the woke ideas on their populations which has brought Marxism full circle, woke politics prevents liberalism and free speech, and the core group promoting this agenda are the extreme ignorant liberals in government, business and the rich emanating out of Hollywood, while actual enlightened liberalism is on the defensive. This is causing a massive split all around the world with the resurgence of the extreme right. Historically, in many countries, it is the left wing liberals who vote; the stupidity of present governments is not only increasing the popularity of the right but is also bringing the right wing grass roots to the vote. Unless governments stop catering to minority groups and the ills of the past we will see a continuing swing to the Right and may God help us all.

Urban dictionary definition of woke, which has its roots in African-American slang: The act of being very *pretentious* about how much you care about a social issue – Jackie Cameron. This quote says it all.

Well as you can see England was not really my cup of tea and the crunch for me came when Mariana wrote her Dental exams. She had to write, if I recall correctly 11 exams including 2 oral exams. She failed one of the oral exams due to the question; 'What is your opinion of the article in the BDJ on page 33 in the March 2002 edition?' (The BDJ, 'British Dental Journal', being a monthly magazine). Not knowing the answer she was failed and then informed that she would have to rewrite all of the 11 exams, not like, as is common in UK universities, rewriting only the failed subjects. We also became aware that approximately 1,200 people had taken the exam at a fee of £950 and only 96 people passed the exam. Three months later she rewrote the exam after paying another £950 along with approximately another 1,300 people on this occasion, once again failing one of the orals with the question; 'What is the last word on page 152 of the Dental Reference Manual?'
82 people passed. Money making business or what? Once again I was reassured of my dislike for the Education system, its racism and xenophobia of the UK Education Board.

Not too long after this we decided to move, Mariana could take the exams in Spain, which were valid throughout Europe, including the UK and so she spent the next few months preparing for them and travelling to and from the University of Seville in order to do the exams. Meanwhile I hit a problem at work. My DOS, Chris, told me that he wanted to find another job as he felt that he was stuck with no opportunities for advancement, in reply I told him that my family would probably be moving abroad within a year or so. As the next in line, a brilliant teacher and a vast wealth of knowledge he agreed to wait for me to leave. However he was too impatient and while on holiday I was phoned by the owner and informed that allegations had been made against me. I returned to work immediately. Chris made allegations that I did nothing but play games on the computer all day while he did both his job and mine. I obviously denied the allegations and pointed out the fact that Chris had only been with us for less than 2 years and I had been fine running the place without him. However Chris wouldn't relent and so the staff became involved, being taken into the office and grilled for half an hour each on the subject and then asked to write an account from their points of view. This was terrible for Chris as it transpired that the staff did not have much time for him, he was arrogant, belittled the staff and started a relationship with one of the students. However as they were both consenting adults, legally no crime had been committed but just the unspoken rule of not getting involved with students, which we all know happens all the time, but it put the teachers in a state of aggression towards him. Chris did not accept the situation and decided on arbitration through the Unions. By this time I realized that I would have to postpone the move as it was my intention to give notice after the Christmas break, but if I left now it could look like I was in the wrong and could affect my reputation, which, work wise had always been exemplary. The case dragged on for months, the Unions heard and dropped the case, James decided to go to court and the owner became worried about the consequences for the school and made an £8,000 settlement and as the busy summertime rush was close at hand, the owner asked me to stay on for the summer and I did so but took 2 weeks break to go to Spain.

Mariana was already in Spain doing exams and so I drove down with the kids and had a family holiday before leaving Mariana the car and flying back to the UK with the kids. The kids finished their academic year at school, Cristina first year and Daniela first year at secondary school. When school broke up for the school holidays Mariana flew to the UK to pick up the kids while I finished in October before I handed over the school to a good friend Michael and attended a farewell dinner thrown by the staff before once again heading off into wild blue yonder.

Before leaving this chapter I would just like one last comment. All my three girls had decided to take up karate with Daniela, at five years old taking the lead. We went to dozens of karate clubs, had the initial free lesson until my five year old kept on telling me 'that's not real karate' until she finally decided on a club, which taught freestyle karate. She threw herself into it, won many cups and medallions for somewhere in the top three places, entered national competitions where, at 10 years old, she came in 7th National All Styles she was competing against 12 and 13 year olds. The proudest moment of my life with her was when she achieved her First Dan Black Belt at 12 years old, and believe me it was not an honorary title. The exam was over 3 hours, she was the youngest taking the exam, along with one 16 year old and the rest adults. Just the warm up would have had me out of the running! After a myriad of stretching exercises, 5 minutes running, 50 star jumps, 50 burpies, 50 sit-ups, 50 push-ups and other exercises the exam started and she passed! Cristina and Mariana both achieved Brown belt before leaving the UK. Mariana was slow to achieve her gradings due to her busy schedule of work, studying and exams. She achieved her Black belt one year later and went on to become an instructor in Spain.

## Chapter 32

Arriving in Spain Mariana had settled us into a flat and found work for me at a local language school where I started immediately. Almost from the word go I had problems with the methodology. The owner of the business, in my opinion, was more interested in keeping the students there until they left school. Teaching was basically done in Spanish, the books, apart from the exercises were in Spanish. Spanish dominated the sessions. What was done there in 10 years is completed in 2-3 years at all the other institutes I had taught at. One day the owner asked for a chat concerning methodology as he noticed on my CV that I had done a course on it. One day after work he invited me for a drink at the tavern on the corner and we discussed methodology. I was frank with him and told him that a lot could be done to improve the courses and speed up the learning process. The following day when I arrived at work I had been fired and my final payslip was waiting for me. Honesty doesn't always pay. The teachers at the institute were nice and good at their jobs and had advised me to just settle in and then later bring in my method of teaching which was what I was trying to do when he asked for the meeting. I had observed one of his lessons and was told to emulate his teaching. To me it was the worst lesson I had ever observed, and I have spent my teaching career observing, teaching teachers and giving workshops! The class was a group of 8 kids, of about 8 or nine, the level was Lower Intermediate and the hour was spent explaining I, my and mine in Spanish for about 40 minutes, 10 minutes copying English examples written on the board while the last 10 minutes was spent with choral and individual repetition. During the hour if the kids fidgeted, talked or mispronounced any words the result was a string of shouted abuse at the culprit.

All in all I was glad I was fired but was worried about an income. I returned periodically to Brighton to give courses for special needs, for example; military English to European Peace Keeping Forces as well as some basic classes to fill in the days when I was there. One project, a summer camp for Real Madrid junior players, was a total disaster! The owner had greatly underestimated the amount of food 170 teenagers could eat, resulting in the football coaches bringing pizzas, hamburgers etc. and paying out of their own pocket while I negotiated a better food deal with my bosses. This was a fruitless task and led to food riots in the dining room at which point I was relieved of duty amid shouts of John, John, John from the students. As I had not done anything wrong I was transferred to the school in Brighton but at the end of the day I was ripped off financially by the school and approached by Real Madrid to see if I would like to organise a contract for the following 5 years. After contemplation I turned down the offer due to the lack of start-up finances. I then got a job in another language school in Alicante Spain, which was also a disaster, in my opinion due to the methodology and jealousy from the owner's wife.

The next job I got was another summer job in Spain with a Villa Rental Company which led to one of the Villa owners offering me a job as the Buying Manager for a private 3 Star Hotel, accommodating about 700 guests and that is where I am today. I am glad to be out of the teaching business and my home life is great. I am well settled having lived here for the longest time I have ever been in one place and God be willing will spend out the rest of my days here.

One last note is that I consider myself to be practicing Christian and have come to terms with different denominations. However I must point to the anti-Christian community that Christianity is a peaceful religion but like all religions it does have its fanatics who pick and choose which parts to follow. The Christian faith is a strict faith but also a compassionate one. For example on homosexuality and 'devious sex' it states: 'Or do you not know that the unrighteous will not inherit the kingdom of God? Do not be deceived: neither the sexually immoral, nor idolaters, nor adulterers, nor men who practice homosexuality' – 1 Corinthians 6:9. 'You shall not lie with a male as with a woman; it is an abomination' – Leviticus 18: 22. So now all the homophobes are jumping up and down in glee while the anti-Christian groups are up in arms about intolerance BUT the bible also preaches, in both the Old Testament and the New Testament, tolerance, respect and love - Exodus Chapter 20: "You shall not give false evidence against your neighbour. You shall not set your heart on your neighbour's house. You shall not set your heart on your neighbour's spouse, or servant, man or woman, or ox, or donkey, or any of your neighbour's possessions.' Mark Chapter 12 verse 31 says: 'The second is this: 'Love your neighbor as yourself.' There is no commandment greater than these", and John Chapter 8 verse 7: "let he who is without sin cast the first stone." These are the precepts of Christianity and anyone claiming to be Christian who does not follow this is on their own rocky path.

The only thing I disagree with about Christians is when they ask other Christians to help them commit a sin knowing it is wrong to do so. As an example a few years ago a gay Christian couple asked a Christian bakery to bake their wedding cake, all the while knowing that in Christian law regarding homosexuality made it a sin. The baker had no bad feelings towards the couple but would not bake the cake as it was a grave sin the couple was asking the baker to partake in, so he refused, was taken to court and lost the case and finally had the verdict overturned. My question to you is this; did the Christian gay couple act in a Christian manner? You can always get service elsewhere and nobody has any right to force people to do things against their will or beliefs.

Christians and most other religions are religions of peace. All religions have fanatics who resort to violence and murder. We are here to forgive not perpetrate the violence and hate. If you cannot forgive an act ignore it until you can or let God show you the way.

Goodbye, God bless and I hope you have enjoyed my tale.

The End, for now.

Bakkie – pick up or open backed van

Boma – A small settlement in the African bush, originally used by the colonial governments for policing and governance of the districts.

Bwana – domestic servants name for the master of the house

Eweh – polite form of 'hey you'

Medem – domestic servants name for the mistres of the house

Picannie – small, often used to refer to children of all races in colonial days

Sjambok – short leather whip with a stiff handle and flexible end

www.ingramcontent.com/pod-product-compliance
Ingram Content Group UK Ltd.
Pitfield, Milton Keynes, MK11 3LW, UK
UKHW021052270726
13967UKWH00012B/588

9 781739 943912